# Latinos at the Golden Gate

# Latinos
## AT THE
# Golden Gate

CREATING COMMUNITY & IDENTITY

IN SAN FRANCISCO

## Tomás F. Summers Sandoval Jr.

*The University of North Carolina Press / Chapel Hill*

© 2013 The University of North Carolina Press
All rights reserved
Set in Utopia and Aller types by codeMantra
Manufactured in the United States of America

The paper in this book meets the guidelines for permanence and durability
of the Committee on Production Guidelines for Book Longevity of the Council on
Library Resources. The University of North Carolina Press has been a member of
the Green Press Initiative since 2003.

Library of Congress Cataloging-in-Publication Data
Summers Sandoval, Tomás F., Jr.
Latinos at the Golden Gate : creating community and identity in
San Francisco / Tomás F. Summers Sandoval Jr.
pages cm
Includes bibliographical references and index.
ISBN 978-1-4696-0766-5 (cloth : alk. paper)
ISBN 978-1-4696-2726-7 (pbk. : alk. paper)
ISBN 978-1-4696-0767-2 (ebook)
1. Hispanic Americans—California—San Francisco. 2. Hispanic Americans—
California—San Francisco—History. I. Title.
F869.S39S757 2013
305.868'073079461—dc23    2013002818

THIS BOOK WAS DIGITALLY PRINTED.

For Benito, Lili, & Graciela

# Contents

# Illustrations

# Acknowledgments

Researching and writing this book have left me with a profound sense of gratitude for the many people who have supported me through this long process. My earliest research on San Francisco began under the guidance of Waldo Martin and Ron Takaki. I am forever grateful to Waldo for his warmth, accessibility, and stellar editorial skills. He was more than a great advisor. His demeanor helped me feel at home in a place that more often felt foreign. His commitment to the success of students of color provided me with the support I needed to successfully complete my graduate education. Ron was a treasured mentor whose seminars provided me with a dynamic intellectual community as well as the benefit of his keen academic advice. At nearly every stage in the writing and editing process his voice rang out in my head, "What about the voices?" He challenged me in so many ways and nurtured in me the desire to do work that matters beyond the confines of the academic world. Carlos Muñoz Jr., Diane Shaver Clemens, and Richard Allen also extended themselves for me in ways that helped shape me as a teacher and as a historian.

My time at Berkeley connected me to a group of people who shared with me their intelligence, creativity, and friendship. Ron Lopez met me on my first day of orientation and was always generous with his oddball and loving brilliance. He and Jason Ferreira became more than friends; they are family. I owe them each a lot for their role in shaping my intellectual growth. Charlie Bertsch, Birgit Brander Rassmussen, Jess Bravin, Nzingha Dugas, Monica Rodriguez, Hatem Bazian, and Pamela Jennings each did their part to make my time at Cal one of the most memorable and meaningful times of my life.

Mark Simpson-Vos at the University of North Carolina Press has shown a consistent interest in and unwavering support of my work. I feel lucky to have found such a welcoming and professional home for my first book. The review process made the book better in a number of clear ways. I am especially appreciative of Matt Garcia's editorial advice and guidance during these final steps. I am grateful to other friends and colleagues who have also read drafts and provided advice along the way. Ron Lopez, Jason Ferreira, Horacio Roque Ramírez, Chris Carlsson, Stephen Rubio, Pardis

Mahdavi, Erin Runions, Anne Dwyer, David Reichard, David Hernandez, Erualdo González, and Denise Sandoval gave important feedback. Mike Miller was generous with his time, skills, and memory on more than one occasion, including offering a detailed reading of the entire manuscript. I have also been lucky to have had the help of various students along the way. Victor Torres has taught me as much as I could ever have taught him. Callida Cenizal, Becka DeSmidt, Kari Mah, Jacob Cohen, Mindy Hagan, Mayra Gradilla, and Stephanie Roman each helped make this an easier process with their intelligence and effort.

I have benefited from the expertise of numerous librarians. The staff of the San Francisco Public Library, in particular those who work at the San Francisco History Room, are the finest public librarians I have ever seen in my life. They handle each and every inquiry from each and every visitor with the same level of respect and attention, whether a lost person off the street or a famous academic. I am grateful for their help, their resourcefulness, and their consistent and ever-present smiles. My thanks go out to the staffs of the Bancroft Library at the University of California, Berkeley, and North Baker Research Library of the California Historical Society in San Francisco. Jeffrey M. Burns, of the Archives of the Archdiocese of San Francisco in Menlo Park, was a tireless resource, always willing to share his deep expertise. I am forever grateful for his help. My thanks go out to Spence Limbocker and Lincoln Cushing, who both helped secure images.

An assortment of people made time in their busy schedules to share their life stories with me as part of the research process. Ultimately, the kinds of decisions that are necessary in writing a book made it impossible to include all of them. Nevertheless, the following individuals impacted this book in clear and important ways: Mike Miller, Dorinda Moreno, Esperanza Echavarri, Jim Queen, Elba Sanchez, Sam Rios, Debra Varner, Steve Arcelona, Manuel Vasquez, Eduardo Sandoval, Juan Pedro Gaffney, Eduardo Morales, Judith Sandoval, and Helen Lara Cea.

Pomona College is a model of support for its faculty's intellectual development. I have benefited from its generous faculty grants as well as the fellowship of my colleagues in the History Department and the Chicana/o-Latina/o Studies Department. Ray Buriel, Jose Calderón, Miguel Tinker Salas, Rita Cano Alcala, Maria Soldatenko, and Gilda Ochoa not only have kept the latter alive and pertinent despite all the odds but also have built a supportive academic community of fellow teachers, scholars, and activists. Sid Lemelle, Helena Wall, Sam Yamashita, Ken Wolf, Victor Silverman, Bob Woods, Gary Kates, April Mayes, Angelina Chin, and Arash Khazeni are dedicated intellectuals who have provided a strong home for my growth. I am also thankful for Gina Brown-Pettay, the backbone of our department, who has been helpful beyond measure. Maria Tucker, Sergio Marin, and Rita Shaw remind me daily of why it is we do the work we do. I am grateful to them and the many students who are part of our Draper Center. My colleagues at CSU Monterey Bay—in particular Rina Benmayor, Ernie Stromberg, David Reichard, Renee Curry, Diana Garcia, Frances Payne Adler, Deb Busman, Annette March, Gerald Shenk, Donaldo Urioste, Qun Wang, Ilene Feinman, Josina Makau, Debian Marty, and Amalia Mesa-Baines—showed me warmth and community. They continue to impact my teaching and scholarship in important ways.

My family has been the foundation upon which I have built any success in life, whether personally or professionally. Aida and Tom Sandoval are two amazingly loving, caring, and supportive parents. Their commitment to family, as well as their dedication to education, has made me who I am today. Denise and Emily have always been friends to me as much as they have been sisters. I'm lucky to have them in my life. We grew up in a family of five where none of us had a college education. Today all five of us have bachelor's degrees, four of us have M.A.s, and two of us have Ph.D.s. Two of my parents' children are now professors of Chicana/o studies. That transformation was made possible by our love and support for each other, every collective step of the way. That love includes many others who round out my family. Dolores Rojas and Esther Sandoval are two amazingly resilient women, as well as loving grandmothers. My mother-in-law, Shirley Summers, never fails to model the kind of compassionate professionalism that makes our world better. Jacques Zalma, Eric Summers, Shari Summers, and my nephews, William and Daniel, are sources of everything that is important.

When I began research on this topic I was a single, childless graduate student living with a rotating group of very close friends: Jesse Garcia, Joshua Stanbro, Eddie Lazaro, Gabriel Emanuel, Spencer Chow, Dan Garcia, and Kristin Cahill. Brian Collins, John Yasmer, Brittany Walker Pettigrew, Jon Pettigrew, Grace Emanuel, Maxine Burkett, Adrienne Hale, Jessica Hawk, and Albert Ortaliza rounded out my makeshift family, both in the Bay Area and beyond. I thank them all.

I complete this book as a husband and father of three. The best thing that ever happened in my life was meeting and marrying Melinda Summers. She is my partner and my friend, a consistent source of acceptance, strength, and love in all I do. Our three wonderful children—Benito, Lili, and Graciela—make every day exciting, unpredictable, funny, tiring, educational, challenging, and, above all else, loving. This book was written while they played, yelled, grabbed the keyboard, or demanded I show them a YouTube video instead of type. It is also a record of my time spent away from them and Melinda. I am grateful for the perspective they have all provided me during this process. They have my love, forever.

# Latinos at the Golden Gate

# How Do I Get to San Francisco?

*Latin Americans and the Golden Gate*

"This doesn't just affect Mexicans or Central Americans, documented or undocumented," explained one San Francisco day laborer in the spring of 2006. "We are all affected." Addressing other local *jornaleros* at a meeting of the San Francisco Day Labor Program, the undocumented man was referring to the Sensenbrenner Bill then working its way through Congress. The legislation, an effort to further criminalize undocumented immigrants, politically mobilized millions nationwide.[1] The fifty or so members of the day labor group had met to discuss the controversy at La Raza Centro Legal, a grassroots organization dedicated to providing accessible legal services to the Latino community. Centro Legal brought together a broad coalition of Bay Area organizations and residents already organized in opposition to the draconian congressional attempts at "border security." The *jornalero*'s passionate plea for unity was repeated throughout the city's network of progressive advocacy organizations, articulating that spring's political struggle in a much larger context. As he worded it, "This is against us—this is against Latinos."[2]

The same refrain of mutuality had echoed in the city decades before, in December 1985, when San Francisco became another in a growing list of municipalities around the nation declaring themselves "cities of sanctuary" for Guatemalan and Salvadoran immigrants.[3] Members of the Latin American community were joined by a diverse group of San Franciscans in this successful movement, a multifaceted effort to pressure the city's Board of Supervisors into taking "a moral position" on the humanity of refugees. The formal resolution forbade local law, health, education, and social service agencies from assisting Immigration and Naturalization Service (INS) agents in the fulfillment of their duties with respect to Central Americans, while condemning the Reagan administration's policies in those countries. The board's affirmative vote made the city one of the national epicenters of a growing grassroots effort to end U.S. military involvement in the hemisphere. For San Francisco, already home to tens of thousands of immigrants from El Salvador and Guatemala, the measure also had particular local appeal: supporters hoped the symbolism of the stance would translate into tangible changes in how "illegal" immigrants were policed within the city's borders. Opponents waged an equally passionate effort, complicating the city's reputation as a bastion of unrivaled leftists. One city supervisor called the measure "inappropriate," the mayor said it would require her to "violate her oath to uphold the law," and an editorial in the *San Francisco Chronicle* characterized it as a "plan for anarchy."[4] The measure passed nonetheless, an assertion of solidarity between the city and the struggle of Central American refugees. One local activist proclaimed that it "signifie[d] the city of San Francisco and the people from El Salvador and Guatemala are in this together."[5]

These multiple expressions of identity, solidarity, and interconnectedness are the heart of *Latinos at the Golden Gate*. In its simplest form, this is a story detailing the social and political experiences of multiple generations of ethnic Latin Americans in San Francisco and their efforts to forge lives of dignity and meaning.[6] It pays special attention to those moments in the past when a diverse population of mostly Spanish-speaking migrants coalesced to express panethnic solidarity and identity rooted to the geography of the city. Though fluid and contingent, these expressions of pan-Latin community could cut across lines of difference, such as those marked by nationality and immigration status. Ultimately, they helped integrate Latinos into the cosmopolitan imaginary of the city itself. When activist and advocacy networks in the city respond to modern attacks on immigrants, they also draw on a rich history of Latin Americans' forging substantive connections to each other and to the city by uniting in common cause. And so central to this study is an examination of this emerging and evolving pan–Latin Americanism as an experience lived through institutions, organizations, and movements.

## Empire and the Golden Gate

For generations, San Francisco has promoted itself as a cosmopolitan city, tolerant of difference and welcoming of a diverse stream of migrants from all over the world. The city enjoys an image as an exception to traditional urban race relations in the United States, "an oasis of equal treatment for restless migrants from Malta to Samoa."⁷ Yet, as generations of San Franciscans have also shown, these optimistic narratives are selective at best. They illuminate a distinct past while also belying the complex histories of dislocation, racial violence, and struggle that delineate the space between experience and imagination. This book locates its stories within these spaces, where the battle between image and reality shape the lives of everyday people.

These historical dynamics buttress the stories of Latinas and Latinos in the city while also tending to obscure a set of forces beyond the Golden Gate that inform global contexts and local communities alike. In 1769, when sixty-four men set out to find Monterey Bay for the Spanish Crown, they became the first nonindigenous people to gaze upon the San Francisco Bay. Nearly two centuries of Spanish imperialism in the "New World" preceded the Portolá Expedition, as did a history of sea exploration, whale hunting, and trade. This "journey of European 'discovery' of a place that had never been lost"⁸ connected the Golden Gate to Spain, to its other hemispheric colonies, and to a set of interests that forever altered the lives of the indigenous people who had made the region their home. Subsequent waves of migrants would further propel a course of events creating what became known as simply "the city." Many traveled under the banners of imperial Spain and the Catholic Church, others with the mission of Manifest Destiny and a thirst for gold, and still more with the hopes of finding prosperity in the modern metropolis. Latinos traveled in contexts shaped by these same forces when they followed a coffee shipping line to San Francisco, used networks in the city to mobilize for political struggles in their homelands, or sought to build community after dislocation from what was once home. However migrants understood the context of their hemispheric movements, those movements had everything to do with political and economic structures rooted to the city. And so this San Francisco story is also one of the inextricable entanglements of imperialism.

The broad story of *latinoamericanos*, whether in the parts of the Americas designated as their "homelands" or as part of the diasporic conditions increasingly marking Latin American lives in the present world, is marked by the effects of empire at every turn. The deliberate course of U.S. economic domination of Latin America has incited movements of both capital and humans northward, nurturing a population of Latinos in the Bay Area for more than two centuries, a local presence older than the city itself. As a result, perhaps no other North American urban locale has enjoyed as continuous and diverse a flow of Latin American migrants as has San Francisco. In motivation and purpose, in structure and form, these forces have animated the city's past, whether in the "discovery" of the bay and the subsequent settlement of Yerba Buena; the war of conquest waged by the United States against Mexico; or the rooting of the city within the organized extension of U.S. capital in the hemisphere. The movements of Latin Americans they have incited have relied on an interconnectedness that is neither passive nor benign. Rather, as Fredric Jameson reminds us, these global "relations are first and foremost ones of tension or antagonism, when not outright exclusion." Latin American migrants have responded to these tensions and their resultant diasporic conditions in myriad ways, including their expression of collective Latino identities and their formation of a visible community. This coalescence of distinct populations representing multiple Latin American nationalities and ethnicities, as well as the sense of their interconnectedness within the discreet geographic space called San Francisco, are dependent on "the preexistence of economic and communicational channels and pre-established circuits."[9] With these understandings as a backdrop, this local story speaks to possibilities in other places, as well as in other times.

This story adds nuance to enunciations from other scholars who have excavated the complex history of U.S. hegemony in the Spanish-speaking hemisphere. Specifically, it harnesses the well-established analysis that "U.S. power has been brought to bear unevenly in the region by diverse agents, in a variety of sites and conjunctures, and through diverse transnational arrangements."[10] This understanding helped recast the optimism contained by San Francisco's economic history, which celebrated its expansive connections throughout the Pacific. Within these networks of profit are dense collections of assumptions, not the least of which is "a pervasive belief that Latin Americans constitute an inferior branch of the human species."[11] This belief undergirds projects seeking to establish and sustain U.S. economic dominion over Latin America, often at the expense of the latter's sovereignty. In their diasporic conditions, Latinos are living products of these structures connecting the United States and Latin America and the ideologies animating them. My interests here are to portray some of the rather seamless connections between this condition of U.S. hegemony and the (im)migration process. Rather than portray them within the bifurcated model of "push" and "pull" forces, I am more concerned with how they work together, how histories of U.S. neoimperialism and domestic immigration constitute each other. From this vantage point, Latin American migration to the United States is recast as a "social consequence of imperial economic expansionism."[12] In these ways, this story is consciously part of what Manuel Pastor has described as a "convergence of themes and issues" in Latino and

Latin American studies, works exploring the links between Latin American political economy and Latino experiences in the United States.[13]

I thus seek to further historicize a discussion that has been largely framed by social scientific studies of present-day communities.[14] The presence of a diverse Latin American–descent population in San Francisco is understood as a product of the particular transnational linkages between the bay and specific parts of Latin America. These interconnections subsequently inform the experiences of Latinos once arrived at the Golden Gate as they respond to racialist pressures and economic marginalization within the city. It is this material, lived experience—informed by U.S. economic imperialism in the hemisphere as well as the interrelations between varied racial or ethnic groups in the city—that animates the narrative of Latinos in San Francisco over more than a century. Cognizant of the limits of pan-ethnic formation, however, this story also explores how new identities can simultaneously exacerbate historic divisions among Latin Americans with respect to race or ethnicity, nationality, and class, while also authentically representing collectives of individual lives. *Latinidad* does not necessarily reflect or create a totalizing or transcendent commonality. It can be, as Nicholas De Genova and Ana Y. Ramos-Zayas contend, "quite fractured and selective . . . whereby some Latinos [are] nonetheless excluded from other Latinos' assertions of a pan-Latino identity."[15] The ways Latin Americans in San Francisco fostered, accessed, employed multiple versions of panethnicity were never separate from the sometimes divergent historical pathways between and among them. Recent studies question utilizations of panethnicity by interrogating the ends such phenomena serve, reminding us that "ethnicity is never free of larger interests."[16] Yet the dangers of asserting "harmonious pan-ethnic Latino identity" extend beyond its tendency to obfuscate. Also troubling is the "potential to perpetuate intra-Latino exclusions and injustices" by homogenizing the diversity of Latin American and Latino experiences.[17] In the case of San Francisco, Latino panethnicity has often struggled with these limitations, nurturing an array of historical expressions. Among these have been moments of effective panethnic community, nearly always contextual and based on specific "intergroup social relationships."[18] The forces undergirding and informing these interactions, in international and local contexts, are foundationally important.

## The Challenges of Community and Identity

Stretching from the Gold Rush to the post–World War II era of social change, *Latinos at the Golden Gate* details the historical processes giving rise to San Francisco's diverse population of Latin American migrants, and the ways they and their descendants forged and expressed community over time. Specifically, I investigate these multiethnic populations in distinct historical contexts, ones marked by ethnic coalescence and collective identity, or what Felix Padilla termed Latino ethnic consciousness—"a process through which two or more Spanish-surnamed ethnics cross their individual group boundaries to seek solidarity as a wider Latino unit."[19] In this book, I refer most often to this situational pan–Latin American ethnicity as *latinidad*. For simplicity, I label its adherents "Latino" and "Latina" although, as we will see, the terms used to convey *latinidad* have varied over time and in the contexts supporting their usage. Further mitigated by the equally powerful constructs of race, ethnicity, class, and generation, the existence of this collective identity has often been a "viable strategy in the everyday processes of community formation." As early as the late nineteenth century, Latinos in San Francisco have utilized what researchers of the late twentieth century have described as "a wide array of distinctive forms of collective assertion and visibility . . . that retain nationally inflected particularities and simultaneously cultivate a shared sense of Latinidad."[20] This simultaneous and situational expression is indicative of the daily social, cultural, and economic interactions of Latinos, both with a larger San Francisco polity and with each other. As ethnic studies scholar Yen Le Espiritu reminds us, "Ethnicity is forged and changed in encounters among groups,"[21] and San Francisco *latinidad* is no different. Indeed, employed to both foster and reflect Latino community, this panethnic identity—connoted by terms as diverse as *hispanoamericano, raza, Latin,* and *brown*—emanated from shared cultural and linguistic characteristics, from an increasingly common lived experience shaped by periods of conflict and informed by the processes of racial formation, as well as from a collective desire for change.

The many ways Latinas and Latinos have manifested those solidarities from within the neoimperial context, then, is a necessary element of this story. The role of the Catholic Church figures heavily in this story as the Latin American–descent populations in various periods of San Francisco's past have utilized its spiritual beliefs and practices to forge unity. The church has always played an important role in Latino community formation.[22] In San Francisco, Latino relationships to the church have both reflected and constituted community. In the late nineteenth century, when elites within the Spanish-speaking population created a "national parish" for the diffuse groups of Latin Americans in the city, their goal was to unite "la raza española" into a cohesive unit. In this instance, the equally transnational institution of Catholicism helped animate community formation in multifaceted ways, not the least of which was by constituting a weekly faith community within the church's walls. In an alternate example, in the mid-twentieth century, when Latinos had begun to firmly establish themselves as a visible barrio in the Mission District, their emergence as a community could be witnessed through the cultural transformation they initiated in one church. Helping to further nurture the development of a meaningful ministerial practice among the clergy by supporting a progressive and Latino-focused impulse already taking root in the archdiocese, Latinos utilized the varied resources of the church to foster unity, meet economic and spiritual needs, and well as mark a terrain as their own. In these ways and more, the Catholic Church and religious faith join a host of other institutions and practices—the Spanish-language press, culturally specific business districts, mass political struggles, and youth movements—to both create and express panethnic Latino community.

The idea of community I employ is not a simple one. Academics have long complicated the many uses of this term, including our collective failures to recognize its subtleties. On one level, community has often meant a group of people united in their geographical location. Certainly, by locating this story within the municipal and county boundaries of San Francisco, California, this notion of community is integral to my project. At the same time, community has also been employed to refer to groups of people who share a social identity, not necessarily tied to (but neither wholly dislodged from) a geographic place. Any discussion of racial or ethnic populations under this concept also makes substantive use of this understanding. I came of age academically in a period when the rich possibilities of Benedict Anderson's book *Imagined Communities* had informed reconceptualizations in the fields of urban, Chicana/Chicano, ethnic, and cultural studies. His often quoted observation that "all communities larger than primordial villages of face-to-face contact (and perhaps even these) are imagined" frames nearly all inquiries into community history.[23] While these visions of community in the imaginary are significant, and often the central focus of the story, I have made efforts to examine the instances of tangible community far more frequently. In so doing, I do not mean to suggest a utopian understanding of cohesive togetherness in the reading of the city's Latina and Latino past. I do mean to excavate moments when the members of this population themselves envisioned and even built "horizontal comradeship" as a means of surmounting (or uniting) differences in nationality, ethnicity, and/or class. In this way, the story of Latino San Francisco can be seen as an articulation of an "imagined community," however unstable and inconsistent that project (or its results) might have been over time. However, as I attempt to highlight in the following pages, these articulations also marked an unfolding set of material experiences where "community" was a lived reality.

## The Crisis of the Present

Though fundamentally a historical narrative located in the past, in substance this book engages our dynamic present in significant ways. Latinas and Latinos are at the center of an undeniably transformative period in U.S. race relations, when questions of national identity, civil rights, citizenship, and equity infuse nearly every facet of their existence in the United States. Our collective inability to understand the histories of migration, integration, and adaptation in the United States are more than gaps in our understanding of the past; they help constitute our future shortcomings as a multiracial, democratic, and humane society. By illuminating the history of Latin American–descent populations in San Francisco, *Latinos at the Golden Gate* adds to the growing bodies of scholarship detailing Latino adaptations to life in new social and political settings. The expression of new, collective identities offers alternative ways of conceiving racial integration and assimilation in the U.S. past, dynamically exhibiting the creation of "new social subjects."[24] Latino mobilizations into visible communities provide fresh understandings about the challenges facing the urban United States in the twenty-first century, as their struggles for respect and survival simultaneously expose the limits of and possibility of pluralism in the modern city. Indeed, this history transcends the limits of a social history confined to one city; it contributes to the larger story of the making of "Latino America."

In the first decade of the twenty-first century, Latinas and Latinos have achieved a level of national visibility unimaginable in earlier periods. In the 2010 Census, our numbers grew to more than 50 million, or 16.3 percent of the total U.S. population. Perhaps more significant, the "Hispanic" population accounted for 56 percent of the nation's total growth from 2000 to 2010, casting Latinos as the likely foundation of future demographic growth in the country. Most Latinos continue to live in only nine states, with 76 percent of the total residing in California, Texas, New York, Arizona, Colorado, Florida, Illinois, New Mexico, and New Jersey. However, of the ten states recording the largest Latino population growth rates over the last decade, all are outside of the traditional immigrant gateways, with top eight located in the South.[25] And while most of this nation's Latinos have their roots in Mexico (63%) and to a much lesser extent Puerto Rico (9.2%), the population growth of those from El Salvador, Guatemala, and other Central and South American nations has been astronomical. From 2000 to 2010, the Salvadoran population in the United States grew by 152 percent, with Guatemalans (180%), Dominicans (85%), and Colombians (93%) exhibiting similarly high rates of growth. Though the ethnic Mexican majority is unlikely to shift on a national scale, in a number of U.S. metropolitan areas they are not the dominant Latino group, or they comprise a much slimmer majority than their national totals.[26]

And yet, reflecting the profound limits inherent in these demographic shifts, Latinos remain socially and politically marginalized, intractably segregated, and largely misunderstood. Nationwide, hate crimes against Latinos rose by 40 percent from 2003 through 2007, as exemplified when four white teenagers in Shenandoah, Pennsylvania, beat Luis Ramirez, an undocumented immigrant, to death.[27] Amid a flurry of local and statewide legislation targeting the rights of immigrants, education officials in Arizona banned a Mexican American studies program in Tucson, depicting it as a platform to "promote the overthrow of the United States Government."[28] These racially infused reactions are hardly rare or confined to remote locales. Latino ascendancy on the national stage has been met with an equally robust rise in anti-immigrant and anti-Latino racism within the federal bureaucracy. As part of the "war on terror" and its concomitant desire to "protect our border," the United States is currently engaged in one of the most frightening periods of mass incarceration and deportation in its history. In 2009 alone, the Department of Homeland Security apprehended more than 600,000 foreign nationals, 86 percent of whom originated in Mexico. Setting a record high for the seventh year in a row, the United States deported more than 393,000 people, with most coming from Latin America (72% were "removed" to Mexico, 7% to Guatemala, and 7% to Honduras).[29] Shockingly, the vast majority of those detained and deported have committed no crime. They are apprehended merely for committing the civil violation of entering, residing, and/or working in the United States without proper authorization. In a pattern begun during the Bush years and continued without abatement in the era of Obama, many are detained for months—even years—without the benefit of legal representation or the right of review. Housed in facilities run by private corporate entities, many of their fundamental, internationally recognized human rights are violated—such as the freedom from arbitrary detention, the right to adequate health care while detained, and the ability to communicate with the outside world.[30] In this period of profound crisis an understanding of the past is more than an intellectual curiosity; it is a political necessity.

## Voices from the Past

While the implications of this narrative are beyond the local, the story contained within this book is, at heart, a community history. My primary goal has always been to tell this story *for* Latinas and Latinos in San Francisco, the people whose lives are represented in these pages. Surprisingly, this is the first historical monograph written about the general Latin American-descent population in San Francisco.[31] In a city known for its social heterogeneity and longstanding cosmopolitanism, where historical works have detailed most ethnic or racial groups in the city, this absence motivates my work.[32] In many corners of academia, the goal of excavating a community history, even when that story has not yet been recorded in a written form, is not in itself a worthy scholarly endeavor. The same is not true from the vantage point of the people whose lives we study as academics. The preservation of collective memory informs how we live in our present conditions.[33] It connects our present hopes and struggles with the legacies left by others. Perhaps most important, it enables us to envision a future based on our comprehension of this union of the past and present. Indeed, few things historians can do hold more significance for everyday people than retrieving and preserving a community's history.

To tell this story I put on center stage the voices of the people themselves. Each chapter begins with words written or spoken by a Latin American or Latino in San Francisco. During the research process I made a special effort to find sources containing these voices whenever possible. Letters and diaries, newspapers, public testimonies, and other documents often contained the thoughts and feelings of Latinos as they experienced life in the Bay Area. These comprise the heart of the social history contained in these pages. Of course, the historical record for this topic is also filled with profound gaps. In addition to the loss that comes with the passage of time, multiple fires and destructive natural disasters have further abated the data available to historians of San Francisco. As a final challenge, during the entire period under discussion, Latinos never composed more than 15 percent of San Francisco's total population, and more frequently they were less than that. Scattered sparsely through the area and highly marginalized, the Spanish-speaking rarely appear in traditional sources for historical study (mainstream newspapers, court and municipal records, etc.), which hardly seem to recognize their existence in the city, let alone provide a window on their daily lives. Accordingly, I purposefully reconstruct the story of Latino San Francisco through its most visible moments, when glimpses of the daily lives of everyday people emerge most completely from the records of the past. For the twentieth century, oral histories have helped fill in those gaps. Beginning with another oral history project in 1995, I have conducted more than thirty oral histories with San Franciscans. Most were everyday residents—working-class men and women who lived, worked, and struggled in the city. Only a small fraction of them are quoted here, but each, as part of a collective, has impacted this study. As oral historian Alessandro Portelli reminds us, "the unique and precious element which oral sources force upon the historian . . . is the speaker's subjectivity." All of the people who took time out of their busy lives to share their living memories help foster my own sense of this community through their subjective reference point. After all, an oral history "tells us less about events as such than about their meaning."[34] Their meanings, sometimes contested but often speaking with a remarkable unity of voice, directed my inquiry in innumerable ways, from identifying topics worthy of further research, to finding small enclaves that have long disappeared from any official memory, to locating archival sources that would have otherwise remained unearthed.

While I am not formally a part of the community in question, I do have a close relationship with it. In the summer of 1994 I arrived in the Bay Area as a graduate student. Having been born, raised, and educated in Southern California, I initially felt isolated and alone as I made the necessary adjustments to a new environment. Seeking the familiar, I decided to make one of my favorite meals—*enchiladas rojas*, or red sauce enchiladas. My local grocery store in Berkeley provided most of the ingredients, but I reached a culinary roadblock when it came to finding the dried *pasilla* and *ancho* chilies I used to make the sauce, unquestionably the most important ingredient. In my short time in Northern California I had already made a handful of visits to "the city" via the use of the Bay Area Rapid Transit (BART) system. Almost all of those initial trips were to the Castro District, entailing a short walk from the 16th Street Mission District BART station. Walking down 16th for the first time, the assortment of markets with displays of fresh produce and the familiar smells of the streets of a barrio immediately struck me as familiar. On subsequent walks I noticed the small *taquerías* and *panaderías*, bars blasting oldies and Vicente Fernández, and the church—Mission Dolores, the eponym of the district—overflowing with Sunday visitors. And so I ventured to the city once again, to the Mission, with the goal of finding my missing ingredients. I didn't need to walk more than a quarter of a block from the station before I found a local grocery store selling a selection of dried chilies. As I stood in line it occurred to me that for the first time I didn't feel out of place in the Bay Area. In the Spanish being spoken around me, in the look of the overstocked corner grocery, and in the smells of the foods in my hands and on the shelves, I had a profound sense of the familiar if not the familial. While the barrios I knew from my upbringing differed from the one I stood in now, the cultural composition of the Mission allowed me to feel at home, if only for a moment. At the same time, I recognized a distinct current of difference flowing through this community. Though I could not yet fully identify or articulate it, what my L.A. perspective labeled "difference" in the Mission is as important as the sameness binding it to other locales in the Chicano and Latino United States. As the impetus to my epiphanic encounter with the neighborhood, food also first illustrated the particularity of this neighborhood's story to me. The Mexican and Mexican American favorites of my youth—the *pan dulces*, the dried chiles, the oversized burritos—were all in ample supply in the Mission District of the 1990s. However, those Mexican flavors also share gastronomical space with popular items from Nicaragua and El Salvador. By no means rare in most Latin American enclaves, the presence of Central (and to some extent South) America in San Francisco is abundant. Restaurants offering Central American *empanadas* or *pupusas* revealed the presence of a large *nicaragüense* and *salvadoreño* population in the district.

Though the theoretical comprehension would not follow for some years, in those early visits to San Francisco's Mission District—the city's primary Latino barrio—I began to unpack the complex and interdependent relationships of geography, ethnicity, and community for the first time. My fascination with these cultural traits of the Mission District propelled my initial curiosity. They were further fed by my partial integration into a community with a powerfully rich and dynamic memory. At nearly every turn I have been amazed at the level of collective historical memory that lives and breathes in San Francisco. In casual conversations with people on the bus or BART, in formal oral interviews in their homes, and in the pictures, documents, and ephemera housed in innumerable "private archives," the people of San Francisco have done much of the research for a thousand books waiting to be written. This is more noteworthy in that these same years have witnessed profound dislocation and destruction at the community level, consequences of unfettered development, gentrification, and the "march of modernity." In some ways, of course, the crusade to preserve the past is a result of these processes—forces communicating the preciousness of stories through their very disregard of them.

My initial entry into the study of Latinos in San Francisco came simultaneously with my entry into the world of cultural and industrial geography. Though my journey in these academic realms never amounted to more than a tourist's expedition, I remained very intrigued by works exploring the spatial alongside race, class, and gender relations. As I developed my own sense of what "community" meant for Latinas and Latinos in the Bay Area, these definitions and scholarly explorations played, at times, foundational roles. Noteworthy among these works was Doreen Massey's *Space, Place, and Gender*, where the debates over concepts such as "place" and "space" first entered my thinking. Her explanation of how the "spatial is social relations 'stretched out'" made my first steps into this past as much about the study of a distinct geographic location (the place of San Francisco) as about the interrelations between people contained within this city. Her book framed these social relations as more than just events in the past. They became the vehicle imparting meaning into and onto the place for the people who lived there, meaning-making processes occurring over a century and in particular ways suited to the dynamic realities of those times. This union of time and space (or "space-time") promoted an understanding of the spatial "as an ever-shifting social geometry of power and significance" that "inherently implies the existence in the lived world of a simultaneous multiplicity of space: cross-cutting, intersecting, aligning with one another, or existing in relations of paradox or antagonism."[35] These understandings resonated with the history of community and identity I discovered, one marked by multiplicity and dynamism over time. If a common thread existed within the span of time it was the "geometry of social/power relations" that structured the local and "stretched beyond— the global as part of what constitutes the local, the outside as part of the inside." This context, one that "challenges any possibility of claims to internal histories or to timeless identities," forced me to think about this story as playing out in spaces much wider than those contained by the city's forty-seven square miles.[36]

As I participated in a diffuse but collective process of excavating and preserving the meanings of the past, my initial goal was to tell the very specific story of how the Mission District "became Latino." The processes undergirding Latinization as well as it limits and fissures not only interested me but also constituted something of importance to the community I had begun to know. I thought this would manifest as a sixties and seventies story of spatial and cultural transformation, including identity and institution building, mass movements, and community formation. As I became more involved in the research process I explored further back in time. The more I bore witness to the emerging movement against gentrification and to the repeated commemorations of loss taking place in the Mission District at the turn of the twenty-first century, the less the recent past of the Latino Mission District seemed like history. This story still breathed and lived, producing more questions and fewer answers, and sending me into an increasing number of archives. What I discovered there were the stories not often told, and sometimes no longer remembered. The story of the *La Misión*, which began for so many after their arrival in the city following the Second World War, had deeper roots. By reconstructing the history of Latin American–descent migrants in San Francisco from the Gold Rush to the early 1970s, I intend *Latinos at the Golden Gate* to serve as a kind of prologue to the present community. Although I cover a broad expanse of time and a diverse collection of human lives, at no time did I entertain the fantasy that this book is complete. I have written it, rather deliberately, with a profound sense of its limits, as well as with the hope that others will someday fill in the gaps and further develop our understanding of this rich past.

As I write these words and, more than likely, as you read them, someone in Latin America is leaving their home. They are beginning a journey northward, a journey whose end is less than certain. If they survive the many perils along the way—an exploitative smuggling industry, hunger and dehydration, exposure to the elements, a highly militarized border—some will successfully enter the United States. A complex of forces has shaped the context of their movements to the United States and will continue to do so within it. Their unfolding stories are, likewise, impossible to dislodge from this nexus of power. Such was the case with the nine-year-old Honduran boy found near Los Angeles railroad tracks in 1998. When a police officer took him into custody, he learned the boy had migrated in search of his mother. For three months he had struggled and survived, "guided only by his cunning" and the knowledge of where she had migrated to earlier. His one question to everyone he met had been: "How do I get to San Francisco?"[37] As the stories contained within this book show, this single question has intersected with the lives of thousands of Latin Americans for almost two centuries.

## CHAPTER ONE

# But Things Will Soon Take Change

*Race and Power in Gold Rush San Francisco*

"Without a doubt, the country is very rich," wrote a young Peruvian from San Francisco at the height of the Gold Rush. Constituting an early wave of gold seekers, Peruvians, along with Latin Americans from ports in Mexico and Chile, provided their fellow countrymen firsthand evaluations of the widespread claims of easy work for instant wealth in California. While this *argonauta* found that the mines "daily revealed themselves to be more full" of gold, he also believed only "those adept to hard work" should risk this change in occupation, declaring that "many of those who have come from faraway lands, without a goal other than mining gold, would have been better having never left their homes." His reckoning with hard work for dubious return was not the only experience shaping his view. The lack of safety, he wrote, "here reduced to a pair of guns in the pocket, infuses terror: there is no more law than the one the North Americans call 'Lynch law.'"[1]

While numerous observations and encounters likely framed this Peruvian's assessment, Latin American experiences with violence and justice in early Gold Rush California were not always so hopeless. On July 15, 1849, "a large party of armed Americans" violently attacked Chileans and other Latin Americans throughout San Francisco. Described as "an association or society of young men" by the local press, the gang called themselves the "Hounds" and had recently developed a reputation for attacking "defenseless and ignorant foreigners."[2] On this night they committed numerous offenses, including sacking tents occupied by Chileans, stealing or damaging their possessions, and physically abusing the residents themselves. By the next morning, the Hounds had stolen approximately $6,300, caused thousands more in damage, and assaulted thirty-eight men and women, raping at least one, and shooting at least two.[3] Far from naturalizing these acts of violence against "foreigners," the following day, a throng of residents responded with outrage. Gathering in the plaza that afternoon, unofficial local leaders organized "the largest public meeting ever held in San Francisco." The amazingly efficient caucus resulted in the creation of a legal infrastructure to address the crimes, including the election of a judge, a district attorney, counsel for the defense, and a grand jury. The mass meeting also organized attendees into a volunteer police force of 230 men to round up the perpetrators and agreed to the establishment of a relief effort for the "sufferers by the riots." Less than one month later, the newly designed legal system of the city convicted several members of the gang, including their leader, a man named Samuel Roberts.[4]

This chapter excavates these seemingly contradictory positions—where Latinos are objects of both racial violence and municipal protection—analyzing their emergence from within the story of the California Gold Rush. Indeed, the multinational and panethnic features of Latinos in San Francisco have their roots in these tumultuous times. The lure of gold motivated the movement of Latin Americans—*patrones* and *peones* alike—as early as 1848, often months before the same phenomenon touched other parts of the globe. Chileans, Mexicans, and Peruvians, in particular, benefited from proximity as well as preexisting networks of communication and travel between their ports and the Golden Gate. In turn, those networks played significant roles in the city's dynamic economic transformation during the period, as this once distant outpost of the Mexican Republic emerged as a "Pacific metropolis" and a center of U.S. trade in the Pacific.[5] New commerce between San Francisco and distinct parts of Latin America resulted, facilitating further migrations of those seeking wealth and a new life abroad. In short, San Francisco became an urban metropolis with a transnational reach, grasping the markets and people of Latin America. This chapter explores these connections for the ways they enabled the later growth of Latino community in the city.

More important, this period also determined how Latin Americans and their descendants encountered the city, how the new and ever-shifting social order integrated and marginalized them, shaping the contours of later struggles to forge community along linguistic and religious, if not cultural, lines. Latin Americans encountered both violence and prosperity in Gold Rush San Francisco. In "a time and place wherein diverse peoples competed over resources, notions of social order, and definitions and distributions of wealth and power,"[6] Latin American experiences simultaneously exhibited the possibility of pluralism and helped define its limits. Although the multiracial promise of full social integration did not manifest itself equitably, its expressions were not rare. In time, however, this possibility gave way to powerful and all-too familiar forms of racial hierarchy, locating "whiteness" as an undisputed norm while marginalizing others, including Latin Americans, in a complex schema of diminishing rights.

The unique social position indicated by these simultaneous reports of the application of "Lynch law" and the legal protection of group rights is hardly an aberration of the time. It suggests the instability and multiplicity of Latin American life in San Francisco. Within the social and legal fabrics—materials woven in the early statehood period—Latin American residents of the city enjoyed a unique status among the "foreign" (non-U.S.) born as something of a naturalized feature of the frontier terrain, deserving of some rights within the new social and political systems. While the swift attention given to the events of July 1849 suggests an assortment of forces (ranging from the need to protect private property to the fruitful conditions for mob action), it also clearly reflects a measure of social integration, as both formal and informal leaders met racially motivated acts of violence with concern, facilitating the creation of legal proceedings. Simultaneously, as demographic change begat familiar "forms of social and economic organization"—helping to make San Francisco "look and feel American"[7]—Latin Americans often served as but one object of a racialist system taking root. By the mid-1850s, while the Spanish-speaking exerted a measured though diminishing political and economic influence in other parts of the state,[8] in San Francisco they had been more quickly relegated to the subordinate position characteristic of a nonwhite population, living in a society ever more reflective of the ways power intersected with deep-seated ideas of race, class, nationality, and gender.

## Before the Rush

Mineral discoveries aside, San Francisco Bay seemed destined for commercial development, though the scope of its potential escaped even the most prescient observers of the early nineteenth century. In 1841, the commanding general of the northern district of Alta California—Mariano Guadalupe Vallejo—with his rich history and deep knowledge of the region, lamented the distance between economic potentials and realities in this, the northernmost sector of the Mexican Republic. California, he wrote, "is a country that is so promising but which can accomplish nothing; for its happiness is conditional, and its misery positive." Distance and the troubles of the early Republic inspired Mexico's neglect of California, and this, in turn, had begun to foment resentment on the part of many *californios*, the Mexicans who called the land their own. By the 1840s this was accentuated by the growth of a modest economy marked by trade in otter and beaver pelts, hide and tallow, whaling, and other forms of commercial enterprise, all highlighting the potential promise of development. Mexico's inattention, then, coexisted with the region's emerging integration in global economic networks spanning the Pacific, ones in which ships sailing under U.S., British, and various European flags at least minimally connected China, Mexico, the Sandwich Islands (Hawai'i), and Chile to ports like San Francisco. Such economic realities certainly informed analysis by Vallejo, already the wealthiest man north of Monterey. In his estimation, however, a glaring limitation countered the natural attributes and commercial potential of the bay, stifling its future. "Its geographic location, the mildness of its climate, the fertility of its soil, amenity of its fields, the safety of its ports, among which that of San Francisco deserves to rank among the principle ones of the world, its navigable rivers and inlets, etc. guarantee it a state of prosperity which it is not permitted to attain, due to its lack of population," he wrote.[9] Less than a decade later, "a tide of humanity"[10] washed ashore in San Francisco and other parts of California, reshaping its future in profound ways and unleashing the potential Vallejo had foreseen. Although Vallejo himself lost more than he gained in the aftermath, to our modern-day ear his analysis resonates like a prophecy fulfilled.

The history of Latin Americans in San Francisco is inseparable from the Gold Rush. However, if not for an earlier set of economic forces giving rise to trade networks between Latin America and San Francisco, that golden phenomenon might have transpired quite differently for the Spanish-speaking. A component of Vallejo's projections, these networks would later mature to constitute both the foundation and direct byproduct of the city's unique position under U.S. dominion, when the port city served as the "capital, for fifty years, of the western empire" and a base for securing U.S. influence abroad.[11] The mass movement of wealth-seekers, which gave rise to so much of California's uniqueness—in both fact and hyperbole—solidified San Francisco's position in the hemisphere by making it the first major "American" city of the West Coast, and the entrepôt of U.S./California trade and commerce in the Pacific. By 1848, mere months after the conclusion of the war in which the United States appropriated California by treaty, most newcomers and new commerce to the territory were drawn to the Golden Gate as their entry point.

San Francisco's commercial position took shape throughout the early nineteenth century. In his iconic history of California, Hubert Howe

Bancroft analyzed the 1830s in Yerba Buena—the name the Spanish and Mexicans used for the small outpost and anchorage point in the bay—as "monotonous and uneventful."[12] With only a handful of structures on the peninsula by the decade's end, his assessment as a European American is unsurprising. However, the San Francisco Bay, and the Yerba Buena outpost in particular, did not escape all attention in this period. Somewhat protected from coastal winds affecting nearly all other natural ports along the Pacific Coast, the anchorage point near Telegraph Hill provided support to robust regional commerce. As Richard Henry Dana described in his 1835 visit to the bay, "boats manned by Indians, and capable of carrying nearly a thousand hides apiece, are attached to the missions [in Santa Clara and San Jose], and sent down to the vessels [at Yerba Buena] with hides, to bring away goods in return."[13] The depth of Yerba Buena, and its location relative to the shallower tributaries connecting the bay to these hide sources, nurtured this nascent trade. Whalers also made Yerba Buena a regular stop in the 1820s and 1830s. Coming from France, Britain, Russia, and the United States, these hunters worked off the coasts of California, stopping at the Golden Gate to gather provisions before heading back out to sea.[14] Whaling ships from New England, in particular, used the port as a temporary home decades before the Gold Rush. They forged direct economic networks that linked their financial success in the U.S. East to the Golden Gate, as they built the shared knowledge of navigating from their home market around the horn to California. These networks were harbingers of things to come.

Of course, transnational commerce carried with it a looming threat. Mexico's loss of Texas in 1836 communicated an early warning to the young Latin American Republic of the possible consequences of allowing a foreign commercial presence, especially one with origins in the United States. In the late 1830s, one Mexican official said of his country's northern neighbor, "Instead of armies, battles, and invasions, which raise such uproar and generally prove abortive, [they] use means which, considered separately, seem slow, ineffectual, and sometimes palpably absurd, but which united, and in the course of time, are certain and irresistible."[15] San Francisco certainly proved his point. As a result of these commercial networks and other enterprises, a small settlement of "Yankees" and Europeans joined the slightly more numerous Mexicans in Yerba Buena by the early 1840s, receiving grants of small lots and further encouraging new construction.[16] The same networks facilitated U.S. control during the war, and the movement of people and goods after 1848.[17] When the news of gold discovered at Sutter's Mill began to spread, New England merchants became among the first groups to profit from trade to San Francisco. In some cases, their "blubber hunters" were even converted into cargo vessels.[18]

Formal U.S. occupation of California and its northern bay represented the most important development in this early period. During the course of the U.S.-Mexico War, Yerba Buena and most of Northern California passed into U.S. hands with minimal formal violence. Though U.S. forces occupied and controlled San Francisco by midsummer 1846, the process of fully transferring and transforming the territory still lay ahead. The U.S. military oversaw this process, asserting control over the territory and bay while also furthering its position in the competition for economic profit. Displacing Mexican government officials, U.S. military commanders assumed positions of power while controlling as much of the local government system as possible. In these actions they sought to create an air of peace and consistency among the Mexican and, to a lesser extent, Indian populations of the districts of the area. After some dispute over which military representative would rightfully lead, Stephen W. Kearny, the brigadier general responsible for the land conquest of the soon-to-be U.S. Southwest, assumed the position of military governor over the entire territory of California. He took up residence in Monterey, a former capital of the territory under Mexican rule. In March 1847, Kearny issued a proclamation expressing "instructions from the President." A reprinted version ran in both English and Spanish in every issue of the fledgling San Francisco–based newspaper the *California Star* beginning the same month. In it, Kearny pledged "to respect and protect the religious institutions of California" and "protect the persons and property of the quiet and peaceable inhabitants." Finally, he expressed the wish of the U.S. government to extend the rights of a free democracy, absolving "all the inhabitants of California from any further allegiance to the Republic of Mexico" and announcing that they would be considered citizens of the United States.[19] Reflecting the kinds of mythical history promoted by the mission of Manifest Destiny, Kearny characterized U.S. occupation as an end to a past history of violence. California, he said, "suffered greatly from domestic troubles; civil wars have been the poisoned fountains which have sent forth trouble and pestilence over her beautiful land." Now that "the Star Spangled Banner floats over California," progress and development could be unleashed to the betterment of all "natives of the land."[20]

Kearny's proclamation assigned meaning to set of historical events that were still unfolding. Kearny gives us a fuller understanding of the project of war after military events have ceased. His words, laden with imagery and racial assumptions regarding all parties involved, are a powerful reminder of the conscious way the United States formally approached the work of extending its domain. Kearny knew the goal of bringing the territory under full control of the United States was far less a military battle than a political one, a contest of ideas framing past and future actions. Rather than allow the violence and conflict in the region to be attributed to the active military campaign he led, he relocated it in California's Spanish and Mexican pasts, predating his arrival. He characterized U.S. expansion in an exceptional manner, depicting it as a harbinger of peace and order. In his role as occupying military commander, Kearny crafted the parameters of inclusion and exclusion in a society not yet formed as he pledged to protect the inhabitants, "against all or any of their enemies, whether from abroad or at home; and when he now assures the Californians that it will be his duty and his pleasure to comply with these instructions, he calls upon them all to exert themselves in preserving order and tranquility, in promoting harmony and concord and in maintaining the authority and efficiency of the law."[21] Instrumental to this phase of the empire-building process, Kearny took control of naming and describing the U.S. project, how it related to peace and conflict, and how it remained focused on "law." All these strategies would prove valuable in framing a base on which future actions could be judged, contextualized, and regulated.

Using this powerful imagery, Kearny—as the official representative of the United States—articulated the national commitment to realizing the promise of California, for both native and newcomer, terms now undergoing a tumultuous redefinition. Despite assuring the local population of the protections that came with U.S. occupation, in the months immediately following his statement, the interests of the "others who have found home in her bosom" would seem to predominate, often at the expense of "the natives of the land." For example, nine days after issuing his first proclamation to the people of California, Kearny published another. This time, he released beach and water lots along the east front of the town for sale to the public.[22] The land in question became among the most valuable in the city as the site of the official port, protected from the open sea and in perfect position for business both within the city and with other parts of the bay. Kearny's replacement, Governor Richard B. Mason, and the appointed *alcalde* of San Francisco, George Hyde, continued this process of land sale as a means of generating revenue for the town, though *californios* held title to much of the property being sold.[23] By the end of the summer of 1847, more than 1,200 lots had been surveyed and made available on the open market. The most inexpensive sold for $12, the most coveted (along the coast and future port) sold for as much as $600 at auction.[24] A local regulation stipulated that no one man could buy more than one lot, but a commentary in the *Star* lamented the reports of speculators arranging the purchase of several lots "by buying other men's names."[25] The history of land speculation in San Francisco had begun.

The transfer of land from the "natives" to the "newcomers" reflects a pattern marking the military occupation period. Though war had not ceased, and no agreement for peace had even begun to be negotiated (let alone written), the United States made it clear that California would be "American," as well as what this would mean in practice. Rather than provide for the wartime governance of the territory, military governors were providing for the eventual transfer of the territory into U.S. hands. Changes in this period reflect their success in attaining this objective. In August 1847, a local report detailed the growth of the population by "at least one hundred percent," identifying 375 total "whites" and only 26 "Indians."[26] These numbers suggest a drastic decline in the Mexican and Indian populations once recorded as residents of the area. As the numbers of U.S. citizens grew—their ownership of the land secured and protected by the military government—the numbers of the former residents dropped inversely. Among the "white" population, the published survey recorded thirty Mexican Californians and two Mexicans born in other parts of Mexico. These thirty-two, the author wrote, "constitute the entire Mexican population."[27]

As striking as the decline in the Mexican population and the movement to smoothly transfer ownership of property, the continued growth of commerce also heralded the dawn of a new day in San Francisco. In no small way a motivation for the expansionist war, the anticipated end to hostilities inspired grand U.S. economic plans. In a letter published in the *California Star*, U.S. vice president George M. Dallas wrote, "The war with Mexico should be turned to good account. It may be made to produce consequences far more important than the mere acquisition of territory. If properly ended, it must lead to an almost boundless enlargement of our commerce to new channels and spheres of trade, and to great markets for our produce and manufactures."[28] This vision, once implemented, formed the material structure of empire for San Francisco. In the ensuing decades, it promoted transnationalism via the continued establishment of economic connections between the port and distinct parts of the world, connections nurturing a unique cosmopolitanism. As local residents officially renamed Yerba Buena after the bay called "San Francisco," the small hamlet also witnessed an almost immediate growth in ship-based commerce. According to Bancroft, between 1847 and 1848 San Francisco had become the primary port of entry to the territory, "doing more business probably than all the others combined, and attracting some attention as a Pacific metropolis threatening the supremacy of Honolulu."[29] In the year ending in April 1848, records indicated the arrival of eighty-five merchant vessels in the port. They traded goods to and from markets around the hemisphere, primarily in Hawai'i but also in the Mexican port of Mazatlán (in the state of Sinaloa), Chile, Oregon, and the United States proper.[30] In this brief period—two years before the news of mineral deposits in the American River would circumnavigate the globe—the port and pueblo of San Francisco had thus begun to emerge as a "Pacific metropolis" and a center (with Latin American ports like Valparaíso) of Pacific trade.[31]

In the years during and following the Gold Rush, the free movement of people and goods would eclipse any that western history had yet witnessed and alter the San Francisco landscape for all, including Mexican *californios* and Latin American newcomers. For many of the Latin Americans traveling through these networks, San Francisco became their first home in the new "U.S. West." There, the commercial possibilities that moved them from one part of the hemisphere to another also promoted the creation of networks to facilitate their survival and success: fellow Spanish speakers who could provide information, food, shelter, and even transportation to the goldfields. After working their fill, or to escape the harsh winters of the gold regions and take a break, many found their way back to the town of San Francisco, their original entry point into California. This migration, buttressed by a robust commercial relationship between San Francisco and Latin American ports, gave birth to the town's first pan–Latin American community.

## California Gold and Latin America

The January 1848 discovery of gold by John Marshall and a team of workers under the employ of John Sutter built on this past. The formal conclusion of the U.S. war with Mexico nine days after the discovery provided the stage for the transformations which would follow, but gold most certainly provided the historical impetus. In the spring and early summer of 1848, the discovery seemed to be of minor significance until word slowly spread, first to the towns of California and then West, South, East, and beyond. If the legendary tale is to be believed, rumors had already infected the small population in San Francisco by late spring, when Sam Brannan—a Mormon sojourner who would later rise to business and civic prominence in the fledgling metropolis—provided a boost of credibility by riding through the countryside and into town with a sack of nuggets and dust, exclaiming: "Gold! Gold! Gold from the American River!"[32] An exodus overtook the town as people dropped what they were doing to go test their fortunes. U.S. soldiers in Monterey and elsewhere abandoned their posts, and the various ships in harbor lost most of their crews to desertion. Even the *California Star*—the region's only newspaper—ceased publication in June when its editor and staff left for the diggings.[33] Throughout the summer, the reports of mineral discoveries spread via word of mouth until late fall, when they also began to appear in U.S. newspapers. In December 1848, President James K. Polk told Congress of the "abundance of gold [in California] . . . of such an extraordinary character," legitimizing the rumors of instant wealth and further fueling the mass movement of the subsequent year.[34]

Seemingly overnight, more than 100,000 people made their way to the goldfields, primarily in the northern and eastern parts of the territory. Tens of thousands entered California via San Francisco, infusing a growth none could have anticipated. In the next three years, San Francisco grew from a town of fewer than 1,000 to a city of more than 30,000 permanent residents from nations all over the world.[35] Thousands more would pass through the city temporarily, either on their way to the goldfields or while waiting for a ship to return home. The majority of newcomers would come from the eastern seaboard of the United States: Pennsylvania, New York, and New England. The quest for instant riches, however, promoted a distinctly diverse population surge for both California and San Francisco. In national terms, Mexico, England, Germany, France, Ireland, and various South American republics were but a few of the places newcomers abandoned in search of wealth. Breaking with the pattern of most "frontier" settlements, California's population in 1850 contained a high proportion of foreign-born (in this instance defined as not born in the United States), easily over 25 percent.[36] San Francisco drove much of these trends, with a census in 1852 placing the foreign-born at over half of the city's total population.[37] No matter their origin, the majority of new arrivals saw themselves as temporary migrants seeking to "get rich—preferably quickly—and return home."[38] Of those who chose to stay, most settled in San Francisco, by 1860 home to more than a sixth of the state's population.[39]

Established commercial links and geographic proximity combined to favor Latin American gold seekers, efficiently moving both information and people within a shorter timeframe. Latin American ports circulated the rumors of gold noticeably earlier than the news traveled in the United States, even corroborating reports as ships under their flags returned from San Francisco with proof. The first ship to purchase gold in San Francisco, for example, sailed under the Chilean flag. When the *J.R.S.* returned to Valparaíso in August 1848 its captain brought with him a crew depleted of all its young men and geological evidence of why so many had deserted.[40] While the news caused anything but a mad rush—the news from the *J.R.S.* escaped mention in local newspapers—less than one month later a ship departed the same port filled with Chilean *argonautas*. With a travel time of only about 60–70 days, the distance between Chile and California (a mere 6,700 miles, compared to more than 19,000 from New York) proved advantageous, with many *chilenos* arriving before those in the eastern U.S. had even heard the news.

Some Latin Americans also benefited from a functional proximity, erected on the trade and commercial connections spanning the earlier decades. Interestingly, these linkages extended beyond the nautical. For example, even before 1848, Alta California represented something of a refuge for displaced Mexicans from the northern state of Sonora. Attacks by Apache and other Native Americans hostile to Mexican settlement made life unpredictable and dangerous, sometimes as far inland as Hermosillo and Ures, and economic and class realignment wrought by mission secularization in the 1830s left many laborers unprotected in other ways.[41] Known for their mining skills and knowledge, Sonorans also came to Alta California to employ their expertise. When an earlier gold discovery was made near the former Misión San Fernando Rey de España (in present-day Southern California), Sonorans were recruited to work the placer, and did so to some success. The migratory and economic interrelations between Sonora and California were extensive, which some found threatening to U.S. hegemony. For instance, when Colonel Richard B. Mason crafted a temporary civil government in late 1847, he closed California to further Sonoran migrants and required those already in the territory to report their business to U.S. officials in Monterey or Los Angeles.[42] Bonded by "commerce and a complex web of family and social relationships" predating U.S. acquisition, however, many in Sonora "viewed California as a natural extension of their state."[43] These economic networks coupled with Sonora's healthy export economy to transform the geographically isolated state into something of a cosmopolitan society, awash with news from Europe and North America as well as entrepreneurs from France, Britain, Germany, and the United States.[44] While U.S. citizens, Sonorans, and the native-Mexican descent population of *californios* in California were the first to receive word of Sutter's find, a multitude of migrants from Sonora—including Americans integrated into the local economy—were perhaps the earliest to make the journey northward.

The emergence of a pan–Latin American descent population in Gold Rush San Francisco rested on these types of interconnections, shrinking the distance between California and Latin America via established migratory routes as well as commercial and informational exchange. After October 1848, when Mexican newspapers provided definitive reports on the mineral wealth of California, the "great migration" of Sonorans worried state officials concerned about the loss of labor and the vanishing buffer of settlers on their insecure frontier.[45] All told, as many as 10,000 Sonorans made the journey north, the successes of the early gold seekers propelling later migrants. As one *sonorense* estimated, "everyone had a son, brother, uncle, father, cousin, husband, or relative working in the bonanza." These migrants represented anything but a monolithic wave. Men formed the largest contingent, yet it was not uncommon for entire families to make the journey north.[46] Indicative of this, as well as of Sonorans' tendency toward collective enterprise, contemporaries in California regularly testified to "gangs" of Sonorans traveling as families and in convoys as large as several score, often for safety.[47] Businessmen venturing to profit more from California's commercial prospects than its mineral ones added to this diversity, with many relocating to exploit new markets for their products. Sonoran merchants and ranchers represented some of the first to profit from the discovery in 1848. Most *sonorenses* earned their reputation for success in the more physically demanding and highly competitive diggings. When journalist Bayard Taylor arrived in the summer of 1849, he witnessed "Sonorians" visibly profiting while others struggled, outpacing rivals to such a degree that "Americans employed Sonorians and Indians to work for them, giving them half the gold and finding them in provisions."[48]

Contract employment shaped the migration and labor of more than a few Sonorans, in some cases even facilitating the prospect of wealth for both parties. How many Sonorans came as free laborers and how many came under some form of contract is impossible to determine accurately, although most likely came unencumbered. Various forms of contract labor were already familiar to *sonorenses*, with "free labor" often existing "side by side with indentured labor" in the Mexican state. Laws regulated servitude, delineating diminished citizenship rights for servants, regulating the contracts for their labor, and protecting against their flight.[49] Contracts requiring unsupervised travel and work over such long distances, however, demanded "a degree of loyalty" suggestive of more personal relations between both parties, albeit ones still steeped in hierarchy. Sonoran elites benefited from these relations, sending trusted servants to California to dig for them, while making necessary allowances. Antonio Uruchurtu, for example, contracted with some of his servants "for a term of six months to be employed at the location or locations which their employer should find convenient to assign their work in the Alta California territory, today part of the United States of America." In his agreement, Uruchurtu agreed to provide his servants horses for transportation, room and board, and a salary of $8 per month, while also agreeing to one free day a week (in addition to Sunday) when the workers might enjoy "the fruit of their own labor." The parties also agreed that in the event of a "case of good fortune," the servants would fulfill their contract to him or else be further bound by a work commitment upon their return. Similarly, Juan Camou sent eight of his servants under contract, agreeing to pay them ten pesos "for 24 days of work every month, and a ration of corn." While this contract allowed for a larger number of "free days," the gold his servants found during those days remained with their employer's share, to be returned to them only at the end of their contract.[50]

These features of economic and social life in Mexico also characterized Chile during the same period, shaping its own exodus of gold seekers. After independence from Spain, a transnational shipping economy transformed port cities like Valparaíso and Talcahuano into cosmopolitan centers for trade and commerce. In the month before the *J.R.S.* returned to port with its sample of gold, twenty-five non-Chilean ships "called" at the port, "all engaged in routine business." Fourteen sailed under the British flag—the British being most common visitors to Chile at the time—with six from the United States and the remaining five from France.[51] Chile's own merchant fleet had extensive connections to ports throughout Latin America, including California, selling metal, grain, flour, lumber, and coal to ports in Mexico, Peru, Ecuador, and New Granada (Panama and Colombia).[52] Chile's climate was similar to California's, and centuries of Spanish colonialism had shaped an economy composed of agriculture, ranching, and mining. Its large class of laborers was composed of both *inquilinos*—workers for large landowners who were given land in exchange for their service—and "unattached, landless, and mobile people who engaged in seasonal labor and lived more precariously," called *peones* or *gañanes*.[53] These laborers' fortunes were dependent on a host of unpredictable factors, the dictates of a small *hacendado* class among them. Not surprisingly, then, the prospect of independent wealth attracted not only a large share of *inquilinos* and *peones*, but also semiaffluent families aspiring to become regional elites.

In November 1848, Valparaíso began to bid farewell to hundreds of *chilenos* bound for California. In less than one year's time, more than 3,000 set sail, most of them from the poorer classes.[54] The initial wave of

Spanish-speaking migrants was comprised of independent miners who survived, as historian Susan Lee Johnson notes, through the joining of households to split profits, divide work, or share domestic costs.[55] A mix of *inquilinos* and *peones*, these laborers possessed little more than the physical ability to forage for wealth and status. Newspapers also reported the departure of more than a few notable citizens among the masses, men making the journey with more than hopes and dreams. As reported, one traveled with "four *indios*" and several more with "groups of ten or more *peones*."[56] The class diversity of South American sojourners framed the contexts within which they migrated to and labored in California, with contracted laborers—hired by those with enough wealth to organize gold-seeking teams—joining independent miners in the diggings. Vicente Pérez Rosales provides one example. Born into a "prominent family" with both land and wealth, Pérez Rosales received a formal European education in his youth but witnessed the decline of his familial fortunes in adulthood. Eager to reclaim them, he engaged in various profitable enterprises ranging from trade to mining, but prospects in California seemed to hold greater promise. Along with three half brothers and another relation, he traveled with two *inquilinos* and three *peones*. His journals describe neither the terms of their contract nor the roles each laborer performed, but both classes are clearly represented as "subservient to Pérez Rosales."[57]

Latin Americans thus found themselves the beneficiaries of an advantageous state of connectivity, linking them to San Francisco with a greater ease and frequency of travel than those in the eastern United States enjoyed. After all, as Carey McWilliams has noted, California remained largely isolated from the United States in 1848, "2,000 miles removed from the western edge of the frontier."[58] Situated either beyond a stretch of land not yet integrated into the nation, or across two vast oceans, California and San Francisco were both land and sea frontiers.[59] The sea routes from Mexico and South America to San Francisco, however, provided passage without crossing through a remote borderland. This benefited the first Latin Americans who came as miners as well as those who came as merchants. When the Peruvian newspaper *La Aurora* announced the discovery in November 1848, it suggested some of these alternative ways to profit. "The most needed articles," it read, "such as clothing, *barretas*, knives, shoes, etc., have risen extraordinarily in price."[60] Chilean accounts confirmed the inflationary effect for local merchants. "It is true that everything, absolutely everything, had begun to leave Chile, and with extravagant prices, because Californian customers had ample gold to pay, and the circumstance had to be taken advantaged of."[61] When Pérez Rosales arrived, he found stores loaded with Chilean jerked beef, gunpowder, brandy, and flour—a sack of the last commodity fetching its "weight in gold."[62]

Although longer in distance from the eastern seaboard of the United States than overland passages, the speed and reliability of the Latin American sea routes also brought the first gold seekers from the United States. For those in the eastern states, the journey to California could take place via one of three possible routes: by one of various difficult overland passages; by ship around the South American continent; or by ship to the Isthmus of Panama (or other location), overland to the Pacific, and then by ship again to San Francisco. Overland through the width of the North American continent, the passage could be difficult and long. On a horse, a traveler could expect a two- to three-month journey, while by wagon the trip could take three to five months. More significant, the elements and the prospect of contact with unknown Native American tribes made survival less than certain. The passage by ship, while longer if one chose to go around the continent, offered the passenger greater comfort, safety, and certainty than did land.[63]

Framed by this context, the relationship between California and Latin America in this era nurtured an interesting phenomenon. Simply put, for many coming from the Atlantic states, California existed on the other side of Latin America. A journey to the port of San Francisco meant boarding a ship in one of several ports in the eastern (or southern) United States, sailing southward, and passing through one or more parts of Latin American countries. Passengers choosing the shortest route would disembark in one of several Caribbean ports and rely on Latin American residents to guide them through jungles and forests to the Pacific, before finding passage on another ship heading northward to the Golden Gate. If they chose the longer—but often safer—route, they were still likely to stop in at least one Latin American port (usually Valparáiso or Talcahuano in Chile, or Acapulco or Mazatlán in Mexico) before arriving in San Francisco. Either way, passage to San Francisco meant passage through Latin America, as well as encounters with Latin Americans. This reality of travel to California and San Francisco sheds light on the fundamental ways power and race—to say nothing of class, gender, and nationality—were constructed in Gold Rush–era San Francisco. For many of the forty-niners, their experiences in Latin America (and even California) would be their first with non-Anglo- or African-descent populations. In their journals and letters, they did little to hide their preconceived prejudices, as they applied their ideas of manifest superiority to the new situations in which they found themselves. Once these travelers settled in San Francisco, they would recreate and reconfigure their imported racism, thus continuing to transform the roles afforded Latin Americans in the city.

The journey of Nelson Kingsley is representative of many of these trends. Kingsley left New Haven, Connecticut, for San Francisco as part of a joint financial venture in March 1849. A seemingly religious and prudish man, Kingsley would later write of his anxiety as the bark *Anna Reynolds*, on which he had booked passage, prepared for the journey around "the Horn." During its journey, the ship stopped in numerous British- and other European-controlled ports. The trip through the Strait of Magellan excited him and his associates as they headed toward the Chilean port of Talcahuano, near Concepción. There, they set foot on dry land for the first time in weeks, able to fortify their supplies with fresh food and water.[64]

Kingsley's first impressions of Chile and the people of Talcahuano and Concepción are fairly positive. He was almost surprised at the cultural and economic dynamism of the busy port, in stark contrast to the assumed simplicity of Latin America. Kingsley met Chileans, European emigrants, and others from the United States. He listened to classical music played by a local, wealthy woman while visiting her family. He also observed life and culture in smaller towns away from the bustling port. In Concepción for the anniversary of Chilean independence, Kingsley and some of his associates joined in the celebration. He wrote in his journal, "They are much in favor with Americans who are free like themselves."[65] However, Kingsley was also quick to compare the society he encountered with his beloved United States, writing that the Chileans fell "far short of the true light of Democracy. No one is allowed to vote but the aristocracy and Church & State are hand-in-hand."[66] With the cultural zeal of a people who defined themselves as a model of civilization, and a passionate belief in the ingenuity of his own country, Kingsley sprinkled his journal with his assessments of Chileans' limitations, describing them in contrast to the inherent potential for progress he identified in their position as a port of growing significance, as well as in their natural resources. In short, all they really lacked were North Americans. "It seems that yankees [*sic*] do better here than the natives as their aptness is much admired by people of this country as concerns business of any kind. And a thorough-going, business like, yankee can do well here, although they are somewhat prejudiced against foreigners."[67] Of Concepción he wrote, "A Yankee mechanic can do well here with good behavior, as virtue is a scarce article among them and where it is found is cherished by all."[68]

Like that of many other forty-niners, Kingsley's passage through Latin America and into California also brought him into contact with Catholic societies and customs for the first time. Reflecting the prejudices and biases of the kinds of anti-Catholic rhetoric of the times, Catholic traditions often fascinated Anglo-Protestant minds. One wrote of the "formalities and rites of the Catholic Church in all their bigotry and supstition [*sic*]."[69] Kingsley suggested that the Chileans' faith made them uncivilized or even inhuman. "A day or two since I saw a man carrying a small box with a number of women and children following him which proved to be the corps [*sic*] of a small child. All seemed to be merry on their way to the burying place."[70] The Catholic faith, seen as a remnant of "old world" ways of thinking, inspired one U.S. observer to write, "Chile is at the present time three hundred years behind us."[71]

Undoubtedly, travel through Latin America often proved challenging and exasperating. Major ports were crowded with gold seekers, pawns of their own ignorance of the region and an inflationary economy providing profitable opportunities for locals. One New Englander sardonically described how his party "got our lodgings on the ground floor of [a] bamboo hut, without any blanket but just as we lay in our wet clothes, paying 25 cts each for the privellege [*sic*]."[72] When passage entailed a land crossing through Central America, migrants relied on locals to facilitate their safe and quick passage, a relationship easily exploited for profit. The same New Englander angrily wrote, "This is one of their modes of swindling: to agree to deliver baggage at Panama [City] in season for the steamer, and then purposely delay it, so that the owners must either go on without it or wait in Panama a fortnight as I did."[73] Crowds and poor living conditions also brought the rampant spread of disease, fueled by the convergence of diverse germ pools from across the globe. Taken together, these conditions most surely colored their more negative assessments.

Further complicating their relationship with the region and its people, many U.S. gold seekers experienced a profound sense of competition with Latin Americans, in particular those they saw as racially nonwhite. Testament to the ways nationalism and racialist assumptions strengthened a more basic condition—the advantage of time and place enjoyed by the Spanish-speaking—one New Yorker even tried to stem the tide of "natives." While anchored in Valparaíso, Abel Biggs tried to convince his ship's captain to be more careful of the regional passengers he accepted but found his racial interests outweighed by the demands of the market. "This evening the Captain and myself had quite a long and rough talk about taking on so many of these natives. I told him that we was all very opposed to his taking on so many deck passengers but all the satisfaction we got from him was that did not carry a d—d for us and he should do as he pleased," he wrote.[74] This competitive spirit likely stewed as men awaited passage in port cities, congregating with the other passengers from around the globe. Kingsley remarked that "the Californians are predominent [*sic*] in this town at present," in reference to all the North Americans and Europeans who were en route but had not yet arrived. The freshly concluded war further informed their competitive spirit, inspiring some to view themselves as colonists. One such sojourner, Jacob Stillman, stopped in Peru in 1849 before heading to San Francisco. Upon hearing the latest from the bay, he wrote in his journal: "The news from California is very exciting the rush from all quarters is astonishing. They say that there are not enough Americans to hold the country, which is in a state of anarchy; that 8,000 Mexicans from Sonora are driving our people before them. Wait until our fleet of California boys now in the Pacific gets there, and you will hear of fun."[75] For others, a stay in Latin America, coupled with their own sense of racial superiority, fueled a cautionary tone with respect to many of those en route. John Lacourt, in a letter to the governor of California, wrote that "having lived long enough among these people he begs to inform his Excellency that the Chilians [*sic*] and the rest of South Americas [*sic*] are the worst possible race to populate a new country," adding that "a great many expeditions are fitting out from Chile to California."[76]

## Latin Americans in California

By January 1849 the rush had reached epic proportions in Latin America, with more than twenty advertisements for ships departing for California appearing in *El Mercurio* and *El Comercio del Valparaíso* alone.[77] Chileans, Peruvians, Mexicans, and other Central and South Americans made their way to San Francisco and then the goldfields. To escape the harsh winter and take a break from the diggings, or to escape once they had worked their fill, many found their way back to the bay, their original entry point into California. These migrants and their families—among the residents who animated the newfound dynamism of San Francisco—also gave birth to its first pan–Latin American community. While "gold rained on the city, passing from hand to hand" with ease and frequency, and fortunes were easily lost on the exorbitant costs of survival or in its many gaming houses, thousands of Spanish-speaking people participated in developing a city that grew at breakneck speed.[78]

Spanish-speaking *argonautas* facilitated each other's assimilation into this confusing world, often before many had even made the trip northward. Letters sent from San Francisco, regularly published in local newspapers, prepared gold seekers for the struggles and opportunities in what lay ahead. A February 1849 letter cautioned that "one suffers greatly when he does not speak English." Another from the same month celebrated the business climate, noting that Latin American "wheat, beans, barley, nuts, cheeses, jerky, and alcohol" sold for an inflated price.[79] Most described their journey, as well as their experience of finding lodging, supplies, and transportation once arrived. A Chilean doctor told the story of his first day ashore in January 1849, when he proved unable to find a place to sleep in San Francisco, even after hours of searching. Returning to the dock to find a ship to sleep on, he encountered another *chileno* who brought him to his "home"—an eight-by-three-yard room "with all the charm of a stable" and some twenty other men sleeping on the floor.[80] Some reported the state of local politics, others of the women they encountered, and still others of the "prejudice against South Americans."[81] All detailed their experiences mining for gold.

Fierce competition marked daily life in the diggings and in the city, inspiring outbreaks of lawlessness to which an almost nonexistent legal system struggled to respond. While the fledgling California press made little mention of Latin American deaths in this early period, Chilean historians estimated "around 200 unpunished murders." Among them were upper-class Chilean men who "disappeared in California without anyone ever knowing their fate."[82] Racial attitudes often informed these tensions, as one "forty-niner" divulged in his journal. Detailing a stranger he almost shot until he realized it was another "American," he wrote: "At a distance he looked verry [sic] suspicious. I supposed him to be an Indian or a Mexican."[83] Clearly, relations "between the races" were anything but smooth. The rabid and widespread competition for wealth nurtured tensions among all gold seekers, but the early success of Latin Americans, coupled with Anglo notions of their racial composition, exacerbated this situation even further. Pérez Rosales recounted coming upon a fellow Latin American about to be hanged for thievery, merely because "a spade had been lost, and since among the miners there was no one capable of the theft but the 'son of a nigger,' as the Americans used to call the Chileans and Spaniards, the robbery was attributed to him."[84] Instances of "dagger and revolver justice" in the mining regions gradually converted San Francisco into something of a refuge by the summer of 1849, as the population of Latin Americans began to swell with miners seeking return home.[85]

Official representatives of the United States did little to ease these tensions, in some cases even exacerbating them. A widely circulated letter sent by General Persifor Smith to the U.S. consul in Panama "capped the list of the injuries to the peaceful and defenseless."[86] Smith viewed the gold in California as the property of the United States and saw "foreigners" as thieves. "As nothing can be more unreasonable or unjust, than the conduct pursued by person not citizens of the United States, who are flocking from all parts to search for and carry off gold belonging to the United States in California," he wrote, "it will become my duty, immediately on my arrival there . . . [to punish] those who offend."[87] Published in Peru and Chile, and well-known in Mexico and California, the letter served as a catalyst to violence against "foreigners" in the mines.[88] Undoubtedly, it also delineated the limits of possibility for scores of Latin Americans considering the journey.

The substance of interracial relations, and the ways nonwhites were afforded rights and privileges within the emerging social, political, and economic systems, took on a familiar tone with the growing influx of U.S. migrants. In this way San Francisco differed from much of the rest of the state. Traditional understandings of the role of Mexicans in postwar California— especially the *gente de razón* (upper-class) *californios*—depict their loss of power as more gradual than swift. Especially in the southern half of the state, Mexicans and the Spanish-speaking continued to exert some authority and influence, most notably in elected office. In places like Los Angeles and San Diego, the initial influx of newcomers varied in its effect on the Mexican majority population, allowing for some measure of continuity for many *californio* families. Santa Barbara in 1855 represents one extreme, with Mexican Californians controlling nearly all political offices—from the municipal to the county to the state.[89] In much of the state, the landed *californios* "gamely combated Anglo encroachment into California, effectively utilizing the legal rights that U.S. citizenship extended to them," allowing for their continued, though uneven, integration into the social fabric.[90] Granted to them in the 1848 Treaty of Guadalupe Hidalgo, citizenship stood out among these rights, but recognition of their deeper inclusive potential also came regionally. For example, the 1849 California Constitutional Convention deliberately protected the rights of Mexicans over those of native Indians and blacks. This distinction did not require a wholesale revision of longer-standing assumptions about "whiteness." Instead, granting the *californios* "whiteness" in order to extend to them U.S. citizenship stood as something of an "unintended consequence to conquest,"[91] a recognition that alleviated more contradictions than it created. Enjoying the designated quality of "whiteness," the Californian Mexicans may not have been treated as perfect equals within the new U.S.-dominated power structure, but they were certainly treated better than many other nonwhites and experienced a slower decline in status.[92]

The case of San Francisco, distinguished by scope and speed, presents an exception to this narrative, while also displaying a complexity characterized by unevenness and inconsistency. A result of the massive population influx of the Gold Rush, the severe competition in the mining regions, and the noticeable and exceedingly common lack of correlation between the stories of California's gold and the realities observed by the forty-niners, San Francisco evolved more quickly into a space in which less contested ideas of racial fitness determined rights and access to power. As the city began to distinguish itself from the rural mining and northern mountain regions, these familiar racial schemes buttressed the wider project of constructing a West Coast urban center of the U.S. empire. A brief survey of the political machinations of 1849 partially illustrates the point. As trade grew and the prospects for wealth became evident, the new arrivals to the town sought a government more responsive to their interests and better equipped for growth. Often, as in the case of land transfers, this process came at the expense of the interests of the settled Mexican population. Yet it would be wrong to portray it as nothing more than common disenfranchisement. From the summer of 1847 to the end of 1848, five different men served in the position of *alcalde*.[93] Marked by "continuous and bitter controversy," the records document a steady stream of letters to the governor in Monterey asking for the removal of one man and the appointment of another. This habitual political competition grew only worse in 1849 as the townsfolk—many of them recent arrivals—began to hold regular elections to choose judges and a town council. Unlike the elections of the same period in Los Angeles, Santa Barbara, or San Diego, the results in San Francisco awarded political control to an all-white, all-U.S.-born, slate of candidates.[94]

While the names of the candidates and the winners reflected the racial homogeneity typical of the U.S. political system, a widespread and general lack of voter participation only exacerbated the situation. The immense pull of the mining region eclipsed most other activity in San Francisco, making it into a way station for many and the long-term home of only a few. For example, in one local election in January 1849, only 95 total votes were cast.[95] However, the draw of digging for gold was not the only force creating this lack of participation. In an election later that summer, a group of residents protested the results to the governor of the territory. As proof of the election's invalidity, the group noted "that sufficient notice had not been given; that the franchise had been limited to the town, whereas it extended to the district; and that Mexicans and other classes of residents had been denied the right to vote."[96] The governor agreed, ordering a new election the following month. Hence, the Mexican population of San Francisco found itself in this transitional status as newly arrived "whites" assumed some level of municipal and statewide control. While instances such as the elections of 1849 reveal the extent to which local Mexicans were unable to use the political system to their advantage, the same events suggest that factions in the town were willing to include Mexican voting rights in their political frameworks, at worst, only for the purposes of overturning the results of an election.

If the Mexican population of San Francisco enjoyed any advantage in the newly forming city it may have been that Yankee newcomers assumed them to be a part of the landscape. While numerous forty-niners recorded their impressions of California in their journals and letters home, often commenting on some aspect of life tied to the presence of Mexicans or "the Spanish," none were surprised to find them there. After all, San Francisco and California had once been part of Mexico. Many assumed they would find California imbued with a certain "Spanish character," even more so after journeying so far away from an "Anglo-Saxon" society and then passing through a Latin American one. Many of their journals reflect this by noting changes in dress, diet, or habit, minor forms of cultural exchange and adaptation promoted by life in a new land. One observer romantically recalled that "nearly all the residents of San Francisco in those days rode horseback, used the Mexican saddle and all the jingling accoutrements; wore the vicuna hat, or broad-rimmed glazed sombrero, and the comfortable, convenient, protecting serapa [sic]."[97] In an 1849 letter, J. K. Osgood wrote, "Our costume is not yet decided upon, the disposition to ape foreign customs leading some to adopt the Mexican poncho or blanket, a very graceful garment when concealing a commanding figure."[98] Depending on the observer, San Francisco could possess a kind of liminality, a place of difference where newcomers "could pursue extravagant urges and do things they had thought beyond their capabilities."[99] Significantly, this difference need not be threatening. Even Nelson Kingsley, armed with his decidedly unfavorable views of Latin America and its residents, began using the Spanish names for the days of the week in his 1848 journal.[100]

While the presence of some Latin Americans was naturalized as part of the San Francisco landscape, the racialized perspective on rights and ownership more dominant in other parts of the United States eventually prevailed. Various newcomers viewed the Mexican presence as something to be controlled or overcome, a condition quickly extended to all

Latin Americans. When James Carothers arrived, for example, he found San Francisco to be a "well governed city . . . different from what I had seen in Mexico and on the Isthmus." In his opinion, the city's distinction came from "the genius of the Anglo-American."[101] With a sympathetic tone, one chronicler of the times saw *californios* as almost hapless victims, poor simpletons with a "mental culture . . . of the most childish kind."[102] European migrants also rarely entertained a positive image of Mexicans, often dismissing them as future participants in a world that had ample room for other "foreigners." One Frenchman, for example, wrote the *californios* were "men whose only diversions are gambling, fighting, and perhaps, when times are not so good, banditry."[103] Thus, while they were part of California's past, from the vantage point of other newcomers, Latin Americans would not be so firmly part of what was to follow. In a letter to his father, one Anglo newcomer provided an apt metaphor in describing his first sights of the bay, including "one of the southern bluffs, [upon which] stands the old Spanish fort, which is now in ruins."[104] This is a rich image for understanding the emerging position of the Spanish-speaking in Gold Rush San Francisco, that of a fortress with a colorful history but little future.

## Latino Liminality in Gold Rush San Francisco

The lure of gold made San Francisco into a diverse urban environment. This trait, in turn, added to its mystery and exceptionalism while simultaneously shaping its version of white supremacy. For many accustomed to life amid a more racially and culturally homogenous population, assumptions of racial difference and fitness proved invaluable tools in their effort to grapple with newness by "rationally" organizing daily, multiracial interactions. San Francisco, with its multiracial population and polyglot culture, further solidified such assumptions. One early account communicates the combination of exoticism and informed certainty that could result:

> The every-day aspect of the plaza and streets was of the most curious and interesting kind. Take the plaza, on a fine day, for a picture of the people. All races were represented. There were hordes of long pig-tailed, blear-eyed, rank-smelling Chinese, with their yellow faces and blue garbs; single dandy black fellows, of nearly as bad an odor, who strutted as only the negro can strut, in holiday clothes and clean white shirt; a few diminutive fiery-eyed Malays, from the western archipelago,

and some handsome Kanakas from the Sandwich Islands; jet-black, straight-featured, Abyssinians; hideously tattooed New Zealanders; Feejee sailors and even the secluded Japanese, short, thick, clumsy, ever-bowing, jacketed fellows; the people of the many races of Hindoo land; Russians with furs and sables; a stray, turbaned, stately Turk or two, and occasionally a half naked shivering Indian.[105]

Indeed, as the city presented an opportunity for observers to categorize according to familiar racialist schema, it also provided them with an avalanche of new "evidence" and expertise.

The Spanish-speaking represented a large share of the "curious" population in this period and, as such, did not escape classification. Their internal diversity and American nativity, however, necessitated a rigid categorization to separate the "dignified" from the "rough." The authors detailed

multitudes of the Spanish race from every country of the Americas, partly pure, partly crossed with red blood,—Chilians, Peruvians and Mexicans, all with different shades of the same swarthy complexion, black-eyed and well-featured, proud of their beards and moustaches, their grease, dirt, and eternal gaudy serapes or darker cloaks; Spaniards from the mother country, more dignified, polite and pompous than even their old colonial brethren; "greasers," too, like them; great numbers of tall, goat-chinned, smooth-cheeked, oily-locked, lank-visaged, tobacco-chewing, large-limbed and featured, rough, care-worn, careless Americans from every State of the Union, dressed independently in every variety of garb, not caring a fig what people thought of them, but determined to "do the thing handsomely," and "go ahead."[106]

The mere presence of such a diverse lot of gold seekers, drawn to the city by the same pursuit, threatened notions of racial supremacy. Physically laboring at the same task, and living in a social world not fully yet able to effectively segregate, this cosmopolitan population possessed an almost innate ability to challenge the fluid yet myopic racial caste system prevalent in other parts of the United States. This promise, however, often succumbed to pressures inherent in white supremacist encounters with pluralism. Suggesting at least one strategy employed to relieve these tensions, these crudely phrased descriptions avoid any accidental expression of commonality.

Ultimately, the position of Latin Americans, in general, determined the position of wealthier Mexicans in San Francisco. Complicating the *californios'* initially advantaged status, most Yankees saw few differences between the Mexican "natives" and the South American newcomers, as this entire, diverse population became lumped together under the terms "greaser" or, less derisively, "Spanish." Pérez Rosales observed that the "animus of the average American toward the natives of other countries, and particularly toward the Chileans" promoted simplistic assumptions of racial fitness, collapsing all toward a low station. "A simple and conclusive argument was adduced," he wrote. "The Chileans were descendants of the Spaniards; the Spaniards had Moorish blood; *ergo*, the Chileans were Hottentots at the very least, or, to give them the utmost one possibly could, something very like the timid and humble Californians."[107] As one historian has succinctly noted, "Latin-American immigrants were a sort of catalyst whose presence caused the sudden and permanent dissolution of the social elements."[108]

While San Franciscans with roots in the United States or Europe could utilize knowledge systems casting all "Spanish" as the same, and classify that sameness as nonwhite (hence inferior), Spanish-speakers from different regions of Latin America brought with them their own distinct identities, forged in the nexus of region, race, class, gender, and nationality. Pérez Rosales, for example, coming from the more affluent classes of Chile, viewed Mexicans with a sympathetic elitism. Passing through Monterey and searching for accommodations, he found locals timid and fearsome of visitors, until they realized he was not an "americano." Struck by "the candor with which these poor people speak about the American invasion and dominion of their country," he contended that the Mexicans welcomed the presence of their countrymen. "They believe that they themselves cannot expel those whom they still justly term tyrants; but they also believed implicitly that the Chileans, if they had the mind to, could do so, in view of their determined resistance to the brutal oppression of the Americans."[109] Pérez Rosales further confirmed what had become a widespread belief in Chilean society: that the South Americans, "unwilling to accept the passivity of the Mexicans," had concluded to "head the resistance" against the "gringo."[110] Such a sentiment among Chileans reflects at least a minimal amount of common cause, as fear of the Yankees' racial aggression gave way to a solidarity forged of a shared hatred of "hostile gringos." While this collective image owed more than a bit to hubris, it also contained at least a grain of truth. To observant residents, Chileans—in particular those from the wealthier classes—differed in appearance and habit from the largely mixed-race, laboring-class Mexicans who predominated in California. One traveler found the Chileans exotic and strange, yet familiar. He wrote, "the gentleman and ladys [*sic*] were very richly dressed, the ladys were dressed in white and wore a great deal of rich jewelry, they were short and heavy looking wimin [*sic*] and as white as any American Lady."[111] Adding to the effect, the economy of early Gold Rush California relied heavily on Chilean merchants, who sold everything from food to mining supplies. This dependency benefited Chileans and other Latin Americans in the summer of 1849, when townsfolk rose to defend them against a gang of largely U.S.-born hooligans. The South American reputation for more fully conforming to the dictates of "whiteness" also proved useful throughout the remaining half of the nineteenth century, as a growing merchant class of Latin Americans established themselves in San Francisco.

Not all Latin Americans held tight to their national preconceptions of other Spanish speakers. Ramón Jil Navarro was born in Argentina but spent his early adult life in the Chilean city of Concepción. In 1849 he joined the masses making their exodus to the North, where he bore witness to the lives and struggles of the Spanish-speaking in the new territory. Perhaps as a result of his own cosmopolitan background, his description of the differences between Mexicans and Chileans was rooted less in nationalism than in an analysis of the context in which all Latin Americans found themselves. From his point of view, the Yankee "had enough hate to go around," though his "irrational hostility . . . was especially directed against the Chileans."[112] Though he, too, remarked on the differences between Mexicans and Chileans when confronting Yankee violence, he also remarked on a reason for this difference. "Because they did not speak English they had no way even to put up an argument," he wrote. "That is why they yielded to the abusive arrogance of the Americans." Further informing their response, Navarro believed a Sonoran gave up his position so easily because he was "fully confident that he could find an even richer location." Chileans, who did not possess "the skills of the Sonorans in locating such rich claims, or the luck in making them pay well," protected their claims more vigorously. "Whether this desperation was the reason why a Chilean displayed bravery, or whether bravery was simply inborn in him, the fact was that he would not submit to abuse from the Yankees."[113] In this period, however, as *chilenos* envisioned their role as a "shield for the Mexicans," and a current of "Hispanophobia" surged throughout the state, the foundation of a pan–Latin American sensibility was born.[114]

Differences between segments of the Spanish-speaking population continued to provide for a diversity of experiences in the emerging city, especially when those differences aligned with tried and trusted tools for determining access to power and rights. The case of Latin American women illustrates the ways an assortment of forces intersected. The overwhelming majority of newcomers to the region during the Gold Rush were men. Stories of miners turning solemn, standing in silence while shedding tears at the mere sight of a woman and child; or of the ceremonial excitement of miners finding a woman's bonnet at camp; or of men dancing with other men, as was a common custom in mining camps, all illustrate the impact of the lack of women on the social formation of early California. Unlike emigration from North America, comprised almost entirely of men, the Latin American arrivals also included women and children; families often sought their fortunes together, migrating as complete domestic units, more easily assuring survival and, perhaps, success. Early accounts suggest that many Spanish-speaking women did housework while their husbands and sons engaged in other profit-seeking enterprises.[115] A Canadian traveler described Sonoran "wives and children in charge" of huts "constructed of canvas, cotton cloth, or of upright unhewn sticks with green branches and leaves and vines interwoven, and decorated with gaudy hangings," while the men dug for gold.[116] Others were the wives of affluent *patrones,* accompanying their husbands and servants in the familial quest for greater wealth and standing. The French consul to San Francisco, Charles de Varigny, noted that most of the "principle merchants" from Chile "brought their wives, daughters, [and] sisters."[117] Many also came from the lower classes, perhaps reflecting an equally robust business acumen among their station. A group of Sonorans traveled as a circus troupe throughout the state, profiting from their "feats of physical ability and other entertainment."[118] Of course, more than a few migrated as prostitutes, representing yet another form of transnational commerce. Pérez Rosales recounted a fellow passenger named Rosario Améstica, who "had gone by the names of Villaseca in Talcahuano and Toro in Talca, and that until the day before she had been known as Rosa Montalvo in Valparaíso." As he explained, when the ship's captain, Orella, learned of her presence and activity on his ship, he nearly left her at port, an act that "very nearly caused a revolution among the steerage passengers and led them to the verge of dumping the good Orella into the sea."[119]

Like "Rosario," many women migrated as individuals seeking to profit from the vibrant gold economy through their trade in sexual companionship. Such opportunities could be lucrative, but they also carried the costs associated with participation in a world of myriad physical threats and compulsory labor. Prostitution in San Francisco also flourished under more organized efforts that initially "favored" Latin American women. An account of "hundreds" being imported from Mexican ports and then being auctioned to "bidders" suggests that a formal human sex trade existed in this period.[120] Other sources detail the assignment of particular roles based on country of origin, with Peruvian women being favored in dancing saloons.[121] Latin American women were not alone. Sources also indicate the importation of women from Australia, France, and the Marquesas Islands. Although Native American women of course did not need to be imported, accounts of their being subjected to labor in the burgeoning sex industry are extremely common as well. Among the many negative effects, the ubiquity of Latin American prostitutes led to a common view of all Spanish-speaking women as exemplars of "the fallen image, the center of gyrating revelry and discord."[122] For example, though he based his claim on uncertain evidence, one historian later estimated that "two-thirds [of the women in San Francisco] were harlots from Mexico, Peru, and Chili [sic]."[123] Constructed as a class to serve the sexual needs of miners, these women were naturalized as part of the landscape, with deleterious effects that are easily observable.

Latin American women found employment in activities other than prostitution. In an intersection of race and gender no less vivid than the widespread brothels of San Francisco, many women worked as laundresses. In a society marked by distance from "home" and, hence, from the fruits of domestic labor, numerous opportunities existed for women willing to capitalize on the needs of the reproductive economy. Washerwomen's Bay, located at the cove near Black Point, acted as both home and workplace for "women of every clime and color."[124] Beginning first as a tent city of laundries for the male population of miners, the area evolved into the site of one of the first Chinese laundries and eventually became the home of the largest operation in the city, owned by A. T. Easton.[125] Some Latin American women also profited from men's unwillingness to cook for themselves. A Mexican woman who fed and cared for an expedition party funded by a wealthy *californio* made up to four ounces of gold a day by preparing more tortillas and frijoles than were required for her group and selling the extra.[126] Of course, gender did not limit such opportunities. After abandoning his hopes of making a fortune in mining and other pursuits, even Pérez Rosales opened an eatery in the city called Citizen's Restaurant.[127] Ultimately, ideas of race, gender, sexuality, and nationalism combined to powerful effect in shaping the experiences of Latin Americans in San Francisco, fundamentally altering race relations in the spring and summer of 1849.

Life in a dynamic yet highly unpredictable economy made both the diggings and the city places of optimism as well as shattered dreams. A

climate of desperate competition continued to fuel regular violence between U.S. migrants and Latin Americans, which reached a crescendo
in the late spring of 1849. Undoubtedly violent encounters occurred in
which either or both parties could be reasonably accused as guilty, but
Latin Americans clearly received the worst of it. Average men had begun to
echo the message communicated by officials' actions, exhibiting a sense of
ownership over California and its wealth. In the months following General
Smith's warning to punish the foreigners, the number of Latin Americans
in the city seemed to swell with the accounts of violence in the goldfields.
To many Spanish speakers, it seemed as if those from the United States
"believed themselves to be the only ones with the right to look for gold, as
well as the only owners of this conquered territory."[128] The presence of nonwhites in California—especially in the gold regions—rested at the nexus
of these sentiments, framing the first wave of gold seekers as an "enemy"
profiting in some surreptitious manner. Bayard Taylor, the U.S. writer who
traveled the diggings in 1849, expressed the more generally shared belief
about "Sonorians" when he described them as having come "into the
country in armed bands . . . and [taken] possession of the best points on the
Tuolomne, Stanislaus and Mokelumne Rivers." He continued: "For a long
time they were suffered to work peaceably, but the opposition finally became so strong that they were ordered to leave. They made no resistance,
but quietly backed out and took refuge in other diggings. In one or two
places, I was told, the Americans finding there was no chance of having a
fight, coolly invited them back again! At the time of my visit, however, they
were leaving the country in large numbers."[129] Hardly passive in the face of
widespread violence, some of the exiled sought revenge by "stripping small
parties of emigrants by the Gila route of all they possessed." To observers
like Taylor, however, it was a battle won by the Yankee newcomer. "It is not
likely that the country will be troubled with them in the future."[130]

In this first year of the rush, the city also became home to a more settled population of residents, often "those who had tried gold digging and
been disappointed, visited town, to spend their gains, recruit their health,
or follow out some new pursuit."[131] The population more than doubled in
1849 alone, exploding from about 1,000 to some 25,000 by year's end, one
and all living in a place unlike any other. Described by one historian as a
"boom town of men . . . given over entirely to business, speculation and entertainment," San Francisco was a city of "common canvas tents, or small
rough board shanties," where "only the great gambling saloons, the hotels,
restaurants, and a few public buildings and stores had any pretensions to
size, comfort or elegance."[132] As much as it represented a refuge for Latin

Americans fleeing the violence of the diggings, it did the same for an assortment of "thieves and ruffians," among them the group initially called the Hounds, later renamed the San Francisco Society of Regulators.[133]

A gang of thirty to sixty "young thugs," the largest contingent of the group served in the war against Mexico, the bulk of the New York regiment commanded by Colonel J. D. Stevenson. Their former occupation is noteworthy, as most of the gang arrived in California as part an effort to literally conquer the local Mexican population. Upon their arrival, they found military service uneventful, if not unnecessary, and so they deserted to explore more lucrative endeavors, such as serving as "collectors" for various merchants and as hunters of other deserters from ships in port.[134] From the late fall 1848 until the summer of 1849—when the Hounds attacked Latin American encampments—their primary employment entailed announcing themselves as representatives of the local *alcalde* and then threatening business owners with violence unless they turned over a sum of money. They targeted an assortment of establishments but clearly preferred those with "foreign" proprietors. In the weeks before the escalation, Chileans had become their target so frequently that one resident testified he "thought [the Hounds] was an organization to rob Chilenos and commit other outrages."[135]

The man accused of being their leader, and the instigator of the violence, embodied many of the less savory aspects of life in the city. Samuel Roberts had his roots in New York, though he seems to have been a man with some connection to the sea. He had lived for a time in Valparaíso, where he learned Spanish and worked on a Chilean man-of-war. How he found his way into the U.S. military is not clear, but he arrived in Yerba Buena in 1846 along with his regiment, likely prepared to do battle but never finding a military cause. His fortuitous timing, fluency in Spanish, and connections with early gold-seeking Latin Americans presented him with an assortment of less physically demanding ways of profiting from the rush. In addition to extortion, he spent time procuring goods and information for *argonautas*, as well as providing transportation across the bay. He also appeared to have had some direct involvement in the city's burgeoning prostitution industry, perhaps facilitating the transnational migration of women he knew in Chile. Whatever his role, he often slept at Washington Hall—"the town's most elegant brothel," saloon, and game house, largely populated with Spanish-speaking women.[136] His early arrival gave Roberts and his comrades the advantage of time and, with it, knowledge of how the urban locale functioned and could be exploited.

In July 1849, Roberts and his gang sacked tents in the part of town known commonly as "Little Chile." As we have seen, within days, the residents of

The July 1849 attack on Chileans orchestrated by "the Hounds" is depicted in this rendering in *Century Magazine* (February 1892). The central "Chilean" is incorrectly dressed as a Mexican *charro*.

San Francisco organized a makeshift legal system and then arrested, tried, and convicted Roberts and some of his associates. The anti-Chilean riots stood as powerfully emblematic of the complex of forces within which Latin Americans lived in San Francisco. They signaled both the possibilities the Spanish-speaking enjoyed and the capricious limits set on their lives in this nascent society. All this notwithstanding, the violence also derived from a more discreet set of events, an escalation of local tensions and dysfunctional interpersonal relationships, all of which culminated that summer. As more and more Latin Americans returned to the city to escape the rising violence in the mining regions, and the Hounds expanded their extortion operation, episodic violence between the gang and the Spanish-speaking grew noticeably worse. Testimony collected during the Hounds' trial describes the chain of events beginning in June, when a Chilean storeowner resisted an attempt by the gang to collect on an imaginary debt and shot one of its members.[137] The *alcalde*, having determined the man acted in self-defense, pursued no official charge. Numerous skirmishes between the two camps followed, with both sides believing the other was the aggressor. Perhaps not surprisingly, one Latin American testified that on the day of the attacks, the Hounds "said they had an order from the alcalde to destroy all the tents of the Chilenos." Another declared, "I heard 'kill the Chilenos' cried out."[138]

At about the same time, a *chilena* named Felice Alvarez[139] arrived in San Francisco, apparently having known Roberts during his time in Valparaíso. She fell under his stewardship, and he secured her employment at Washington Hall. By her own account the two got on agreeably until he stole ten ounces of gold from her on July 4, using this to compel her loyalty. She testified: "The prisoner has lived with me since I have been in town—more than a month. Prisoner showed me the ten ounces every day, but would not let me have them. We lived on good terms until prisoner took my money. I told prisoner to go away after he took the money; but he said he would come, and break open the door if I did not let him in. I feared him, and admitted him; he has threatened to break in the door of both houses in which I have resided."[140] Events unfolded to justify her concerns. On July 15, Roberts entered the tent in which Alvarez lived (and, perhaps, worked) and found her in conversation with some men, including a German. Angered at the presence of this particular man, he left and gathered the Hounds. They drank and caused some havoc at local establishments before returning in the late evening to the group of tents the Spanish-speaking called Chilecito. Adorned in their uniforms and playing a fife and drum, they provoked an initial confrontation near Alvarez's tent—where at least one *chileno* was shot—then went on a rampage, sacking tents, abusing residents, and looting goods, sparing only tents whose occupants shouted, "This is an American tent!" or "This is a German tent!"[141]

The next day, in what the local press called "one of those whirlwinds of excitement," residents mobilized to create a legal infrastructure and a posse of "citizen armed police," leading to the subsequent arrests and trial. Less than two weeks later, eight of ten men (including Roberts) were convicted on various charges. Though favorably concluded, the episode demonstrated the racial contradictions embedded in daily life in San Francisco. While city elites—segments of the merchant class, political establishment, and publishers of major newspapers—deplored the "systematic attack upon the lives and the property of this community," a growing segment of the residents violently expressed racial hatred of Latin Americans. The mass of residents who rose to defend the attacked Latin Americans embodied, in word and deed, one pluralistic possibility. In his closing remarks, the prosecutor sought the sympathies of the jury while placing injured "Americans" side-by-side with the injured Latin Americans. He pleaded, "You have to give a verdict gentlemen in vindication of the welfare and safety of this community." While the need to protect private property in a period of mass accumulation certainly drove local residents to act, those actions positioned Latin Americans as part of the "community." With this recognition came rights, including the right to be protected by the law. Further, the recognition of their victimization by the Hounds was not disconnected from its racial overtones, with the local press and prosecutor viewing the "outrages" as an extension of the abuse of foreigners in the mines.

Conversely, the Hounds and their defenders embodied another possibility, one more familiarly labeled "white supremacist." Seeking to mobilize these sentiments toward the defense of the accused, Roberts's attorney blasted the arresting posse for its mixed-race character, charging it "had associated with the *foreigners*—had armed vagrant Chilenos with loaded muskets to patrole [*sic*] the town and to protect American citizens!" Tacitly recognizing the inferiority of nonwhites, he further naturalized the kinds of interrelations that could result. "It is not to be wondered at, then, that collisions should, from time to time, arise between our countrymen and foreigners. Nor could it be denied that foreigners had been guilty of lawless deeds in our midst."[142] These arguments proved unpersuasive in the conclusion of the trial, yet they hardly ceased to hold sway over segments of the population. In the same edition of the *Alta California* that recounted the trial, a section titled "Placer Intelligence" reported something of a growing movement: "The best feeling prevails, except in the matter of foreign encroachment, for our people are united in the determination to expel the vagrants of other nations from the mines, and the movement is a very general one we are informed. The roads through the country are filled with Chilenos and New Mexicans returning from the Placer."[143]

By the middle of the decade, the ways race and nationality informed the local power structure more often mirrored the public sentiment that fueled violence, sentiments increasingly shared throughout the state. Reflecting the growing trend, in 1850 the legislature passed its first attempt at a foreign miner's tax. The law required "foreigners" to purchase a license giving them legal allowance to partake of the "unprecedented privilege" of mining. As an argument for the bill demonstrated, the targets were chiefly the Spanish-speaking. "Tens of thousands have already arrived in our country, and they are the commencement of a vast multitude en route and preparing to come hither, of the worst population of the Mexican, South American states, New South Wales, and the Southern Islands to say nothing of the vast numbers from Europe. Among others, the convicts of Mexico, Chile and Botany Bay are daily turned upon our shores, who seek and possess themselves of the best places for gold digging whether upon their own or on account of foreign employers and carry from our country immense treasure."[144] Criminalized and further subjected to "strife and bloodshed," an estimated "half to three-fourths" of the nonwhites (in this instance, both Latin Americans and Chinese) left the mining regions as a consequence of the tax and unabated violence.[145] Even though pressure from Stockton merchants forced the repeal of the measure—foreign miners took with them their disposal income, leading to an unexpected drop in retail profits. A clear message of racial exclusivity had already emerged in California.

In San Francisco public sentiment would vary depending on the instance of racial vigilantism. When the legal system did respond—as in the case of the 1849 riot—the appointed legal authorities, judges, and jury were comprised of only U.S.- or European-born men. Latin Americans in San Francisco increasingly found their culture under attack, sometimes in not so obvious ways. For example, gambling (the primary form of entertainment in Gold Rush San Francisco) became associated with the presence of Latin Americans in letters, journals, and early histories.[146] In fact, Latin Americans dominated many of the gambling houses, and Mexican and South American gaming styles were the most common in practice. In a society that sought increasingly to reflect Protestant values and nurture the growth of families and permanent homes, city fathers saw gambling as a licentious threat. In September 1850, the city banned gambling on Sundays.[147] By 1855, prominent gambling houses ceased operations as the state legislature sought to ban gaming outright.[148]

In the late nineteenth century Mexicans and Chileans increasingly came to occupy an inferior position, and the legal system rarely protected Latin Americans as it had in the summer of 1849. San Franciscans with the fewest formal rights—such as women and children—often found themselves most profoundly affected. Less than two years later, a Mexican woman entered the police station to report the abduction of her twelve-year-old daughter by a local prostitution ring. Several officers "volunteered" to apprehend and return the girl, keeping her in jail for the night until her mother retrieved her in the morning. Upon leaving the station with the girl, the mother encountered the man who had abducted her daughter in the first instance and "threatened the life of the man."[149] Police then arrested and jailed her. Unable to secure bail, the mother remained incarcerated for a day or so, allowing the man to abduct her daughter yet again. When a warrant was issued for his arrest, the man, Peter McKinney, returned to the station with the girl and a certificate of marriage. "As a man could scarcely stand charged for the abduction of his own wife, the matter was dropped."[150]

The gradual change in the tenor of race relations did not keep Latin Americans from migrating to and settling in the city, and their presence continued to grow throughout the century. Limitations in their economic, political, and social prospects notwithstanding, the sheer strength and profitability of networks between San Francisco and Latin America facilitated migration. In 1852, despite the waning pull of gold, one Chilean newspaper lamented the loss of 824 workers in one month to California. Recruited and shipped by U.S. and Chilean effort, the men deprived South America of what they provided the labor-poor western metropolis—*brazos*.[151] While the city did not always welcome Latin Americans, San Francisco merchants' reliance on trade with Latin America nurtured a continued connection through most of the period. Spanish-speaking merchants further contributed to the increasing settled population, establishing eateries, boarding houses, and other businesses catering to a Latin American clientele.[152] And with six Latin American consulate offices in the city by 1854, and at least one church offering services in Spanish, Latin Americans also enjoyed a measure of formal representation.[153] Still, one might wonder whether a moment of possibility had been lost. As historian Kevin Starr contends, "The Gold Rush represented . . . a wake-up call to the United States that it would at some time in its future have to deal with the global nature of American culture."[154]

If anything, the decades after the Gold Rush reflect a deliberate course of action to destabilize the state's possible pluralist future, institutionalizing a familiar pattern in relations between the races. The uneven ways San Franciscans negotiated this condition animated the experiences of a diverse population of Latin Americans. At the Golden Gate, the limits of legal and social integration helped constitute a community from what once was only a collection of Spanish-speaking populations. In the 1870s, as "Yankees" collapsed Latin American diversity by paying little heed to differences of class and nationality, and as racial violence became more common, an assortment of Latin American elites promoted cohesion and unity in an effort to maintain some standing. As I discuss in the next chapter, they fostered a panethnic identity and community through the commonality of language and faith, all housed in a church.

## CHAPTER TWO

# El Esplendor, Brillantez e Influencia de Nuestra Raza

## Panethnic Identity and the Spanish-Speaking Church

"We who belong to the Spanish race in this city, will never achieve strength or respectability while we do not also have unity," wrote a contingent of San Francisco Latin Americans in 1871. Calling themselves *hispanoamericanos*, the group—comprised of Spanish-speaking diplomats and other local elites—spoke to fellow Latin American residents in the city via a circular letter promoting the cause of community. Bearing witness to various racial and class consolidation efforts, as well as to a clear decline in the Latin American share of the growing population, these spokesmen for the Spanish-speaking sought nothing less than to "reestablish in this great city the splendor, brilliance, and influence of our people." To do so, they solicited funds to build a Spanish-language Catholic church. The endeavor, they hoped, would not only nurture culture and spirituality—since religion was "the soul of Spanish honor"—but also help unify the diverse and diffuse Spanish-speaking population. "Unity," they wrote, "builds strength, and strength begets respect."[1]

Four years later, their efforts culminated with the opening of La Iglesia de Nuestra Señora de Guadalupe, Our Lady of Guadalupe Church, the first Spanish-language "national parish" in California. The church became a vibrant presence among the Latin American–descent of San Francisco, even fostering the emergence of *la colonia*, a Spanish-speaking enclave marked by a concentration of Latino residents and businesses catering to their cultural needs. Though originally the product of elites' fears of a loss of status in the city, the church fulfilled its stated goal of unity by forging—in both physical location and spiritual practice—a visible pan–Latin American community and identity. Based on a shared religion and language, this identity coexisted with the various national and regional identities already present within the population, suggesting the scope of heterogeneity inherent in the unified "new." While this simultaneity often reflected the limits of unity—measured, to an extent, in the interethnic rivalries played out within the church—so, too, did the customs and traditions of the church nurture a palpable cultural cohesion.

Guadalupe Church, as it was commonly called, brought the Latin American ethnic population together as a linguistic and spiritual community until its closing in the late twentieth century. The manifestation of *latinismo* it promoted emerged as a response to hemispheric migration and social exclusion, forces situating Latin Americans as new social subjects in the city. Simultaneously, its panethnicity hinged on the level of cultural continuity it re-created through religious worship, demonstrating Catholicism's ability to "reinforce group identity, [and] engender a sense of belonging."[2] The version of "ethno-Catholicism" practiced at the church not only respected and incorporated Latin Americans' cultural sensibilities but also accounted for their political ones.[3] Often, this meant using the church as a setting for the expression of singular national identities, as opposed to expressions of collectivity. On December 12, for example, the official feast day of the church's namesake, the Virgin of Guadalupe, Mexican Catholics in the city celebrated mass with many of the same symbols, prayers, and songs as did *mexicanos* worshipping in their homeland. Yet these "national celebrations" could also help build broader, Spanish-speaking solidarities—unions unimaginable in the country of origin. At the turn of the century, for example, a "unified" Spanish mass commemorated the national independence days of both Chile and Mexico each September. Like the regular weekly services provided by the church, these celebrations brought Spanish-speaking San Franciscans together, on common ground and for a common purpose, as Spanish-speaking Catholics in the city.

This chapter investigates the rise of a panethnic identity among Latin Americans in San Francisco from the late nineteenth century to the early twentieth. Detailing some of the more pressing qualities of daily life for this population, I explore the ways Latin Americans adapted to their transnational condition and confronted the challenges of racially restrictive norms. These forces fueled the creation of the Spanish-language "national parish" of Our Lady of Guadalupe as a defense and an affirmative expression of a panethnic vision of community. Using the Catholic Church as a focus, I argue that the city's heterogeneous Latin American–descent population found in Guadalupe Church a space to forge a situational form of *latinidad,* a shared Latino identity. The birth of the church, a product of the collective efforts of a Spanish-speaking elite, reflected the broader race and class tensions marking life at the local level as well as the possibilities framed by transnational life and culture.[4] Its power, however, extended well beyond these concerns. By the early twentieth century, the church represented the heart of an emerging physical and spiritual community, a linguistic and cultural space where Latino Catholicism could be practiced and improvised. This bond of shared religiosity and perceived "togetherness," identifiable to local Latin Americans and the broader San Francisco polity, wove diverse nationalities together in this urban environment in more than cosmetic ways.[5] By 1906, when an earthquake and a fire left much of the city in ashes—including Guadalupe—San Francisco's Latin American–descent population had become a constituency whose place in the rebuilt city, unlike the ethnic Chinese, seemed assured. The rebuilt edifice demonstrated their organization and unity, an architectural testament to their financial and political capacities. For the generations who followed, Guadalupe Church provided the spiritual and cultural resources Latin American migrants required as they sought to navigate the challenges of life in the urban West.

## Transnational Life in the City

The role played by Catholicism in constituting Latino San Francisco is inseparable from the nineteenth-century patterns of interaction between Latin America and the city. These patterns, in turn, were initially framed by the sea. In the two decades after the Gold Rush, the San Francisco–based Pacific Mail Steamship Company built a near monopoly on Pacific trade with the United States, in particular with respect to Asia. These lines also sustained San Francisco's connections to Latin America, both directly and as a route from the eastern states, a nexus built through trade and commerce. The completion of the transcontinental railway in 1869—though framing an optimistic outlook for Pacific trade in general—threatened the long-term position of the steamer company and its historic networks via the Spanish-speaking hemisphere. The ensuing decade witnessed a brisk competition for the steamship line, culminating with the Union Pacific and Central Pacific rail lines seizing effective control of Pacific Mail by 1880. Though San Francisco's position as a significant port throughout the Pacific was further secured as a result, its previously dependent connections to Latin America were now loosened by more direct access to the eastern seaboard via rail.[6]

Though it no longer occupied as central an economic position, Latin America remained commercially connected to San Francisco in the post-Gold Rush era. These networks, in turn, further accentuated the city's cosmopolitan character. In 1870 nearly half (49.3%) of San Francisco's population was foreign-born. A decade later, despite a small decline in the ratio (to 44.6%), San Francisco ranked second overall in the nation by this measure.[7] Though migrants from all parts of Latin America continued to compose part of that diversity, their collective numbers increasingly shrank relative to those of other foreign-born groups. For example, in 1880, while one-fifth of the city's immigrants came from China, only 1.9 percent (2,017 in absolute numbers) came from Latin America. Indicative of a post–Gold Rush shift, nearly three-quarters of these originated in Mexico, with the entire continent of South America constituting most of the remaining quarter.[8] This trend took root in a city experiencing a general population increase, further solidifying its place in the West and making the city one of the most populous in the nation. San Francisco's population grew by more than 260 percent between 1860 and 1870, from 56,802 to 149,473. A decade later, it had grown to 233,959.[9] More than half of the city's population was still native to the United States; arrivals from other parts of California accounted for more than 60 percent of San Francisco's overall growth, with those from New York, Maine, Massachusetts, and Pennsylvania making up another 24 percent.[10] These trends reflect the strength of Gold Rush–era migration patterns in the railroad age, and put the share of Latin Americans into perspective. For most of the late nineteenth century, Latin American San Franciscans found themselves in much the same situation as that of Mexicans in the rest of the state: they were increasingly marginalized demographically.

Newcomers may have eclipsed them in numbers, but Latin Americans continued to live and work in San Francisco. The historical record is partially helpful at best when we try to reconstruct daily life for Latin Americans in the city, but it may be safe to assume that much of the violence directed toward them during the peak of the rush subsided. As early as 1852, one South American sojourner described those earlier times as "abnormal in every aspect, and what happened then has little or no significance in terms of the excellent relations that exist today between Chileans and Americans."[11] Whether this translated into anything meaningful for the majority of Spanish speakers is hard to assess, but a smaller group of elites certainly began to benefit, while also participating in the formation of a unique transnational condition. Whether in business, politics, or social life, wealthier Latin Americans maintained deep ties to their countries of origin as they simultaneously created settled lives in San Francisco. Navigating their positions within the "trade diaspora" encompassing the Pacific, merchants established commercial houses linking the city to southern ports and business interests.[12] Those with means sent their children to live, study, or work in the Bay Area, connecting them to business concerns run by others, often from the same towns. Political causes in Latin America found bases of financial and moral support among the settled populations of their citizens living at the Golden Gate. And, in the most dynamic demonstration of this condition, many Latin Americans lived transnationally, traveling regularly between the city and their homelands while nurturing relationships spanning borders and the Pacific.

The remnants of numerous Spanish-language newspapers illuminate the broader phenomenon. In the last half of the century, Latin Americans published nearly twenty Spanish-language newspapers in San Francisco, seeking to reach a population eager to remain connected to *la patria* as much as to their adopted home. Newspapers like *El Sud-Americano* (1855), *La Voz de Méjico* (1862–66), *La Bandera Mexicana* (1863), *La Voz de Chile* (1866), *El Tiempo* (1869), *El Tecolote* (1875), *La República* (1881), and *El Cronista* (1884) fed readers a steady diet of politics and life in Latin America. *La Voz de Méjico*, for example, reported on the European intervention in Mexico, as well as the movement of French troops into Puebla.[13] Most provided accounts of minor yet regionally important happenings in Latin America, such as the turmoil over the Chilean colony of Magallanes or the swearing in of a new governor of Sonora.[14] While the coverage of international affairs primarily involved Mexico and only a handful of South American nations—suggestive of the composition of the city's Latin American population—the Spanish-speaking press did not ignore the broader Spanish-speaking world. In one example, *El Cronista* updated readers on the struggle for independence in Cuba.[15] As these publications informed the Spanish-speaking about their former homelands and Latin America more generally, each also printed the latest news of cultural events and social gatherings in the city. Articles on the vacation plans of prominent citizens, local baptisms and marriages, and upcoming visits by noted politicians and cultural figures provide a further, though limited, window on the daily social world of Latin Americans in San Francisco. *El Tecolote* even printed updates on rumors of local marital indiscretions.[16]

These journalistic remnants of the Spanish-speaking population do more than provide evidence of the myriad ways they lived across borders and cultures; they also record the ways San Franciscans created and nurtured transhemispheric connections. Reports from Latin America came via two methods: through letters sent by traveling readers who could offer their firsthand accounts of Latin American happenings and through reprinted stories previously published in major Latin American papers. The latter method underscores the persistence of meaningful connections to Latin America. While editors likely reprinted these stories informally—often noting whether the newspaper in question arrived on their desk via the most recent ship to enter port or through correspondence with a traveling San Franciscan—their regularity helped collapse the distance between the two locations. More important, republishing linked the success of a journalistic enterprise in San Francisco to an editor's ability to receive legitimate and trusted news from Latin America in a timely manner. Thus, as in the case of San Francisco and Sonora, the "continual comings and goings of Sonorans to the port" nurtured an "informational interchange" between the two, with the regular republishing of articles from the official state paper of Sonora dependent on the ability to cross borders. In turn, these movements helped elite and entrepreneurial Mexicans, in particular, to simultaneously "live and operate in two worlds."[17]

The same can be said of letters from travelers. Speaking to a readership with both existent and emerging business ties to parts of Latin America, most of the periodicals printed letters from San Franciscans assessing the commercial prospects for growth in Mexico or further south. These writings were hardly benign in their political goals, often suggesting an organized effort to dominate Latin American economies and political systems in a manner described by some as "peaceful conquest."[18] Even for businesspeople less aware of a broader colonialist project, such letters facilitated individual economic enterprise. The letters from Latin America provided entrepreneurs with the firsthand accounts they needed to distinguish between rumor and fact, and thus make informed economic decisions in potentially destabilizing situations. Letters written to Alberto G. Packard, the editor of the Sonoran-focused weekly *La República*, illustrate the point. One writer, on a trip to the Mexican port of Mazatlán, informed Packard's readers of the latest news relating to the Sonoran wars against the Apaches. The Sonoran military had the situation well under control, he reported, noting that the military leadership had "been the target of unjust attacks" by a U.S. press out to sell papers.[19] Of course, travel could also entail movement within the United States, even within California. When one sojourner visited California's Central Valley, he wrote *La República* to inform its readers of the gubernatorial nominee selected by the Democratic Party of Kern County. Another letter from a Mexican in Tehachapi, California, described German migration to Colima, Mexico. Still another letter recounted the plans being made by "los mexicanos de Bakersfield" for their local September 16th celebration.[20]

Information derived from both domestic and international travel nurtured the binational character of Spanish speakers in San Francisco while furthering the growth of the transnational business sector. The news did more than sustain the presence of Latin America in the imaginary; it provided the necessary market and political knowledge to form tangible connections between the region's commercial centers and San Francisco. As they assumed the roles of interlocutors, commercial elites and entrepreneurs enabled these transnational structures and animated them through their daily lives. The information they provided San Francisco publishers extended the apparatus of which they were a part, facilitating the ability of local newspapers to also act as informational intermediaries in the Spanish-speaking hemisphere. This service carried with it a market value beyond the Spanish-speaking, a fact not lost on the editors of *El Cronista*. Calling attention to its low subscription rates, the weekly regularly included an English-language assurance to "merchants and all businessmen" that its rates "enable everyone to subscribe, and give [*El Cronista*] a most thorough and extensive circulation both in the United States, Mexico and Central America." Touting their paper as "the best Spanish advertising medium of its kind in this city," the publishers offered to translate any ads submitted in English or French into proper Spanish.[21]

The Spanish-language press in San Francisco laid the groundwork for the formation of a cohesive community identity, using a shared language and transnational condition as its tools. This identity, however, only tangentially reflected a pan–Latin American sensibility. Most often geared toward a single nationality, this generation of periodicals reflected their national leanings in ways even beyond their names and Latin American press sources. *La Voz de Méjico*, for example, crafted both a commercial and political form of transnationalism via the Mexican nationalistic project it helped mobilize in San Francisco. During the French intervention in Mexico, the paper kept its readership abreast of the events unfolding in Veracruz, as French, Spanish, and British officials sought to recoup debts owed them.[22] As the others returned across the Atlantic, and the French marched toward Puebla, *La Voz* provided delayed coverage of events, including what it described as "our triumph against the French" at the Battle of Puebla.[23] "¡¡Viva Méjico!! ¡¡Viva la Independencia!! ¡¡Vivan los valientes soldados Mejicanos!!," the paper exclaimed. This limitation, however, also suggests that the strength of these newspapers was their ability to nurture lives where interests straddled borders. As the exiled government of

Benito Juárez sought financial and political support from abroad, two San Francisco–based papers—*La Voz de Méjico* and *La Bandera Mexicana*— became increasingly committed to aiding the restoration of republican rule in their homeland, publicizing, for example, the creation of Juntas Patrióticas across the state. In the words of the San Francisco junta, expatriates established these groups with "the noble desire to directly or indirectly help and defend our country."[24] Beginning in 1862, that support took the form of monetary donations. At first contributing to a commemorative tribute for the victory of General Ignacio Zaragoza over the French, fundraising campaigns evolved to more directly serve "the war effort" of the exiled government. Juntas "raised funds to provide medical care for wounded soldiers and support for the widows and orphans of Mexican soldiers killed in battle," as well as secure the return of former prisoners of war from France and to award medals for acts of military valor.[25]

Suggestive of its role for the expatriate population of Mexicans and other Latin Americans in California, San Francisco was the center of the juntas' statewide but locally driven fundraising campaigns. With the support of the consulate office and the Spanish-language press, locals in the city created the Junta Central Directiva de la Sociedad Patriótica Mejicana. Serving as a central managing unit for the varied campaigns, and acting as a collector and remitter of funds, the group chose Manuel E. Rodríguez, editor of *La Voz*, as its treasurer. In early 1863 he sent a "modest offering" of $1,040 to the effort.[26] Such endeavors had broad support from consulate officials, who sought "to maintain the allegiance of [the nation's] sons and daughters residing temporarily (presumably) in *México de afuera.*"[27] Not surprisingly, the context of war and the defense of republican rule in Mexico further animated their efforts. Through the coordinated effort of Matías Romero—the pro-Juárez Mexican minister assigned to Washington, DC—consuls general and a small band of semiclandestine agents promoted a multifaceted campaign to secure further support. In addition to raising funds and supporting the creation of patriotic clubs in the States, they "forwarded to Mexico tons of ammunition, hundreds of thousands of guns, medical and other military stores."[28] Though the historical connections are difficult to fully unpack, it is likely this coordinated effort benefited the creation of more than a few outlets of Spanish-language journalism in San Francisco.

As Latin Americans nurtured an economic and political transnationalism between their homelands and the San Francisco Bay, individual lives embodied even more. The case of Fernando Montijo powerfully illustrates how transnational entrepreneurs and their families carved out lives spanning borders. Montijo was born in the Sonoran port of Guaymas in 1854, into a family that owned land and minor commercial interests, marking their presence among the lower strata of the local elite. The family's prospects were bolstered by Montijo's uncle, Agustín Bustamante, "one of the most important merchants in Guaymas." Along with a partner, Bustamante managed a commercial operation connecting Guaymas to Los Angeles, San Francisco, and even New York. He and his partner divided their time between Sonora and California, with the latter making his permanent residence in San Francisco. Availing himself of the opportunities presented by these "familial networks," Montijo arrived in San Francisco at the age of twenty-three and began working for his uncle's business in the city.[29] Once in the Bay Area, Montijo lived an increasingly bicultural life. While his business dealings and relations with local Mexican elites marked a high level of fluency within the "class and social hierarchies prevailing in Mexico," he also acculturated to life in the cosmopolitan city. Along with other Sonoran youth in San Francisco—young men similarly benefiting from extended familial networks—he "took advantage of all the diversions offered by the port city, including theaters, concerts, dances, and a nightlife marked by regular visits to bars and well-known brothels." His letters to friends visibly communicated the degree of his biculturalism, demonstrating his immersion in and mastery of both formal and colloquial English. Equally noteworthy, his correspondence "exhibits a bilingualism typical of a person functioning within two cultural and social realities," regularly "code switching" between English and Spanish to communicate his sentiments.[30] Upon his return to Sonora two years later, Montijo's correspondence with friends further suggested the scope of his connections to San Francisco, with the city providing a measuring stick against which life in Guaymas could be compared.

Though most Latin Americans did not migrate to San Francisco as members of an entrepreneurial elite, multiple transnational connections continually marked the lived experiences of others. The life of Hipóleta Orendain de Medina serves as an example. Born in Sonora during the war with the United States, she migrated to San Francisco with her widowed mother and younger sister toward the end of the 1850s. As the story was passed down to Orendain, her mother was an heiress to a silver mine in Mexico but spent much of her fortune organizing an army of Mexican nationals in San Francisco and funding their failed military campaign to liberate Mexico from the French.[31] The Orendain family maintained other connections to Mexico, and the young Hipóleta corresponded with acquaintances in Sonora throughout her teen years. In one reply a young woman in Mexico wrote to Orendain, "I also remember you." Making a reference to earlier conversations between the two, she expressed her hope "that you are happy surrounded by all the young miners."[32]

When she was twenty-one, Hipóleta Orendain married Emilio Medina, a "musician, editor, and diplomat," and similarly a more prominent member of the Spanish-speaking population in San Francisco. Though her husband remained active in the city—he published a Spanish-language newspaper in the 1890s—the Census of 1870 notes her as a widow, with only her children and younger sister listed as members of her household. The historical record provides an illuminating though limited view into the life of Orendain de Medina, who supported four daughters by working as a dressmaker. While it seems unlikely she ever traveled to Mexico in her adulthood, her personal artifacts include an extensive collection of "calling cards." Reflecting a common practice among socialites, the scores of small cards provide a small glimpse into the social world of which she remained a part. Among the "callers" were prominent figures such as Miguel G. Pritchard (the consul of Mexico in San Francisco) and General Francisco Leyva (military veteran of the war against France and one-time governor of the state of Morelos); well-known local professionals such as Dr. E. Maldonado (a Spanish-speaking dentist); and various callers suggesting her husband's evolving professional life. Other cards are handwritten, perhaps by visitors who exhausted their supply or could not afford a more formal demonstration of their presence. Though physically rooted to San Francisco throughout her adult life, Orendain de Medina maintained social networks marked by a dynamism spanning national borders.

## Racial Troubles and the Religious Cause

The organized movement to create a Catholic church for the Spanish-speaking existed within this nexus of a flourishing transnationalism and a relative demographic decline. Indeed, when we see Catholic religious practices and institutions themselves as objects spanning borders, the effort to create Guadalupe Church appears as nothing less than an extension of these dynamics. In the late nineteenth century, however, this institutional project also responded to more immediate concerns. Local racial tensions animated calls for unity under the auspices of Catholicism, as Latin Americans in the city communicated an uneasy relationship to ever strident U.S. racial norms. As Laura Gómez contends, with legal "whiteness" balanced by a social reality marked by "otherness," Mexicans in the United States were "uniquely situated as 'off-white.'"[33] The benefits of this position notwithstanding, the demographic ascendancy of the U.S.-born whites in California accentuated overt efforts to marginalize local Mexican ethnics. Even wealthy elites faced losing their position as they were increasingly integrated into the racialized laboring class.[34] The racial milieu of nineteenth-century San Francisco, however, presented other alternatives. While Latin Americans comprised less than 2 percent of the city's foreign-born population, the growing population of Chinese immigrants (which increased from 16 percent to more than 20 percent of the foreign-born total in the 1860s) kept San Francisco's Spanish-speaking from being the primary target of late nineteenth-century racism. The place of Chinese at the Golden Gate communicated in vivid detail the liabilities of being situated as distinctly nonwhite. These demographic and social realities fomented a context in which the two groups were sometimes pitted against one another. A brief news article in 1878 titled "The Mexican Must Go" described the extent to which the "Mexican colony of this city is being depopulated" due to an exodus of the "industrial classes." Lamenting the loss of willing laborers, the author contended that the returning Latin American emigrants "all complain that they are unable to compete with the Chinese."[35]

Though more than economics undergirded the crusade against the Chinese population in the city, the nativist tide against their presence was driven to a crescendo by their inequitable integration into the local labor market. The sharp rise in the Chinese population between 1860 and 1870, and the racially segmented wage system that predominated, facilitated the growth of industrial manufacturing in San Francisco, with lower-paid Chinese workers comprising "nearly half the workingmen employed in the city's factories" by 1872.[36] Anti-Chinese movements targeted these workers as a threat to free labor and, hence, to republicanism, with parallels often drawn between the "celestials" and slaves. Latin Americans likely benefited from this racial discourse, which cast the Chinese to the lowest end of the racial hierarchy and fostered "innumerable campaigns of persecution even more systematic and cruel than those which had been directed against the Spanish-Americans."[37] Indeed, regular violence against Chinese immigrants grew common in San Francisco, often escalating into mob action, as on July 24, 1877, when a major anti-Chinese riot drove an untold number from the city. The vitriolic nature of the racially motivated campaigns certainly provided some cause for alarm among the Spanish-speaking. The Spanish-language press often reported incidents of violence against Chinese workers, in one case noting how "boys employed in the tobacco factories are accustomed to assaulting *los chinos* who pass down Commercial Street around midday."[38] Formal Chinese exclusion in 1882 did little to alter this pattern of recreational violence, since in "sanctioning racism, it perpetuated racism, and by sanctioning racist policy at the highest levels of government, it helped legitimize racist action at every level of society."[39] Even with the passage of the restriction law, the Chinese population in the city continued to grow (from under 22,000 in 1880 to over 31,000 in 1890), in addition to becoming further concentrated in the ever shrinking segregated zone of Chinatown.[40] Taken together, Latin Americans and their descendants in San Francisco had less to fear concerning their place in the city than did Chinese residents, though such consolations provided more tension than relief.

The intersection of these varied forces, although difficult to assess, may have nurtured an assimilative impulse among San Francisco's Latin Americans. For the wealthy, in particular, assimilation hinged on the ability to frame their cultural connections to European civility (and hence, their non-Chineseness), as well as their ability to participate in the city's elite social life. The strategies of women like Dulce Bolado Davis, who descended from Mexican *californios* but recounted her family's history by distinguishing its connections to Spain, are better understood in light of these forces.[41] While little is known of her family's struggles to maintain its standing, Bolado Davis represented its success. Coming of age in the late nineteenth century, she attended a school for girls run by a French woman. While she admitted they learned very little academically, she praised the woman for teaching them "culture and refinement."[42] The Bolado family participated in upper-class life, remaining actively engaged in the broader social sphere. Bolado Davis remembered "there was quite a colony of French and Spanish families; each had a reception day and friends came together with delightful formal informality to indulge in nothing more exciting than the lost art of conversation."[43] Such practices may have helped to distinguish the family from working-class Latin Americans, as it further associated them with the European-descent mainstream. The effects of this on a new generation of San Franciscans born to Latin Americans were undoubtedly many, not the least of which was the gradual loss of their connection to Spanish-speaking culture. In her evocation of Woodward's Gardens, a retreat marked by elite respectability, Bolado Davis recalled the grounds "full of statuary, birds, animals and a boat in a lake of lilies" with the same exotic wonderment as she remembered after seeing "Spanish students" in the venue's music hall.[44]

The unstable racial climate also fostered uneasiness among working-class Latin Americans, those on the other end of the social spectrum from men and women like Montijo, Orendain de Medina, and Bolado Davis.

Clearly, the greater the social distance between Latin Americans and Chinese the greater the likelihood that the former would benefit from being "off-white." For that reason, the long-standing representation of Latin Americans in the entertainment ventures in San Francisco's vice districts was an area of concern. The transnational sex industry, which took root in the city during the Gold Rush, continued to flourish throughout much of the mid- to late century. Brothels, melodeons, and fandangos remained among the most vibrant demonstrations of "the immigrant character of the city," where Latin Americans were often both laborers and clientele. Fernando Montijo—with deep connections to the transnational merchant class in the city—spent much of his free time in the city with prostitutes. In letters to one "madame," he asked that she send his regards to "María la China, Clara la Irlandesa, Pauline la flaca y Antonia." The sex industry constituted such an important part of his experience in the city that when he returned to Guaymas the town seemed "abominable" by comparison.[45] Indeed it must have seemed so to anyone who grew accustomed to the sex industry in San Francisco—marked by its full integration into urban social life as well as its diverse structures, patrons, and laboring classes. In addition to brothels, for example, melodeons provided performances involving "bawdy songs, skits, and dances, principally the cancan; and, in a few places catering principally to Mexicans and Negroes, obscene poses by 'finely formed females.'" Another sex entertainment establishment "offered the bawdiest and most obscene shows" and hired only French and "Spanish women."[46]

The campaign for a Spanish-speaking church arose to ameliorate these tensions marking migration to and resettlement in San Francisco—namely, the ascendency and institutionalization of new forms of racialist politics, an assimilative tendency among some elites, and a vice district involving (and implicating) Latin Americans. The strategic decision to pursue a religious cause demonstrated an acute recognition of the Catholic faith's potential to nurture and assert a more palatable presence of the Spanish-speaking. Employing Catholicism to foster unity and bridge population divides built on the city's strong Catholic tradition. Catholicism, after all, had come to San Francisco Bay with the first Spanish visitors in 1769. The system of colonialism that created the city invoked a "religious purpose," albeit one "that concealed the political and territorial motivation behind it."[47] The nineteenth-century transformations incited by gold eclipsed the church's centrality in the lives of local Mexicans, as the financial and cultural realities of the "new" city dominated. Yet, for those who remained, the church quite literally structured their community. Though not substantial in population, a small pueblo of Mexicans remained clustered around Mission Dolores throughout the 1850s.[48] Detached from the core of the new urban center of the Pacific, it struck one visitor as emblematic of a more primordial time: "About one hundred and twenty persons live around the Mission. Most of them are Mexicans, Indians, or half-breeds; Europeans and Americans are in the minority. There is no business activity here beyond the raising of garden produce which brings in quick returns. Everything else is at a standstill. An alcalde, a combination of mayor and justice of the peace found in Spanish countries, is the sole person in authority."[49] In an era marked by the prolonged process of conquest, prejudices based on race and religion helped define the lines between inclusion and marginalization. Not surprisingly, Mexicans relied on institutions that could provide them some protection from the legal, economic, and cultural assaults waged against them by the new majority. The Mexican pueblo surrounding the mission served as a testament to the ability of the Catholic Church to provide that safety, if not in reality, then at least symbolically. Unquestionably, the institution also provided some sense of continuity between the Yerba Buena that was and the San Francisco that was in process of "becoming." If it had served the Spanish-speaking once before, could it not do so again?

As a group of Spanish-speaking elites ascended to various positions of leadership among the population they later called "our people,"[50] they sought to exploit this tradition for the benefit of their entire community. The group was largely comprised of the heads of various Latin American consulates and other prominent people whose work or political position fostered the transnational character of Latin American life in the city. In the early 1870s, their collective effort took the shape of an crusade to raise funds for the building of a Spanish-language Catholic church. In a "circular letter" seeking the support of "all the *raza española* living in the city and surrounding area," they lamented the profound decline in the social status of their population. A Spanish national church, they reasoned, could operate as a tool to achieve multiple ends, including enhancing the spiritual lives and the social standing of their community's members. Accordingly, they sought a parish whose charge would be to serve the Spanish-speaking population as a whole and, in the process, foster its sense of fellowship as a community.

They framed their goal as means to an end as much as an end in itself. In their letter, members of the leadership described their desire to create a "grand effect" among the Spanish-speaking, "a powerful and energetic echo to animate the timid."[51] Undoubtedly, an enhancement and expansion of their own influence constituted at least one of the many re-verberations of this echo. As numerous historians have argued, Mexican consulates have historically played an active role in communities of ex-patriates in the Southwest.[52] By fostering a continued national allegiance they helped assure the stability and health of their national state in times of crisis, as in the earlier example of the French intervention in Mexico. Con-suls and their offices also played a "central role in organizing community life" for their constituencies through their support of fraternal organiza-tions and cultural institutions abroad, ranging from "celebrations of Mexi-can holidays to the formation of Spanish-language schools."[53] In San Fran-cisco, this kind of consular activity predated similar efforts in other parts of the Southwest. Largely because of the deep financial and commercial connections between San Francisco and multiple parts of Latin America, the consulates of nearly every Latin American country had an office in the city by 1852. By the late nineteenth century, the political culture's use of an overt racialist discourse and a growing tendency toward assimilation likely caused some concern in the consulates. Accordingly, the project of a Span-ish-language church also responded to more local concerns, as these po-litical elites and the business interests they supported sought some form of organized community to provide a voice in financial and municipal circles.

The varied motivations and intentional strategy of these elites are re-flected in their fundraising letter of 1871. "In this city," they wrote, "those of us who are of *la raza española* will never achieve strength or respectability if we are not united, and there is no unity without a core. This core must necessarily be religious, otherwise it is impossible to produce the strong union that is so indispensible."[54] As they mobilized the "core," the authors did not avoid a forthright confrontation with the challenges facing the cre-ation of a "strong union." In the letter, they detailed the "main objections" to the building of such a church. These "objections" are better understood as logistical challenges, but the rhetorical tactic of addressing an imagined opposition provides an interesting perspective on these elites' view of the wider population. Most of their perceived objections related to the status of the Spanish-speaking in the city and their capacity to undertake such an effort. "That our race is not visible, in either number or in financial abun-dance," was the first "objection" in the writers' estimation. In addition to widespread poverty, they acknowledged the phenomenon of assimilation ("we are losing the distinctive character of *nuestra raza*") and the lack of demographic concentration ("living scattered in various parts throughout the city") as other formidable challenges. The solution to them all became the construction of a Spanish-language church.

The circular not only recognizes the tensions marking life for "la raza española" in the city but also communicates a distinct strategy to ease them. In the minds of this efforts' leaders, religion was a cause the larger (non-Latino) polity would view as legitimate and good, one "so powerful that it can stand up to all opposing causes."[55] The political landscape of San Francisco Catholicism made this calculation both logical and safe. In this period, San Francisco was home to the "largest [Catholic] parish west of the Mississippi"[56] and a site served by three skilled administrators from the Gold Rush to the Depression: Archbishops Joseph Sadoc Alemany, Patrick W. Riordan, and Edward J. Hanna. Demonstrating the strength of the city's Catholic community, when Riordan assumed leadership of the archdiocese (which at the time encompassed all of Northern California), he was able to retire a $600,000 debt, build a new cathedral, and construct and open a new seminary, all within his first fifteen years.[57] Never far from the machinations of City Hall, Catholic influence was not limited to church leadership. Four of the six mayors who served between 1897 and 1934 were Catholic. At the turn of the century, when an anti-Catholic organization began distributing propaganda, Catholic interests coalesced in the birth of a new men's club and the first printing of a politically inclined church newspaper, *The Monitor*. Among the supporters of the club was William Sullivan, a future chief of police.[58] For Latin American elites, the goal of constructing a Catholic Church meant connecting with this solidifying influence and, potentially, playing a larger role in the city's political destiny.

The consuls envisioned a common, unified, pan-Latin identity as well as a pathway to greater influence in the city, not only for their offices but for all Spanish-speaking Latinos in the city. In their circular letter they framed their cause as a response to the loss of status experienced by "our race" and "our people," expressing what David Gutiérrez has called an "affirmative sense of themselves as an ethnic minority of a larger society."[59] Their Catholic faith, described as "the soul of Spanish honor," represented the base of their cohesion. As they made their case, they portrayed what they sought to foster. They used terms not limited to any one nationality—such as *la raza española* and *hispanoamericanos*—and described Latin Americans as being collectively "sensitive, generous, noble, and able to live in abnegation without limit."[60] The most overt form of collective identity promoted was that of *hispanoamericanos* united through the commonality of daily life in late nineteenth-century San Francisco. The general lack of standing and effective power helped constitute this common condition, as did a shared condition of vice and criminality. So, too, did the loss of "our native tongue" and the "erosion and perversion of our culture." "Is it not a crime," the writers of the circular letter asked, "to contribute to our apathy and indifference regarding the loss of the distinctive character of our people?"[61]

The writers also recognized other challenges facing the collective effort of San Francisco's *raza española*. Chief among their concerns was the divisiveness of "nationality [and] political opinion." Indeed, the primary challenge of and need for the unity they sought was the internal diversity of the Spanish-speaking population. Though Mexicans made up the majority of San Francisco Latin Americans at the time, representatives from Central and South American consulates led the drive for the church. Present to a larger extent in the city than in other urban centers in the United States, the diversity of Latin Americans in San Francisco reflected the historical transnational networks connecting the bay to multiple ports in the hemisphere. Cognizant of this diversity, church advocates based their movement on the shared "heritage" of language and religious faith. In seeking to benefit the "Hispanic American residents and visitors to this ever growing city," they invoked the "evangelical doctrine . . . to propagate the faith" as well as an emotional plea for Latin Americans to unite—a sense of their collective "fraternity."[62] In this context, their strategy can be seen as a counterstance to the marginalizing effects of empire. As Aims McGuinness argues in his book on Panama during the same period, confrontations with "a concerted Anglo-Saxon onslaught" helped inspire nascent forms of "pan-Latin theorizing" in parts of Latin America. Though the developments bore little fruit in terms of formal diplomatic alliances between concerned nations, they did represent something meaningful "in the realm of political imagination."[63] In San Francisco, such panethnic mobilizations were less theoretical and more organizational. Pan-Latin mobilization constituted an affirmative step toward individual and group survival, deliberately aware as its leaders were of the struggles faced by Latin American immigrants in a city imbued with "American" notions of racial superiority. As people participating in an economic context reflected and nourished by increasing U.S. economic hegemony in the hemisphere, pan-Latin mobilizations confronted the necessary separation from the familial and familiar as the city's Latin Americans sought an alternative, responsive grouping. When local Latin American leaders asserted a collective identity as the basis of their cause—in effect, *latinismo*—they both challenged the evolving processes of marginalization and assimilation they confronted and also tacitly framed an understanding of their collective experience as determined by the broader contours of life in the U.S. racial milieu. At the same time, their version of pan-Latinism could strengthen itself by connecting to legitimate concerns about the future of their home countries.[64]

In addition to the broader political and social strategy of "unity," the creation of a national church would also serve the very pragmatic purpose of religious ministry to the Spanish-speaking. Without a priest fluent in Spanish, the Catholic Church of nineteenth-century San Francisco could never fully serve the spiritual needs of Latin Americans. The circular based most of its argument for the national parish on this very fact. "Those who come and then return, as well as many who remain here permanently, will never know more English than they do now," reasoned the authors. Quoting the logic of St. Paul they asked, "How can they believe (or have faith) if they don't hear? How can they hear if there is no one to preach?" They continued, "And how can someone preach to them (we say) if they don't understand?" When it came to the administration of the sacraments—such as last rites—the circular made its strongest plea. "A messenger (stunned and only slightly aware) runs from church to church and from priest to priest before finding one who knows Spanish, while our compatriot, our friend, or perhaps even our loved one dies without the comfort of our holy religion and without a word of consolation."[65]

These cultural arguments, framed as they were by spiritual need, provide an alternative way of understanding the campaign to build the church. The consulates envisioned the institution as a vehicle both to combat assimilation and to promote a distinct version of cultural instruction. As they confronted "detractors" who argued against a culturally specific church and acquiesced to the gradual loss of the "distinctiveness of our own heritage" in a sea of Americanism, the authors of the circular letter challenged their constituency's sense of "brotherhood." The opposition, they wrote, "abandon our brethren whom they encourage to adapt or even lose themselves among a people whose character and beliefs these detractors condemn." Their church, in contrast, "would not only preserve the purity [of the Spanish language] and spread its use; it would also help induce many others to adopt our religious belief."[66] While assimilation can certainly be understood as a product of the material experience of empire, so, too, can the battle against it—often expressed as something of a conservative counterstance. Seeking to nurture and preserve a Latin American identity via an essentialized set of cultural practices, the collection of consulships recognized a collective *hispanoamericano* identity as a necessary precondition for their cultural project, as well as for furthering their power in the social and political landscapes.

Ultimately, the various arguments proved persuasive. The circular letter and the accompanying campaign mobilized enough financial support from the local community while also securing the endorsement of Catholic

Church officials in the city. In 1876, only five years after the circular first appeared, Archbishop Joseph Alemany established the national parish of Nuestra Señora de Guadalupe. Located in North Beach, on Broadway near Mason Street, Our Lady of Guadalupe Church formally opened its doors in 1880. Andrés Garriega served as the first pastor, with Antonio M. Santandreu as his assistant. Santandreu became a pillar of the community for more than half a century, serving as pastor from 1889 to his death in 1944. A child named Teresa Castro was the first baptized, while Mr. D. Juan C. Cebrián and Miss Josefa de Laveaga were the first couple married.[67] Rebuilt after the fire of 1906, Guadalupe Church served as the "Spanish" national parish of the city of San Francisco until its closure in 1992.[68]

## Guadalupe Church and Latino Community

In its century-long history, Our Lady of Guadalupe Church embodied multiple meanings for the Spanish-speaking population. Within a generation of its founding, the church had become a symbol of Latin American victory over a past mired in "unfortunate treatment." In a postearthquake history published in its newsletter, Guadalupe Church was celebrated as the end of the era in which "the Spanish-speaking inhabitants gradually lost importance, in part due to their small number compared with the rest of the population and also because they gradually lost their personal wealth, not knowing how to defend themselves against the new methods."[69] The community recognized the church's wider significance in the spiritual guidance it offered to Spanish-speaking Catholics. Undoubtedly, this helped assure a smoother transition to life in a new country with a new culture and language. For Latin American immigrants who spoke little or no English, participating in services offered by Guadalupe Church meant engaging in a form of cultural continuity between their present and past. As David A. Badillo contends, the "immigrant church" in the United States has historically allowed Latin Americans to maintain an "ongoing relationship" with their homelands. While its presence in the United States frames a degree of integration into the new, "they are simultaneously pulled back to their roots" in the language and customs of their religious home.[70] Put another way, Guadalupe Church facilitated the ability of the Spanish-speaking to maintain a closeness to their religious faith (and perhaps their "Latinness") that would not have existed if they could not receive sacraments such as last rites, confession, and marriage in their native tongue. Of course, the benefits flowing from a "national parish" structure extend beyond the individual. A space that nurtures a stable and "secure identity" for

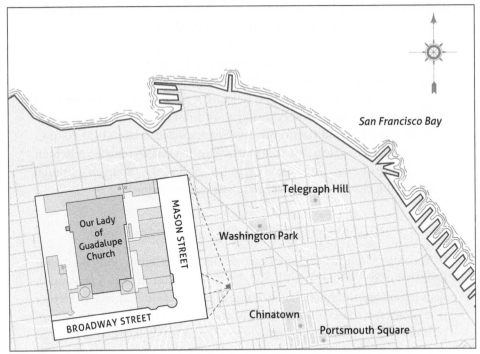

Map of Our Lady of Guadalupe Church and surrounding area, 1906

an immigrant population helps parishioners cease "to be mere objects of ministry" and become a constituency able to "exercise [its] own ministerial role."[71] On the level of community building, then, la Iglesia Guadalupe created a space in which the culture and spirituality of its members became the commonality upon which a strengthened sense of collectivity could be built. Accordingly, the processes of becoming a Catholic congregation and a Spanish-speaking community were intertwined and, in many ways, dependent on one another.

As the institution propagating the cultural, social, and intellectual practices that comprise a religion, the church is fundamental to envisioning a communal religious identity as well as constituting the physical geography of where cultural religiosity manifests. In the case of San Francisco's Latinos, it both reflected and created religious culture and community. To understand such phenomena we must examine the church as much more than a physical building, or even a social institution. At its base the church is a community of people defined by their beliefs and common cultural practices. In short, organized religion fosters "congregation"—what James P. Wind and James W. Lewis have defined as "a body of people who regularly gather to worship at a particular place," requiring both intentional and regular assembly (gathering for the purpose of worship) and a place for that gathering to occur.[72] When these dynamics take root successfully, as they did at Guadalupe Church, the results are visible by secular measures as well. As the central institution in the lives of the Spanish-speaking, Guadalupe Church mimicked the church in Latin America, occupying the physical hub of an emerging residential and commercial community. Representing no less a form of cultural continuity than the celebrations within, the construction of the church further marked the immediate geography surrounding it as "Spanish" or "Mexican," creating something of a symbolic center to which others were drawn. Lying roughly west of Columbus Avenue, and bounded on the north and south by Filbert and Washington Streets and on the east by Jones Street, this smaller sector of the city composed part of the larger district known as the Latin Quarter. Though Latinos were less numerous here than the French, Italian, and Portuguese immigrants who initially gave the area its name, by some calculations more than half of all the Spanish-surnamed population of San Francisco resided in the Latin Quarter by 1880.[73] With Nuestra Señora providing regular religious services and a central community space, even Latinos who did not reside in the barrio made weekly visits.

By the early twentieth century the neighborhood surrounding Guadalupe Church had solidified its ethnic character. The presence of the church organized the population of this barrio, which stretched out along the city grid from the Broadway and Mason Street intersection, in an increasingly common terrain that bore clear indicators of the presence of the Spanish-speaking. By 1920, at least a third of San Francisco's Mexican population resided in what was now called the "Mexican colony" or "Spanish colony."[74] Nestled between North Beach and Chinatown, and just on the other side of "the central artery of San Francisco's vice and tourist district,"[75] Guadalupe Church stood as the enclave's most consistent resident. The church that by definition had no geographic boundaries, functioned more as a de facto "regular" parish. Within a few generations, many (if not most) of its parishioners lived near it. For example, in the 1940s, when almost 350 parishioners signed and submitted a petition to the church, nearly all of them listed an address in its general vicinity.[76] Regardless of where the Spanish-speaking lived, by the mid-twentieth century, Our Lady of Guadalupe Church attracted at least their spiritual presence. A 1936 census report identifies the parish membership at 6,000 strong, representing a sizable percentage of the city's total Spanish-speaking population.[77]

The Guadalupe barrio had more than a physical church to imbue its geography with a sense of "Latin" culture. Throughout the late nineteenth and early twentieth century, a Latin American business district thrived on the same city streets, no doubt an effect of the presence of the church and its parishioners. The foundation of this community existed before the construction of Guadalupe Church, though Latinos were outnumbered by the neighborhood's Italian residents. As one late nineteenth-century observer noted, "Shops with such titles as *La Sorpresa* and the *Tienda Mexicana* adjoin the *Unita d'Italia* and *Roma* saloon."[78] Nuestra Señora catalyzed this phenomenon, primarily with businesses having no connection to the church other than through language. Spanish-language newspapers featured regular advertisements from neighborhood physicians like Manuel J. Urrea and Enrique M. Aldaña. Music schools, jewelry stores, and dancing halls in the neighborhood also advertised their services.[79] Publishers of Spanish-language books and newspapers as well as two printing shops were also located in the barrio. The business district included restaurants, markets, and bakeries specializing in Latin American food. Not surprisingly, periodic church publications also provided an opportunity for these businesses to find customers by offering a taste of the familiar. The City of Mexico advertised itself as a "genuine Mexican restaurant." Panadería Española, El Bule de Oro, and a store owned by a Señor R. Cosio all sold "Mexican foods," including baked goods, meats, and tamales. La Novedad sold desserts and candies, in both large and bulk quantities.[80]

The existence of the Guadalupe barrio, while significant as a visible manifestation of the Spanish-speaking community, also suggested some of the persistent limits to the cultural cohesion and continuity it could provide. While efforts to establish the church required panethnic organization of the Spanish-speaking population in all its diversity, a majority of that population had roots in one nation: Mexico. The cultural dominance of the ethnic Mexican community nurtured a nationalistic rather than pan–Latin American model of community. Such tendencies rendered Nicaraguans, Salvadorans, and South Americans largely invisible. The dynamic reflected itself in the composition of the business district. El Bule de Oro, for example, sought customers by advertising its "complete assortment of Mexican effects, especially in *salsas, chorizos,* and all class of spices for making the best tamales,"[81] recognizably Mexican delicacies. The dominance of such merchants facilitated the ability of a *mexicano* clientele to remain connected to its culinary and cultural pasts in a way that it did not for other Latin Americans. While from a business perspective catering to the "Mexican market" made sense, in the more delicate realm of cultural representation and ethnic unification it could also function as a "Mexican bias." This ethnic dominance could challenge the evolving project of pan-ethnic community, and at times it contributed to rivalry and tension among other Latin American nationalities. The cultural disparity remained as the years progressed. In the thirties, the Xochimilco Café and Azteca Grocery Store suggested the continued Mexican bias in name if not in content.[82]

The Mexican plurality also tended to determine the character of Guadalupe Church. Already named after the "patron saint of Mexico," the church regularly served as a community center for overtly Mexican cultural and political events. Primary among these, the commemoration of Mexican independence allowed *mexicanos*—especially those who had fled the violence of the Mexican Revolution—to celebrate the progress achieved by their *patria* while uniting their *paisanos* in the same customary celebrations as were held in Mexico. An annual mass celebrating the independence of Mexico was held at Nuestra Señora every September. As in Los Angeles, the nationalist organizations hosting these festivities often had direct relationships with the Mexican consulate.[83] Planning for the week-long festivities took an entire year and was overseen by a committee of more than 100 led by A. K. Coney, the Mexican consul in San Francisco.[84]

Guadalupe Church became the venue for larger competitions within the "Mexican colony." A year after the Hidalgo Club organized a celebration of the ninetieth anniversary of Mexican independence, the group met again to coordinate the next commemoration. The growth in the Mexican population and the incorporation of some business leaders into the group meant their plans entailed no financial or other support from the Mexican consulate. Whether this precipitated the rift or not is unclear, but weeks ahead of the festivities Consul Coney accused the club president—Colonel Juan Guillermo Reed—of being an "imposter," saying he never served in the Mexican army.[85] The rift widened as the Hidalgo Club and Coney's Mexican Patriotic Society of San Francisco held competing celebrations within one day of each other.[86] Perhaps reflecting the rise of a more assimilated population, or merely a leadership not beholden to the Mexican government, no record clarifies which group attended the annual mass.

Mexican patriotism and culture rooted themselves to Guadalupe Church via various other events and organizations. The Zaragoza and Hidalgo Clubs hosted an annual Cinco de Mayo celebration, usually entailing a dance as well as a mass.[87] As in communities throughout Mexico, the celebration of the December 12 feast of the Virgin of Guadalupe provided for an annual Mexican cultural display throughout the faith community. A novena or triduum offered to "Our Lady"—a service where the faithful pray the rosary, in the case of the latter, over three consecutive nights—preceded a formal service on the actual feast day.[88] Hardly confined to the walls of Guadalupe, a significant part of the celebration entailed a procession through the barrio to the church. No matter where they took place, the fiestas for the Virgin of Guadalupe became important "because they layered religious veneration and Mexican culture into a celebration for the entire Mexican *colonia* to see and participate in."[89]

The icon of the Virgin of Guadalupe represented a particularly visible marker of the predominance of Mexican cultural celebration at the church. The *sociedades guadalupanas* had existed in local parishes throughout the Southwest since the early twentieth century. Created as associations who prayed to the Virgin Mary, performed some regular duties for the church, and held cultural festivities throughout the year, these societies grew in importance, far beyond a single day in December. As Mexican Catholics fled their war-torn homeland, they reestablished a connection with their spiritual and cultural pasts in their organized "devotion to the central icon of Mexican spirituality." Thus, in these pious associations the *mexicano* parishioners could participate in a religious devotion as well as a celebration of *mexicanidad*. By 1957, in the San Francisco Archdiocese as a whole, seventeen parishes had Guadalupana societies. That same year, in an attempt to coordinate their strength, the archdiocese created a Guadalupana Federation, with Father Luis Almendares serving as first chaplain.[90] At the time an assistant pastor at St. Peter's parish, in the Mission District, Almendares earned the respect of Mexicans throughout the archdiocese for his leadership of the federation. In fact, that involvement was enough to outweigh the fact that Almendares had been born not in Mexico but in Nicaragua.

The Guadalupanas highlighted the kinds of identity and community formation that could be activated by the church. Unquestionably religiously based, their functions "encouraged the attendance of all Mexicans, regardless of class or citizenship status, country of birth, and, in a few cases, even religious affiliation." A more cohesive and recognizable community resulted. Furthermore, as the Guadalupanas forged those bonds through a celebration of ethnic and situational similarity, they "helped ethnic Mexicans resist their marginalization within the American Catholic Church."[91] This process transcended the local as well. Having created a federation, the associations held annual meetings for the entire Archdiocese of San Francisco. Covering more than a dozen counties, this brought together more than 100 Guadalupana members in a yearly display of solidarity and fellowship.[92]

In the city of San Francisco, the Guadalupana society at Our Lady of Guadalupe Church operated at a distance from the more member-concentrated areas of San Jose and Stockton. Still, where the Guadalupanas operated, benefits were to be felt. Women, in particular, found leadership positions within the associations as they far outnumbered men in actual membership. In creating an acceptable sphere for women to exert influence, the Guadalupana societies also allowed for their increased involvement in the Church, an avenue unavailable to nonmembers. While the vast majority of participatory roles for women in the Church built upon their traditional gender roles—maintaining altar accessories, decorating the church with flowers, cleaning the church, cooking for festivals, preparing crafts for sale—the societies themselves could not have existed in any form without the same traditional networks for recruitment and publicity.[93] Regardless of gender, the specific cultural meanings of *mexicanidad* advanced by the *sociedades guadalupanas*, and the numerical dominance of Mexicans in the community, limited involvement to the Mexican segment of the Spanish-speaking population as a whole.

La Iglesia Guadalupe was much more than an institution for the ethnic Mexican population of San Francisco. Salvadoran, Nicaraguan, and various South American nationalities found in the church a space to mark important events in their homelands, celebrate the feast day of local saints, and even mobilize aid drives for those back home. Suggestive of the hopes and calculations with which leaders had created it, the church also forged bonds among the diverse Latin Americans of the city, creating a functional "group solidarity."[94] In both physical and imagined ways the Latin American-descent population in the city joined together weekly in the rituals of the Catholic faith. Regular masses and other offerings of the sacraments were not denominated by ethnicity or nationality but instead were offered to a single community bound by language and faith. As much as Guadalupe Church provided outlets for distinctly nationalistic concerns—such as the annual celebration of Mexican independence—it also nurtured the possibility of even greater unity among groups. At times this dynamic incorporated Latin American nationalism, as in 1904 when parishioners celebrated a single, combined mass to commemorate both Mexican and Chilean independence.[95] In 1921, the centennial of independence united Mexican residents and their consular officials with those of Honduras, Guatemala, El Salvador, Costa Rica, and Nicaragua in a celebratory mass and, later, dance.[96] Other times the symbol of *La Virgen* acted as a unifier. Salvadoran and Nicaraguan celebrations of the Immaculate Conception, just before the feast of Guadalupe in December, connected to the annual

A girls' class preparing to enter Nuestra Señora de
Guadalupe Church to celebrate the Feast of the Assumption, 1924.
San Francisco History Center, San Francisco Public Library.

Mexican devotional in both timing and reverence. As perhaps the only Spanish-speaking institution crossing the boundaries of nationalism and class, Guadalupe Church had at least the potential to perform the kinds of community-building once envisioned by its founders.

Guadalupe Church played a formative role in reshaping one part of the city as a home for the Spanish-speaking, no matter where they originated. As it did, it also helped to secure the presence of the Latin American-descent population in the city. When the 1906 earthquake and fire nearly destroyed San Francisco—turning Nuestra Señora into a pile of rubble and ash—city elites supplanted the democratic government and took command of rebuilding their seat of empire. As Philip L. Fradkin deftly demonstrates, part of their vision for a new city entailed removing certain enclaves, such as Chinatown, racialized as dirty and filled with disease.[97] The continued presence of the Chinese community in San Francisco remained a contested issue for some time, with local business interests emerging victorious when Chinatown was allowed to rebuild.[98] However, in a Catholic-friendly city, the Catholic leadership's cause of rebuilding all of its parishes—including Guadalupe—was never in question. As the twentieth century progressed, Nuestra Señora assumed its multiple roles in the realms of spirituality, culture, and even politics, each time equipping the broader community to cope with aspects of its diversity. For example, shortly after the reconstructed church opened, the local community found itself encountering some of the same problems that marked life for their forebears—namely, crime and violence. Guadalupe Church helped frame a collective voice for local residents, at times even crossing over traditional barriers. In 1915, in a response to local assaults, Mexican, Filipino, and "Spanish" community members asked the San Francisco Police Department to assign an additional officer to weekend evening patrol. The multiethnic and multinational collective threatened to form its own "defense league" if law enforcement officials did not comply.[99]

## The Decline of Nuestra Señora de Guadalupe

In the years leading up to World War II, an increased flow of Latin American migrants to San Francisco further challenged the ability of Guadalupe Church to create unity, exposing the wider Catholic hierarchy's ignorance of the particular needs of the Spanish-speaking. By 1950, the Mexican-born population of San Francisco had reached 5,600, or 4.6 percent of the total foreign-born. However, the population of Central and South

American–born (6,855 or 5.6%) outnumbered them.[100] And at roughly the same time as Our Lady of Guadalupe Church faced the growing presence of non-Mexican Latinos, the parish confronted a leadership crisis. After the death in 1944 of Father Santandreu—pastor of the church for more than half a century—the archbishop appointed Father Charles J. Murphy, a "faithful man" within Catholic circles but also a priest who spoke no Spanish. Although Murphy was assisted by Father Rosendo Villaseñor, a Spanish speaker, this situation must have left the pastor somewhat alienated from much of his flock. When the archbishop transferred Father Villaseñor in 1949—despite the organized protests of hundreds of parishioners—the parish was left without a Spanish-speaking priest at all.[101] For a time it seemed that Guadalupe Church no longer served the very need that gave rise to its existence.

The significance of these administrative decisions was not lost on Father Murphy, who consistently acknowledged his limitations and the problems they created in correspondence with the archdiocese. While the record of his efforts is not complete, it is clear that he advocated for a permanent Spanish-speaking assistant in meetings with archdiocesan representatives. In a letter after one such meeting, he apologized to the chancellor secretary of the archdiocese as he restated his position.

> You must excuse my vehemence during our discussion the other day but I feel strongly on the question of leaving me alone or practically alone in this church. To my mind it is out of the question for these reasons.
>
> A Priest who speaks Spanish and incidentally has a knowledge of English and an automobile is essential as an assistant if this national parish is to continue caring for the spiritual needs of the Spanish speaking people of the city and county. I might note that during the year 1950 we performed 112 marriages and 311 baptisms and that up to this date we have had 44 marriages and 128 baptisms. About 90% of these people are Spanish speaking only and require a priest who can understand their language. I mention a car because we have frequent calls to practically every hospital in San Francisco as well as numerous house calls and funerals. We are summoned by reason of the language.[102]

Presenting many of the same issues as did the 1871 circular letter contributing to Guadalupe's founding, Murphy ultimately mounted a successful argument. In 1951, Father Santiago Iglesias, a *salvadoreño*, was appointed to the parish to assist Murphy. However, the lack of a full-time Spanish-speaking priest during this period is revealing. While the construction and maintenance of Our Lady of Guadalupe Church suggest a continued level of support on the part of the institutional church, that support could also fluctuate and be shaped by the same kinds of cultural ignorance framing life for Latinos in other parts of the state. The two years they went without a Spanish-speaking priest reveals as much.

Father Iglesias later became pastor and served the parish until 1970. His presence surely made a difference to the growing number of *salvadoreño* immigrants as well as the Latin American community at large. Unfortunately, to a few of the long-standing *mexicanos*, the difference was for the worse. Indicative of the kinds of ethnic rivalries that had challenged the community in the early period and would for decades to come, some Mexicans clung to the representational advantage they had enjoyed for half a century. Their ethnic nationalism could play out in church politics as some sought to maintain the "Mexican character" of Guadalupe Church above all else. If an assigned priest came from Latin America and spoke Spanish, the local church hierarchy likely felt it had met the service burden of the national parish. Some local Mexicans, however, insisted their local priest be from Mexico. Though the *nicaragüense* Father Alemendares—whose work with the Guadalupanas placed him beyond reproach for nationalists[103]—faced no overt movement to have him replaced, a contingent of Mexicans did try to remove Father Iglesias from his post. Encouraging the archbishop to appoint a Mexican priest to the parish, a 1953 letter suggested that the national and ethnic disparity between Mexican and Salvadoran was too great. "We have been enduring for a long time the lack of a good understanding priest for our colony. We do not understand why churches of different nationalities like french [*sic*], italian [*sic*], etc., have priest from the old country to attend to their own people but in our church it has been impossible to obtain a Mexican priest for a long time," they wrote. They accused Iglesias of being "very selfish and queer and he does not love Our Lady of Guadalupe." Clearly finding fault with Iglesias because of his nationality, they wrote that "the actual priest at Nuestra Señora de Guadalupe is not the type for our church. In fact, none of the Central or South America priests in the Bay Area are." The letter closed with a clear sentiment: "We hope your Excellency will attend [to] ou[r] petition as we want to keep our Church Nuestra Señora de Guadalupe as it is and as it has been, Mexican for the Spanish Speaking people."[104]

While the views expressed by these and other parishioners contain obvious references to the *mexicano* versus *latinoamericano* rift within the population, other more material forces incited a period of decline for

Our Lady of Guadalupe parish, one beginning as early as the aftermath of World War II. Though the lack of a charismatic priest may have been a problem for some parishioners, nearly the entire community was affected by municipally funded development in the district. In 1950 construction began on the Broadway Tunnel, just in front and west of the church, reducing attendance and permanently dislocating part of the barrio.[105] The arrival of a new population of Spanish speakers, and their settlement in other sectors of the city, flowered in the same period. Father Murphy's death in 1952 added to the picture of a parish in flux. Father Iglesias succeeded Murphy in the positions of head administrator and pastor of the parish. For the Mexicans who had long advocated for a priest from "the old country," Iglesias served the additional role of scapegoat for a parish in decline. Two wrote of Iglesias: "He has chased away the 99½% of the Mexicans from our Church and he is so despotic and ignorant in liturgy that it is impossible to have him any longer."[106]

Despite periods of setback, and the continued challenges of ethnic and national rivalries among the Spanish-speaking, the church and the faith community lasted throughout the century. In some ways the maturation of the city's Latino population signaled the final period of decline for Guadalupe Church. Already by midcentury, several parishes throughout the city incorporated a Spanish-speaking priest into their regular services. By 1960 some 150 Spanish-speaking priests resided in parishes all over the archdiocese, reducing in practical terms the importance of Guadalupe Church as a spiritual service center.[107] Coupled with the dispersal of the mid-twentieth-century migration flow from Latin America, Nuestra Señora declined in significance in the community as other parishes—like St. Kevin's and St. Anthony's or St. Peter's in the heart of the Mission District—gradually grew in the roles they played in the local Spanish-speaking community. Like Guadalupe, these "new" Spanish-speaking parishes both promoted the creation of pan–Latin American community and identity and provided a space within which rivalries and divisions could be played out.

Father Murphy noted the demographic changes to the community surrounding Nuestra Señora as early as 1946. In his annual Parish Historical Report for that year, responding to the query for information regarding the changes in parish populations, Murphy recognized two movements that would continue in subsequent decades. "The Spanish speaking population is leaving the district in large numbers," he wrote. "The Chinese have bought property next to [the] church and are progressively buying the whole block on which the church is located and spreading in the direction of Van Ness Avenue."[108] Later reports described the same. "Year after year the Spanish-speaking families move to way out places, and many Chinese families are moving in."[109]

AS LATIN AMERICANS responded to their unique contexts in the San Francisco Bay, religion helped ease tensions wrought by physical dislocation from the homeland, the pull of assimilation, and the dynamics of late nineteenth- and early twentieth-century racial formation. Nuestra Señora de Guadalupe responded to these conditions while simultaneously playing a definitive role in the history of the Latino panethnic community in the city. As the next chapter shows, national developments within the church also had much to do with these local histories, as did the rise of a cadre of priests with deep concerns for the spiritual and economic well-being of the Latina and Latino population.

Undoubtedly, the physical places of individual churches, sites where the possibilities of intraethnic unity could be at least partially realized, remained among the most enduring legacies of this history. Testaments to this fact, places like Guadalupe Church continued to occupy a special place in the hearts of Latinos throughout the Bay Area, even after their "decline." Until its closure in 1992, Guadalupe Church received regular correspondence from former parishioners who had moved to a different parish in the city or, more often, another city altogether. Many requested that a mass be offered in memory of a loved one who had passed. Often getting on in years and suffering from deteriorating health, others asked that the pastor remember them in his daily prayers. Almost all included a donation of five to ten dollars for their "blessed church." Those donations came most frequently as a yearly commemoration of Our Lady's feast day.

For some, like Señora Vasco, this relationship with Our Lady of Guadalupe Church lasted up to—and beyond—death. After her permanent move from the area surrounding the parish, she sent yearly donations to commemorate the anniversary of her husband's death, the deaths of a short list of friends, and the feast of *La Virgen*. When poor health prevented her from corresponding, letters from her daughter requesting the same prayers and masses replaced the letters in her own hand. As the years passed, her daughter wrote in her own voice, requesting that the pastor pray for her sick mother and, after Señora Vasco's passing, say a mass in her memory. For years afterward, the daughter sent a donation for an annual offertory mass, just as Señora Vasco had done, being sure to add the name of her mother to the list of loved ones.[110] In many ways these letters convey the success of the circular of 1871—"Unity engenders strength"—as a community of Latinos persisted in ways more meaningful than their physical presence in one part of the city. Indeed, as the next chapter shows, the community force of Guadalupe Church extended beyond its own walls.

## CHAPTER THREE

# We Can't Go Home

*Latin American Migration and Community*

*in the Twentieth Century*

"None of us really knew any English," recalled Elba Sanchez of her family's arrival to San Francisco, "which I think is probably the most common immigrant experience." Her father, Salvador Sanchez, had already migrated to the United States without his wife and three daughters, the eldest being Elba. Unable to continue working in the cotton mills of Atemajac, Mexico, he followed the informational and occupational networks connecting Guadalajara to the border and beyond. He first found work in Chicago, but as his daughter remembered the story, "he disliked the weather intensely" in addition to feeling "somewhere so far away" from his family. The migration of others informed his next decision. "Our town was Atemajac, and next to Atemajac was La Experiencia . . . and in La Experiencia my dad had a lot of friends that would come to the U.S. and were now working in San Francisco." For the last time in his life Salvador Sanchez migrated, again without his family. He found a job as a janitor—the same job he held until he retired decades later—and worked for a year and half before bringing his wife and children to join him in the Bay Area.

The transition from Atemajac to San Francisco proved difficult for the entire family, in particular for his eldest daughter. Nearing her teenage years, Elba Sanchez had grown accustomed her familial life in Mexico, the only life she had ever known. The small and diffuse Spanish-language population of midcentury San Francisco was a stark contrast to the weekly family gatherings back home in Atemajac. "We used to have regular Sunday get-togethers," remembered Sanchez, with "forty-something cousins and uncles and aunts, and just people coming in and out of the house, almost every Sunday, somebody's house, they would rotate." Separated from those familiar traditions, the family settled in the Fillmore District, where they were "one of maybe four Latino families living in that block. Everybody else was African American, and there was a Chinese family also that lived on the same street that we did." Unable to speak the language, and surrounded by the unfamiliar, Sanchez and her younger sisters pleaded with their parents to take them back to Mexico. "All they could say was, 'Well, we can't go home.'"[1]

For Latin American migrants to San Francisco in the first half of the twentieth century, the ability to maintain one's culture, language, and social life was not predetermined. Joining a population with minimal visibility in a distinctly cosmopolitan urban landscape, Mexicans, Salvadorans, and others from the Spanish-speaking South did not benefit from the same concentration and cohesion as did the Mexican migrants settling in El Paso or Los Angeles. Though most Spanish-speaking migrants led daily lives marked by substantive interactions outside their linguistic and cultural groups, barrios did exist—most notably the North Beach enclave surrounding Nuestra Señora de Guadalupe, the Spanish-language parish. Additionally, migrants created numerous institutions to meet their social, cultural, and, at times, political needs. In the process, they further fostered cohesion among the diverse immigrant base of their communities.

By midcentury, as early Latin American–descent barrios in the city began a visible decline, a postwar wave of Spanish-speaking migrants made San Francisco their home. Although many continued to live in cultural isolation in neighborhoods like the Fillmore and Bayview, many more began concentrating in the working-class district of the Mission. Drawn to the bay for work opportunities, their presence in the city most often emerged as the product of the evolving pattern of U.S. economic domination in Latin America. Yet, like all migrants whose movements take place in the transnational sphere shaped by the dictates of interests beyond their own, dislocation and resettlement in the city also inspired distinct cultural transformations. As they engaged "home making"—the "processes by which diverse subjects imagine and make themselves at home in various geographic locations"—they also refashioned what it meant to be Mexican, Salvadoran, Nicaraguan, and Guatemalan in San Francisco.[2]

This chapter details the growth of the Latin American–descent population in the early and mid-twentieth century. Demonstrating the scope of San Francisco's economic connections to the Spanish-speaking hemisphere, the migrants of this period continued to represent the internal diversity that had marked their earlier community formations. Heavily indebted to the inordinate influence of U.S. economic and political interests in the region, however, a collective wave of migration from El Salvador, Nicaragua, and Puerto Rico joined one from Mexico to further animate these processes. In excavating these forces and weaving them into the story of twentieth-century migrations, I frame a multifaceted context within which Latinos remade themselves and their community in the new geography of the bay. As a consequence of this amalgamation of economic, political, and social dynamics, a Spanish-speaking barrio took root in the Mission District. I detail how Latinos emerged as new social subjects by harnessing the traditions in this working-class neighborhood, the historical home to generations of European immigrants to the city. Paramount among these traditions were those of the Catholic Church. Latinos challenged the traditional ministerial model of the San Francisco Archdiocese, already an institution of great significance in the Mission, not only by their presence but also by their organized efforts to focus its resources on their cultural and spiritual needs. No example better demonstrates the rise of "Latino Catholicism"[3] in the city than does the story of St. Peter's Church, in the heart of the Mission, where this chapter concludes.

## "Tributary to San Francisco"

In late 1906, just months after an earthquake and fire left much of San Francisco in ruins, an article in the *San Francisco Chronicle* celebrated the completion of multiple railroad lines in northern and western Mexico, "where Californians are opening a rich territory to commerce." The rail extensions spotlighted in the piece connected the interior of Mexico to the Pacific ports of Guaymas, Acapulco, Mazatlán, and Manzanillo, opening "a territory vastly rich in minerals, hardwoods and tropical and semi-tropical products of all kinds—the most fertile part of all Mexico." The author praised this development as a monumental advancement for San Francisco's economic interests. "All this territory is tributary to San Francisco—at its door, with a straight steamer path in between."[4]

Throughout the twentieth century, the economic connections between San Francisco and distinct parts of Latin America continued to mature and diversify, as U.S. business elites and their concerns benefited from an organized campaign of "peaceful conquest" of the hemisphere.[5] Largely entailing the "spread of [the United States of] America's authority through nonmilitary means, through commerce, cultural exchange, and multilateral cooperation," to significant affect, this deliberate endeavor also utilized armed might toward a "nonterritorial conception of empire."

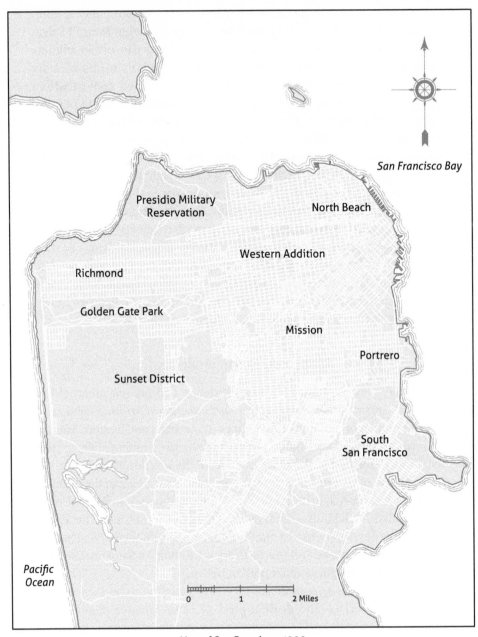

San Francisco Bay

Presidio Military
Reservation

North Beach

Western Addition

Richmond

Golden Gate Park

Mission

Portrero

Sunset District

South
San Francisco

Pacific
Ocean

0          1          2 Miles

Map of San Francisco, 1900

As Greg Grandin demonstrates, "by 1930, Washington had sent gunboats into Latin American ports over six thousand times," in addition to numerous acts of sustained military involvement in Cuba, Honduras, Mexico, and Guatemala, among a host of other nations.[6] In service to its vision of neoimperialism, the United States involved itself in the hemisphere as a "financial trustee," fostering the "idea that national security, overseas capitalist development, and global democratic reform were indivisible goals."[7] With U.S. diplomatic and military assets as their willing allies, U.S.-based financial and corporate interests "came to dominate the economies of Mexico, the Caribbean, and Central America, as well as large parts of South America."[8] As others have shown, the effects of U.S. imperialism in Latin America crippled national economies' ability to adequately provide for their own citizens, leading to the mass uprooting of rural populations. Dislocated from their homes and traditional forms of sustenance, many of these campesinos migrated to the United States.[9]

Despite the 1906 catastrophe, San Francisco continued to occupy a position of some weight in the flowering U.S. hemispheric empire. In the late nineteenth century San Francisco emerged as "the center of the informal and formal financial networks which spanned the Pacific Coast states." Few could rival its status, buttressed by isolation and expansive wealth, as the financial center of the West. This position "foreshadowed the city's emergence as a national center in the twentieth century."[10] The city's primacy in the commercial and manufacturing sectors mirrored its position in the financial markets. By early century, the port of San Francisco ranked second only to New York in both the value and volume of its cargo.[11] With berthing facilities unable to fully meet the volume of business—reflected in regular queues of ships in the bay waiting to unload their cargo—it was the leader among the Bay Area's collection of ports. In 1925 they moved a combined 28.8 million tons of cargo, at a value of more than $1.8 billion.[12] Likewise, from 1909 to 1925, the value of manufactured products in the city increased by more than 297 percent, to almost $530 million.[13] San Francisco not only provided berth to the ships dominating Pacific trade but also produced ships in the largest shipbuilding plant in the West. Home to glass works and perfume producers and the only chocolate factory on the coast, San Francisco, its Chamber of Commerce boasted, sold "every variety of manufactured article."[14]

The city was the preeminent economic gateway for the western states, first and foremost California. Beyond the Golden Gate, ships and rails moved California's goods to market, most notably the fruits and vegetables grown and harvested in the state's fertile valleys. With their city home to the largest fruit and vegetable cannery in the world as well as to an unrivaled transportation network, San Francisco's business leaders understood the connection between their metropolis and the state's agricultural zones. The rest of California, reasoned one Chamber of Commerce publication, "is the backcountry upon which the city depends—the backbone of the metropolis. The fertile valleys of the Sacramento and the San Joaquin, extending some 600 miles in length, as well as the Napa, Sonoma and Santa Clara valleys, all drain into San Francisco Bay. The products of these valleys are shipped to all parts of the world, from San Francisco. Here the raw materials are manufactured into the finished products. These goods are all handled by San Francisco brokers, commission houses and warehouses."[15] San Francisco's importance to U.S. Pacific trade is clear from the top six international destinations for goods exported through its port in 1914: Japan, England, the Philippine Islands, Australia, Canada, and China.[16]

A healthy share of the economic success of the port of San Francisco derived from the U.S. position in Latin America. For example, the United Fruit Company, which exercised an inordinate influence over economic and political institutions in places like Nicaragua, Costa Rica, and Colombia, occupied its own "banana terminal" on Channel Street, moving fruit from refrigerated ships to refrigerated cargo cars. It operated three vessels between Central American ports and San Francisco, transporting both freight and passengers.[17] San Francisco also witnessed an astronomical increase in coffee importation to its port, making it a national leader in the coffee industry. In the first two decades of the century, San Francisco emerged as "the premier port of the world for Central American coffees," with a 568 percent increase in the importation of the product.[18] During the period of the First World War, as coffee imports from Brazil dropped and those from Mexico stagnated, a San Francisco—financed and controlled importation of Central American coffee boomed, rising from 40,000 pounds in 1914 to almost 160,000 by war's end.[19] Celebrating their achievement, groups such as the Green Coffee Association of the San Francisco Chamber of Commerce noted the extent to which their success rested on a merchant-led "bitter fight for supremacy in Central America." The arrival of almost 1.2 million bags of coffee to port in 1919 represented the culmination of "an uphill struggle for more than forty years" resulting in Central American planters' being "almost exclusively financed by San Francisco interests."[20]

City business leaders often looked toward Latin America when planning the city's future economic growth. In some ways, they viewed San Francisco as part of a larger regional economic zone that included the Pacific ports of the Americas. For example, the Chamber compared the city's capacity for trade and manufacturing with that of locations not only in the United States but also in Mexico, Central America, and South America.[21] When local business elites considered the opening of the Panama Canal, they argued that future profits relied on the ability "to fully appreciate what Latin America means to San Francisco and California."[22] In subsequent years these same interests promoted this perspective in an assortment of ways. Both the English- and Spanish-language press recorded regular "investigative" expeditions by San Francisco businessmen southward with the intent of increasing commerce between the city and the Spanish-speaking nations. In 1921, for example, a delegation of business leaders toured the Mexican west coast in search of trade prospects. Receiving a great deal of notice in the Spanish-language newspaper *Centro América*, the delegation of Chamber of Commerce members verified that the hostilities of the Revolution had subsided enough to establish new trade ties. Stopping at the major port of Mazatlán, the San Franciscans were welcomed by a Mexican delegation and treated to elaborate ceremonies, fine dining, and a dance in their honor.[23] In the months after their return, and with the help of the major English- and Spanish-language newspapers, they initiated an effort to advertise "the resources and advantages" of San Francisco and "the glories and magnificence" of California. Organized by the Chamber of Commerce, the Real Estate Board, and "many industrial associations," the campaign included hosting the same sort of events San Franciscans had attended in Latin America.[24]

The transnational connections between San Francisco and distinct parts of Latin America were material, long-standing, and continually evolving. At times the context within which developments took root required less an imagination framed by the profit motive than a simple recognition of the realities of life and business in the early twentieth century. For example, as a consequence of their domination of the fruit, oil, and coffee markets, U.S. businessmen and their families spent much of their lives in various parts of Latin America. Not surprisingly, they also began to build institutions there to meet their own health and educational needs. In the twenties, when Anglo-American business elites began fundraising to build a hospital in Guatemala—"for Americans who chance to fall ill while in Guatemala or in neighboring Central American countries"—they naturally sought money from the business community of San Francisco, "whose knowledge of conditions will undoubtedly inspire a quick and generous response." Rather than "asking for charity in the usual sense of the word," the fundraising effort was framed as "a friendly start toward helping ourselves."[25] For Latin Americans who settled in San Francisco, even those who pursued domestic business ventures without international ties, transnational forces continued to shape family destinies. When a former Guatemalan colonel migrated to the Bay Area and began serving as a corporate official in a local business, he never seemed to envision a life for his San Francisco–born son apart from the Central American nation he once served. When his son was of age, he sent him back to study at his nation's military academy. The son subsequently returned to the States "for the purpose of getting some active service" and joined the U.S. Army in the war against the Philippines before returning to Guatemala as a colonel in its army.[26]

In the early twentieth century, life in Latin America also reflected many of the forceful interconnections built and maintained by U.S. neoimperialism. Capital from the United States funded the construction of railroads, mining, and systems to extract raw materials like fruit and rubber from Latin America, inciting an internal migration along U.S.-owned networks moving goods from the rural regions of the Southern Hemisphere to U.S. ports. In the case of Mexico, as historian George Sánchez has argued, the dynamics framing Mexican emigration and U.S. immigration are nearly inseparable. "The creation of the Mexican railway system was both a product of and had consequences for not just one, but both sides of the border" as U.S. railroads built during the Porfiriato increased Mexican track from 663 kilometers to more than 19,700.[27] These, in turn, reshaped the demographic distribution of Mexican workers and brought both a rise in rural land values and the widespread loss of traditionally communal holdings.[28] As a general "de-peasanting of the land" occurred, the rails also transformed village life in other ways. Torreón, a village of 2,000 inhabitants in 1876, grew to more than 43,000 by 1910, simply by being at the intersection of the Mexican Central Railroad and the International Railroad. The same sort of growth happened in towns like Nuevo León, Sabinas, and Coahuila.[29] The rails also facilitated the movement of laborers northward to the United States. Most of the migrants to Los Angeles in this same period, for example, originated from towns and villages "within a day's walk from the railroad lines."[30] Ports also developed during the Porfiriato, as the nation increased its level of foreign trade "from about 50 million pesos in 1876 to about 488 million pesos in 1910."[31] Many of the same dynamics marked early-century life in other parts of Central America.

Major improvements to the harbors of Manzanillo, Mazatlán, and Salina Cruz, all located on Mexico's Pacific coast, further connected Latin America to San Francisco. When Richard Q. Camplis left Acapulco in 1922, he arrived at the Golden Gate via the same shipping lines exchanging commerce between the two ports. His son remembers that most of the city's

Mexican population then was comprised of "*mexicanos de costa*," coastal Mexicans. Their common origin was reflected in the seafood dishes they ate.[32] The majority of Mexican migrants in this era entered the United States through Texas, with about half remaining there permanently. From Texas laborers could also be redistributed to meet urban and rural labor demands throughout the Midwest and West. Approximately 15 percent came to California.[33] When Salvador Sanchez made his initial journey to the United States, first to the Texas border and then to Chicago, he traveled a well-worn path for Mexican migrants, one that not only connected Mexico to the United States but also interconnected North American urban centers in the nexus of industrial capitalism. Sanchez's further relocation to San Francisco suggests how migrants found themselves at the Golden Gate, even when it was not their initial intended destination.[34]

As a central port in the Pacific empire, San Francisco drew migrant labor as part of a larger network spanning the globe, but always determined by the needs of U.S. business interests. For example, labor contractors like the Alaska Packers' Association searched for cheap labor throughout the hemisphere. They regularly advertised in the city's Spanish-language newspapers like *Hispano América* and ventured southward in their quest. Pedro García, an early-century migrant, recounted how a California-born Mexican "who still shows indigenous features" recruited *mexicanos* from Sonora and Jalisco to work on Alaska-bound salmon expeditions. Marked by "tortures" and "unequalled deprivations"—the men were virtually imprisoned aboard their fishing ships—his experience at sea filled him with anger "against the foreign exploiters and against one's own, who in turn abandon out of ignorance the legions of men whose arms are wanted by Mexican fertile soil." Work as a fisherman in Alaska also entailed regular trips to San Francisco, not only as part of the work route but also as an escape from the horrors of the job. As one contemporary phrased it, "When the Mexican laborer starts to lose faith in finding work, he gradually steers himself to San Francisco, where he roams the wharf, famished as a rabid dog fighting over a scrap of bread."[35]

Many migrants to San Francisco followed a less direct path, though one still intimately tied to U.S. labor demands. Sam Rios's father was born in Torreón, Mexico, one of the towns transformed by railroads during the Porfiriato. Rios's grandmother, who fought in the Revolution, later took her son via the rails and crossed the border at El Paso, Texas. There, the matriarch baptized her child and secured him a birth certificate listing his place of birth as the United States. Rios's maternal family similarly migrated to El Paso, though their journey originated further south, in the city of Zacatecas. Once in El Paso, the paths of the two families crossed. "Apparently, my mom's mom and my dad's mom met each other in El Paso, so they knew each other."[36] Soon after, his mother's family headed to Los Angeles where, a decade later, his father's family arrived. Their paths crossed again, only this time the two teenagers married. The newlyweds found work by following the agricultural circuit throughout California. "From then on, it was nothing more than a trail, from L.A. to Sanger, to Fresno, to Clovis, to Parlier, to, you know, coming up in the camps. . . . So eventually they end up over in the Mountain View area."[37] Once in the fields around San Jose, his family would eventually move to the area's largest city—San Francisco. Reflecting the city's importance to the state's northern agricultural zones, his mother left her work in the fields and traveled all the way to San Francisco's Mission Hospital to give birth to her son Sam in 1931.[38]

U.S. business interests also incited labor migration through far more compulsory mechanisms. Along with the growth in San Francisco's Mexican and Central American populations, the first decades of the century also saw the emergence of a measurable Puerto Rican population in the city. Exported as a source of cheap labor, Puerto Ricans left their island under the direct influence of U.S. sugar interests. Seeking laborers for the cane fields in the U.S. colony of Hawai'i, "recruiters" harvested the dislocated populations in Puerto Rico and sent them to the Pacific on a grueling trip involving sea passage to New Orleans, rail passage to San Francisco, and then another ship voyage halfway across the Pacific.[39] In 1900, more than 50 Puerto Ricans "jumped ship" while in San Francisco. Of the 114 who made the first trip, only 56 arrived in Hawai'i, the rest having engaged in what the press called an "escape."[40] Their decision also indicates the prospect for integration within the city's Spanish-speaking enclaves.

San Francisco's place within the larger hemispheric and national economies translated into opportunities for the highly trained and educated, as well. Spanish-language newspapers that made concerted efforts to foster business ties with the Spanish-speaking hemisphere often featured stories detailing the migration experiences of more prominent individuals and their families, perhaps even encouraging the process. In their telling, these tales often contrasted the stability of the Bay Area to episodic political distress in the Spanish-speaking South. For example, after suffering a "long and distressing trip all over the Central American Republics," one medical doctor "from a well-known family" permanently settled in San Francisco in 1913.[41] Julio Arce, a publisher of newspapers in Sinaloa and Guadalajara, came in 1915. He had been imprisoned in Mexico in the midst of the Revolution before he used the transnational commercial possibilities extolled in his newspapers and migrated to the Bay Area. He later rose to some prominence in the community.[42] A man known as "General Ruelas" was widely known to have commanded in the Porfirian army before coming to San Francisco in 1914. Within a few years he was a professor of Latin American history at the University of San Francisco. Indeed, local press accounts often contended that "one fairly common émigré [to San Francisco] is the political refugee."[43]

## Latino "Homemaking" in San Francisco

By the 1920s, San Francisco's Latin American ethnic population numbered approximately 15,000 to 20,000. The Spanish-speaking were at times celebrated as "integral and fundamental components of San Francisco," their presence linked to a romantic vision "of the days when San Francisco was a tiny Spanish village."[44] The population remained mostly ethnic Mexican, with their numbers increased by a wave of immigration in the first decades of the century. The diversity of the Spanish-language population, however, remained clearly evident.[45] Central and South Americans continued to be a significant portion of the population, with San Francisco the primary California destination for immigrants from those regions. While the Census for 1920 records only 944 "Central Americans" and 871 "South Americans" among the city's foreign-born, both figures eclipsed the tally in other parts of the state. By comparison, only 132 migrants from Central America and 339 from South American resided in the entire county of Los Angeles in the same year. Both figures only earned Los Angeles third place in statewide rankings, with the East Bay county of Alameda coming in second to the West Bay county of San Francisco.[46]

When Latin American migrants found their way to San Francisco, they settled in neighborhoods all over the city. The historical record shows that Mexicans and other Spanish speakers raised families in North Beach, the Mission District, Bayview–Hunter's Point, and the Fillmore District. By and large, however, most in this pre–World War II period congregated in one of two barrios. The first, in North Beach, surrounded our Lady of Guadalupe Catholic Church and thrived as a religious and commercial center until the mid-1950s. Many San Franciscans saw the barrio, recognized by the mainstream press as a "Mexican colony" comprised of "the nomads of the West," as demographic proof of "the active and friendly relations between California and its nearest neighbors."[47] As we will see in the last chapter, the centrality of the church in the daily lives of the Spanish-speaking fostered the growth of this barrio.

Through midcentury, the business district surrounding Guadalupe Church best embodied the presence of Latinos in the city, in particular those from Mexico. Indeed, the largest concentration of "Latin" restaurants in the city existed in the Guadalupe barrio, beckoning migrants and native-born alike to encounter "the spirit of Old Mexico."[48] As early as 1912, the City of Mexico served food to a Spanish-speaking clientele. It was joined by an assortment of establishments selling prepared foods, baked goods, meats, and tamales. The barrio also housed dentists and medical doctors for the Spanish-speaking, as well as the offices of some of the city's Spanish-language press.[49] One of the first Spanish-language movie houses in San Francisco made its home on Broadway, near the church. Called Teatro Verdi, it billed itself as "the preferred theater of the Spanish-speaking," though it also entertained the district's Italian immigrants.[50] A plurality of the city's Mexican and Latin American populations called this neighborhood home.[51]

The other Latin American barrio spread out from the waterfront of the city, just east of the Guadalupe barrio extending southward. Located closer to the city's thriving docks, this smaller enclave emerged as Latinos entered the city by boat or found employment in the various shipping-related and manufacturing industries. Located most enduringly in the area known as South of Market, the barrio (with its dense cluster of apartments) not only provided an initial residence for newcomers but also housed canneries, processing plants, coffee companies, and various other factories that used Latin American–descent workers.[52] Fractured by the building of the Bay Bridge in the late 1930s, and by related development in the immediate postwar years, the South of Market area included the well-known Latin barrio until the Mission District pulled most of these residents away.

Like its North Beach counterpart, the South of Market barrio had its share of local businesses catering to a Spanish-fluent clientele. Health providers like Drs. Arturo V. Samaniego and Gilberto Meléndez both ran practices in the barrio, the first a medical doctor and the latter a dentist. A laundry owned by a Spanish-surnamed proprietor and located in the barrio also regularly advertised its services in the Spanish-language press.[53] Frank J. Vásquez ran the Crystal Palace Barber Shop and Beauty Parlor in South of Market.[54] Euro-American business owners also made an effort to solicit Spanish-speaking patrons by advertising in the same papers.[55] Surrounded by a critical mass of working-class employment, the South of Market barrio also contained its fair share of bars and other businesses offering urban nightlife. A lively Spanish music scene even thrived in many of the establishments. Joe Rocha came to San Francisco when he was only

Julia Bayze at La Mexicana grocery store with owner Peter Arizu, 1947.
San Francisco History Center, San Francisco Public Library.

a teenager in the 1930s. Familiar with hard labor, and never without an opportunity to employ this familiarity in San Francisco, Rocha found the opportunity to work as a musician another profitable advantage of life in the city. He remembered as many as twelve different places where he and other singer/guitarists performed, including clubs like La Casita and the Royal Club.[56] Once he established himself, this entertainment circuit provided enough regular work for Rocha and two or three dozen other musicians. They were more a collective than competitors, Rocha remembers: "If I didn't play with one of them, I played with the other."[57]

With Nuestra Señora and an assortment of older and more reputable businesses as its central feature, the Guadalupe barrio undoubtedly possessed a great residential neighborhood feel than the more industrial enclave near the docks. In many ways, however, poverty and despair connected both. The records of John A. Robinson, an inspector for the Immigration and Naturalization Service in San Francisco, reflect as much. For most of the early century his work focused heavily on the arrest and deportation of the city's immigrant prostitutes, part of a larger campaign to investigate "the white slave market on the West Coast."[58] His journals reveal a thriving prostitution industry involving the lives of scores of Latinas and Latinos as both sex workers and "procurer[s] or pimp[s]." Some were immigrants who had been living and working in the city for more than a generation; some, undoubtedly, had been imported as sex workers. A woman listed as "Paulene Gonzales" told Robinson she had migrated from her home in Guadalajara, Mexico, arriving at the docks at the age of eighteen. Her residence was within two blocks of Guadalupe Church.[59] Many worked in brothels and other establishments near the docks. Robinson's journals show that he made arrests while conducting routine investigations on deportable aliens, often aided by a local member of the Spanish-speaking community who also worked for the *San Francisco Chronicle*. Most frequently, he processed immigrants for deportation after retrieving them from local jails or prisons. His journals provide brief glimpses into the lives of men, women, and children from the Spanish-speaking hemisphere, people whose lives were bounded by the sex industry and U.S. bureaucracies.

Less oppressive structures affected life for the city's growing Latin American–descent population, as print cultures further defined the space between Latin America and the bay. A Spanish-language press continued to thrive in San Francisco, as it had the century before, though twentieth-century organs did not reflect of any continuity of ownership or title. The archival remnants of the surviving periodicals largely continue to reflect a Mexican focus in their coverage of international news and of the local community, though both the titles and mastheads also suggested a growing effort to speak to and for the diversity of Latin Americans. *Semanario Imparcial* proclaimed itself "El semanario de la Raza, por la Raza, y para la Raza [The weekly of the *raza*, by the *raza*, and for the *raza*]" in its early editions. By the late thirties its slogan had become "Periódico Informativo e Dedicado a las Agrupaciones de Habla Español [News Periodical Dedicated to Groups of the Spanish-Speaking]." At times the weekly even published pieces in English, either to reach a less fluent second generation or a wider audience beyond people of Latin American descent. Its coverage echoed the pan–Latin American sensibilities of the masthead, featuring regular news from South and Central America.[60] *Semanario Imparcial* was joined by such periodicals as *Centro América*, *Hispano América*, and *Gráfico Internacional*, all of which shared many of the same tendencies. *Hispano América*, in particular, had close public relations with the non-Mexican segments of what it called "the Spanish colony," in particular, with the Chilean, Spanish, and Peruvian embassies.[61] *Centro América* also published pieces in English, eventually calling itself an "English-Spanish Weekly."[62] The result of transnational connections between the Bay Area and Latin America, these periodicals also reflected the interests of a growing Spanish-speaking business elite in the city. They not only promoted further commercial and financial interaction by connecting the business community of San Francisco with reliable news from Central and South America but also provided intermediary services to connect "manufacturers interested in being represented in Latin America" with reliable commercial agents as well as information about the market.[63]

The same period also witnessed the creation of numerous mutual aid societies, clubs, and associations by and for Latin Americans. Many, if not most, of these new groups—part of an explosion of organizational activity in the Latin American ethnic community—joined members together along nationalistic lines. El Club Azteca de Señoras began in 1912 as an effort "to promote social good feeling among the Mexican residents of the city."[64] The first gathering of this women's group involved music and dances as well as two speeches—one in English and one in Spanish. Among the higher-profile and more enduring organizations—news of its events regularly appeared in both the English- and Spanish-language press—Club Azteca built a reputation within the "Mexican colony" for hosting elegant dances and other social functions, many of which raised money for the poor in Mexico.[65] Testifying to the club's longevity, as well as its integration into the city's social affairs, later city directories list its main office at 605 Polk, less than two blocks from City Hall.[66] By 1921 the club became the annual sponsor of the mass celebrating Mexican independence at Guadalupe Church—an event attended by the mayor, chief of police, and numerous other city officials.[67] The club's size and influence sometimes drew it into controversy. When the club treasurer and a small group of "allies" broke away from the club, they refused to release the club's accounts. Accused by the remaining sixty members of "embezzling $15 and a set of account books," Guadalupe Tsouvas stood trial in 1917. Threats and accusations of violence marked the coverage, with one of her supporters rumored to have said, "If she's guilty, not all these women will leave the [court]room."[68]

Though prominently positioned, Club Azteca was hardly the only social, artistic, and political organization in the barrios. La Sociedad Mutualista

Mexicana Chapultepec united segments of the ethnic Mexican population to host annual celebrations of Mexican independence, often with the financial support of the Mexican consulate. A program for one such occasion reflected a two-day celebration, including dance, song, and a "ladies contest."[69] Club Moctezuma sought to harness the musical talents of the Mexican colony and establish a Mexican-style "Orquesta Típica." Once established, the musicians made themselves available for fiestas.[70] The diversity of organizational efforts within the Mexican colony also reflected some of the fissures within the Mexican ethnic community. Rivalries between groups often played out during the September festivities celebrating Mexican independence. For example, Club Hidalgo and La Sociedad Mexicana Anahuac hosted events similar to the annual festivities of Club Azteca and Sociedad Chapultepec. In 1918, with the encouragement of the Mexican consul, Sociedad Anahuac convened a meeting of San Francisco Mexicans encouraging them to join forces "without hatred, rancor, or passions."[71] The gathering proved unable to surmount the differences among the groups: at least three celebrations took place that September. By the 1930s, however, the once unimaginable collaboration had become the norm for the annual festivities, with five major groups coming together for a dance and celebration.[72]

Nonethnic Mexican groupings were far less numerous, yet hardly invisible. When they do appear in the historical record, most reflect the union of multiple, non-Mexican nationalities. Their smaller numbers made these efforts more successful in the long run, yet such regional ways of thinking also promoted a distinct vision of Central American identity, often at the heart of some groups' purposes. For example, El Comité Unionista de San Francisco, which claimed that it "here keeps alive the love of country and is considered, with filial affection, guardian of the good name and love of prosperity" of El Salvador, sought to bring attention and support to the movement to create a united federation of the Central American nations.[73] The growth of migration from Central and South America left some in the community wondering if there was a role they could play to help young men who "find themselves wandering about alone in a large and cruel city." They began working toward "the formation of a center or club here in the city for the young men themselves" that could better serve "the son of Central America."[74]

The associations and societies serving the Latin American–descent population promoted effective community, providing mechanisms through which the barrios' constituencies could assume a collective voice within the city's wider social and political worlds. As with similar efforts in other parts of the state, such groups (in particular the charitable *sociedades* and *mutualistas*) "expressed the obligation of the elites or the middle class to morally and materially elevate the rest of *la raza.*"[75] In the process, they facilitated group cohesion across generation and class, often promoting the maintenance of culture and national identity. In the barrios of San Francisco, nonnationalistic goals also animated organizational formation. Most notably under the encouragement of Central American newspaper publishers, segments of the population sought to create multinational and multilingual unions within the barrio. At least partially inspired by the pan–Latin American efforts ubiquitous in the hemisphere, they had their most enduring impact with Las Sociedades Unidas Latino-Americanas. This coalition of various constituencies came together and coordinated the annual "Fiesta de la Raza" celebration every October. *Hispano América* called the fiesta, which most often took the form of a dance, "a brilliant and lucid event": "All the companies together should be congratulated on such amazing success, and they must be very pleased to have proved it is possible to unite Latin Americans under one roof."[76]

## Midcentury Migrations

Latin Americans migrated to the city in increasing numbers during and after World War II. The agricultural industry encouraged the migration of hundreds of thousands Mexicans to California, with direct consequences for the Spanish-speaking community in San Francisco.[77] With its port and factories often providing greater job opportunities than the fields, the city drew migrant laborers from the farms in the Salinas, San Jose, and San Joaquin Valleys—places one author termed well within the "sphere of San Francisco."[78] Migration to the city in this period benefited from older trends as well. During the Depression, more than 300,000 "white" workers migrated to the West from the fields of Oklahoma, Texas, Kansas, Missouri, and Arkansas. By 1934, 142 agricultural workers existed for every 100 agricultural jobs.[79] By comparison, the industrial and transportation base of San Francisco's economy left it with "one of the lowest rates of unemployment of any large city and . . . a higher standard of relief."[80] Indeed, by 1930 more than 37 percent of San Francisco's economy was in either manufacturing or transportation, while as a port, it handled more than 80 percent of the state's agricultural output.[81] San Francisco, of course, benefited in multiple ways from the massive irrigation projects transforming the once arid lands of the San Joaquin Valley into thriving agricultural plantations, canning, processing, and moving much of the resulting output—which itself accounted for some 40 percent of the U.S. total.[82] The movement of people was a residual effect. As early as 1919 one official with the California Commission of Immigration and Housing observed that a "very large percentage of the Spanish and Mexican laborers of San Francisco are migratory, here during the winter months and in the fruit and agricultural fields the balance of the year."[83]

For many agricultural laborers, San Francisco represented the urban destination point with a larger *corrida*, or migratory circuit. The Moreno family migrated from New Mexico in the late thirties. The parents lived out of their car as they picked crops to earn money en route, the circuit of agricultural work transporting them far beyond the home they once knew. "They picked all the way to Half Moon Bay," their daughter Dorinda recalled.[84] Life in the fields and, later, in the cities of California, allowed the family to progress economically. By the early fifties, they had saved enough to buy a house. But "we still picked," Moreno remembered. "We'd still go out on the weekends and whenever there was no school."[85] Similarly, Rosa Guerrero crossed the border at El Paso as a small child but was raised in Reedley, a small agricultural town in California's San Joaquin Valley. Growing up, she "worked the fields to earn money while she was going to school so everything she had she paid, she earned it." While in high school, she visited San Francisco during the 1939 Golden Gate International Exposition. And "she fell in love with the city. She said, 'Oh, I want to live here.'" After she married, she and her husband settled in the city, where they raised their family.[86]

Wartime industrial expansion drew workers from the fields in even greater numbers. Providing job opportunities and newly built "temporary" housing units for wartime laborers, communities like Hunter's Point were home to more than 35,000 newcomers.[87] For many, these units represented a move up from the poverty they had known in the fields. For those already accustomed to city life, the units provided affordable rents and proximity to work. With both a mother and an aunt working in the wartime industries, Sam Rios and his family qualified for this housing when they relocated to Hunter's Point. The community "was like family," said Rios, recalling the other Mexican families that lived nearby. However, with the presence of Filipino, black, and Anglo families, wartime housing created something beyond a Latino enclave. "It was a mixed community."[88] The shipping ties that predated the war allowed that industry to recruit workers heavily from Central America, especially Nicaragua and El Salvador.[89] In addition to attracting thousands of new Latinos to the city, the war also changed the community of those already established there. New housing and employment opportunities allowed many families to "get a leg up" during the war.

The stories of professionally trained Latin Americans who made San Francisco their permanent home encompassed many of the same themes as the experiences of "unskilled" labor migrants throughout the twentieth century. When Martin del Campo, an architect from Guadalajara, immigrated to the United States with his wife and two daughters in the 1940s, he moved to Detroit. Del Campo's wife—a U.S. citizen who had met him while studying art at the Academia de San Carlos—had roots in Michigan. But Los Angeles had been his "first idea," and del Campo was generally unhappy with his new life in the upper Midwest. So when a coworker began touting San Francisco over a period of months, del Campo finally broke. "I thought, well, why shouldn't I go to San Francisco?" It was a decision he never regretted. "It was a revelation. Not only did I love the town, but I loved the atmosphere, the people. . . . San Francisco has great attraction to Mexicans. It has such perfect weather and such tolerant attitudes." The Golden Gate provided a fresh start for the family of four, especially the young del Campo, whose artistic trainings and leftist political leanings had made him feel like an outsider in the architectural professional community of the Midwest. "[San Franciscans] were very liberal in their views," he found. "I felt very happy in San Francisco."[90]

By 1950, the Central and South American–born population of San Francisco had risen to 5.6 percent of the total foreign-born. With the Mexican-born population only representing 4.6 percent of the city's total, the Central American presence was establishing the pattern that would come to characterize succeeding decades. From 1958 to 1960, the flow of migrants from El Salvador alone outpaced that from every other Latin American nation, with more than a third of all Central American immigrants to the city beginning their journey there.[91] Postwar *salvadoreños* most often came as a consequence of economic desperation and political turmoil. For example, as a nation marked by coffee monoculture, El Salvador relied on trade to export its primary crop as well as to import the majority of the beans, corn, and other foods necessary to feed its population.[92] This would naturally connect the nation to the rest of the world via shipping routes; its coffee connected many of those routes to San Francisco. With a military government in control of a class-stratified and economically unstable society, the El Salvador of the 1950s and 1960s offered little chance for advancement. Migration, whether direct or in stages, presented one solution. As the San Francisco population of *salvadoreños* grew, it attracted succeeding waves. When a conservative regime overturned the 1972 election of leftist José

Napoleón Duarte and ushered in a renewed period of repression and strife, and when conflicts erupted into civil war nearly a decade later, thousands more used the preestablished networks between Central America and the Bay Area.

Similar forces framed emigration from Nicaragua to the United States. A military dictatorship took power in Nicaragua in 1932 on the heels of a U.S.-backed assassination. General Anastasio Somoza García ruled the nation for more than a quarter of a century before handing power over to his sons.[93] The general political repression and economic hardship plaguing Nicaragua's modern history promoted movement as well. A mid-1960s study of Nicaraguan immigration to San Francisco found that most respondents came to the United States for the economic opportunities, while another large percentage had fled political persecution.[94] Several postwar transportation developments facilitated Nicaraguan immigration. In addition to already established shipping lines, airlines provided service between Managua and San Francisco as early as the fifties. A one-way ticket cost approximately $185 in 1960.[95] The results were palpable. The U.S. Census listed as many Nicaraguans in San Francisco as in all of California.[96] Since travel by other means would have meant a stopover in a city like San Diego or Los Angeles, this statistic speaks to the use of more direct forms of transport, and the ultimate lure of San Francisco, with its preestablished connections to their homelands.

Like migrants that came from all Central American nations, Nicaraguans sometimes traveled to San Francisco through Guatemala and Mexico. These patterns of migration frequently entailed trains, buses, and foot travel. During the journey of more than 5,000 miles, many things could go wrong. One Nicaraguan couple recalled their journey through Mexico with some regret. "His father had fastened the bag containing their papers and money to his wrist with a light chain. While they sat in the cathedral [of the Virgin of Guadalupe (in Mexico City)] listening to the mass, the old man fell asleep. When he awoke later and lifted his arm he found that the chain had been severed and his bag was gone. Without the papers he could not get into the States, so he had to wire his son in San Francisco, then wait until his son could send him bus fare back to Nicaragua to enable him to get a new set of papers. Naturally, the old folks had a low estimate of Mexicans as a whole after this incident."[97] In a strange twist of fate, the same thing had happened to their son when he made the same journey years before. Whether retold as a warning to future migrants of Mexican criminality or an account of what actually happened, such tales were made believable by the difficulties of nondirect travel from Nicaragua to San Francisco.[98]

The diversity of San Francisco's Latino community included representation from most, if not all, Latin American nations. In addition to the six Central American countries and Mexico, Venezuela, Colombia, Ecuador, Peru, Brazil, Paraguay, Uruguay, Chile, Argentina, Cuba, and the Dominican Republic also sent statistically measurable contingents.[99] Puerto Ricans' migration in the postwar period made them the fourth-largest group in the Latino community. A survey of Puerto Ricans leaving San Juan for San Francisco illuminates the shift in their migration process from the earlier period. The study by Ayuda Católica para Emigrantes Puertorriqueños (Catholic Aid to Puerto Rican Emigrants) sought to provide emigration information to local Catholic parishes. Assuming that the Catholic Church would facilitate these immigrants' transition into mainland U.S. society, the group conducted research for every major destination in the United States, primarily the East Coast centers of New York, Philadelphia, and Miami. Though made statistically irrelevant by the fact that many migrants failed to answer some questions, the survey does relate vital information for forty-six Puerto Ricans who entered San Francisco between September 1956 and September 1961.[100] The majority of the Puerto Rican migrants questioned left to San Francisco to reunite with a family member or spouse. While twelve of them responded that they had never been to the U.S. mainland, most had previously lived there for at least one year.[101] Though family networks and familiarity with San Francisco seemed instrumental in creating the flow of migrants from the island to the bay, just under half of them also had jobs waiting for them upon arrival.[102] As the small sample suggests, Puerto Ricans came to San Francisco in the postwar period for many of the same reasons as other Latin American migrants. Using established familial patterns and networks, migrants made San Francisco their destination in order to be with family, find work, or just begin a new life.

As a new Latin America–descent population settled in the postwar city, it primarily chose the Mission District as its home. Their movement of these Latinos was partially shaped by the demise of the two early twentieth-century barrios. The North Beach–based Guadalupe barrio began its decline in the late forties. Temporarily divided by the construction of the Broadway Tunnel, this community was dislocated from itself by development. Adding to this disruption, the ethnic composition of the barrio also began to change in the postwar years as an increasing number of Chinese and Chinese Americans came to reside there. By 1960, Guadalupe Church served a congregation far more diverse than just the Spanish-speaking. The South of Market barrio went into a partial decline in the mid-1930s with the construction of the Oakland Bay Bridge, completely displacing the part of the barrio around Rincon Hill.[103] A more general pattern of south-ward migration accelerated the effects of displacement, with more Latino residents in South of Market migrating southward along the city grid, into first the North Mission, then the Inner Mission. Replicating a pattern es-tablished by earlier waves of Germans, Irish, and Scandinavians, Latinos settled an area close to where they had entered the city, and then migrated into the working-class bastion that was the Mission.[104]

The Rios family moved to the Mission before the war, when the oppor-tunity to own a home presented itself. Growing up in the vicinity of 21st and Harrison Streets, Sam Rios remembered that certain sections of the district had a Latin American identity from the late 1930s. "When I was a kid I used to run up and down 24th Street. And you hardly ever heard anybody speaking English. It was all Spanish. 16th Street was like that, 21st Street was like that, 7th and Mission. . . . You knew they were Mexican en-claves."[105] Though most were not homeowners, more and more Latinos settled in district. Even for those with more migratory life experiences, the district became the center around which their movements revolved. "We went in and out of the Mission. No matter what we did we'd always end up back in the Mission."[106] And they were not alone. Between 1950 and 1970 the "Spanish-surnamed" grew from 11 percent of the district's population to more than 45 percent, making the Mission District the primary Latino barrio in the city.[107]

Many Latinos worked in the city's shipyards, canneries and produce packing warehouses, slaughterhouses, and other factories. Some of these employers—like the Levi-Strauss factory—were located in the Mission, while most others were nearby. The port lay just north, a short ride up Mission Street on the number 14 bus. The same area housed a variety of fruit and vegetable packing warehouses.[108] Most of the canneries were in the Mission District, down 18th Street and on Mariposa, while the slaugh-terhouses thrived in nearby Hunter's Point.[109] Out of the fourteen largest manufacturers in San Francisco, only two were outside of the Mission or the South of Market region just to its north.[110] Unfortunately, the postwar wave of Latin American workers settled in a city undergoing a general de-cline in its manufacturing base. From 1947 to 1963, during the first phase of a general boom in the San Francisco economy, manufacturing jobs in the city *decreased* by 21 percent.[111] This decline in manufacturing was part of a larger shift in the Bay Area, as blue-collar jobs left San Francisco for the four surrounding counties. From 1958 to 1967, while the city lost some 7,000 manufacturing jobs, the surrounding counties gained more than 28,000.[112] These trends, presaging more of the same in later decades, made the city an increasingly difficult place for a working-class family to survive, and yet they did little to curb the postwar migration boom.

Most Latino families who survived in the city did so because they found work. Many, like the Rios men, found employment in the shipyards, which largely provided a stable income and an increase in job skills. Taking advantage of the shortages created by war, both their wives also found work in the shipyards during the forties.[113] Esperanza Echavarri's father worked at a butcher shop on 3rd Street. She remembered that "we'd always have meat that he'd bring, every piece of the meat we ate—because they ate it all."[114] Like many other women, Josephine Petrini worked in the canneries. Sometimes pulling a double shift, Petrini could work up to twenty-hours straight in an attempt to provide for her family. She even performed her sometimes grueling job while she was six months pregnant with her son, evidence of both her financial need and her sense of dedication.[115] Factory work also connected Latinas and Latinos to other working-class people of color. As Petrini recalled, Chinese workers stood side by side with the Spanish-speaking in her assignment. Dorinda Moreno's mother likely experienced the same while working at local fish canneries.[116]

Rather than work for someone else, some Latinos and Latinas built businesses of their own. Sam Rios's grandmother, a self-sufficient woman who provided for her family, reflected some of the ways Latinos created their own opportunities. "She started a little tortilla factory right on 21st and Harrison. And so her and her *comadres* they used to sit around this *comal* and make tortillas by hand. And they would go door to door and sell them. So little by little, they built up a business. . . . My grandmother was always the strong, stable person in the family."[117] After migrating to the city with her husband and three daughters, Guadalupe González was disappointed with the job opportunities for a monolingual Mexican immigrant woman. She began taking English classes and attending beauty school. After graduating, she "found out that they were only willing to give her a job as a shampoo girl," so she decided to open her own shop in the Outer Mission. Every Saturday, her daughters had to choose how to help out. "Our choice was, you go to the beauty shop and you work all day or you stay at home and clean the house and cook dinner. So it wasn't much of a choice, okay?"[118]

Work patterns often mirrored migration networks, as Latin Americans used kinship networks to navigate the city. When one Salvadoran family came to the city with their small child, they lived with a Costa Rican–Mexican couple the young girl thought of as "padrinos."[119] They resided in the South of Market barrio, on Boardman Place, where Spanish-surnamed tenants occupied most of the housing.[120] Later, the girl's mother, aunt, and their *comadres* all found employment working as domestics in a local nursing home, depending on each other for economic and social support.[121] Interpersonal connections were often the foundation of community. When Esperanza Echavarri's family left the fields and came to the city, her father "had a family relation who knew his family [and] that settled here in San Francisco." The family moved in with them for a few years, until they could afford their own apartment in the South of Market area. The matriarch "was always very connected to us. She was always over for our celebrations, and always my mom maintained a very close connection with her."[122]

## "Latino Catholicism" in the Mission

The rise of the postwar community played out in community institutions in the Mission. St. Peter's Catholic Church, in the heart of the district, bore witness to this demographic and cultural shift, as the same dynamics recast it as a Spanish-speaking parish with few rivals. As the Spanish-surnamed population of the city rose to 51,602, a Catholic statistical survey done in the same period revealed 51,235 Latino Catholics.[123] Most of the city's parishes, then, had at least some Latino parishioners. The Catholic churches in the Mission housed the largest concentrations. Mirroring emerging patterns of Latino concentration, by the 1960s, sixteen parishes had Spanish-surnamed parishioners, who made up at least 10 percent of their total congregations.[124] The five adjoining parishes—St. Joseph's, St. Charles's, St. Peter's, St. Anthony's, and St. Kevin's—ran from the South of Market area through the Mission District and had the highest percentages of Spanish-surnamed parishioners. St. Peter's (in the center of this cluster) in addition to Mission Dolores, St. Paul's, St. Teresa's, and St. James's (along either side of the cluster) were the five parishes with the highest number of Spanish-surnamed parishioners. Together, these parishes composed both the heart of the Mission District and of Catholic Latino San Francisco.[125]

The Mission was an immigrant-friendly district for most of the century, and Latinos entered it as members of the Irish, Italian, and other European communities migrated to "better" parts of the city and "more peaceful" suburbs. Latin American residents found affordable homes, a solid working-class character, and sunny weather in the Mission, in addition to a robust set of Catholic churches. In St. Peter's, Latinos encountered a parish with a strong ethnic immigrant past. The church had served as the focal point of the Irish Catholic community since the late nineteenth century, when the character of the "Mish" began to take on a decidedly Irish flavor.

Supporting the community with an elementary school and both a girls and boys high school, St. Peter's shaped the spiritual, intellectual, and, at times, the political life of the district.

No single figure better embodied the power of St. Peter's than its long-time pastor, Father Peter C. Yorke. An Irishman who served the parish from 1901 to 1925, Yorke was a priest known for his oratory, his command of the written word, and his dedication to the Irish-Catholic cause. As editor of *The Monitor*—San Francisco's archdiocesan newspaper—he rose to "citywide fame in the 1890s by 'vanquishing' the anti-Catholic American Protective Association."[126] Coupled with his active support of unions (witnessed in the 1901 Teamster's strike) and of Irish independence (reflected, among other ways, in his creation of the pro-Irish newspaper *The Leader* in 1902), Yorke had near mythic status among the Irish of the city as "the defender of Catholicism against hostile attackers, the champion of labor, and the pro-Irish advocate."[127] Two years after his death on Palm Sunday 1925, the parish community began holding the Annual Yorke Memorial Mass at the 11:00 A.M. Palm Sunday service.[128]

The Latino newcomers benefited from their church's Irish immigrant history in more than spiritual ways. While the Irish American church and its clergy may have exhibited an anti–working class tradition in other parts of the Southwest, in the Mission working-class values and Irish ethnic identity could not have been more united.[129] The Mission District gave birth to more than half of the city's unions, and more than a few of them had members from that same Irish community.[130] The class realities of the district only reinforced that identity, with the Mission widely known as an immigrant entry point to the city. One priest recalled how locals "used to say that it was the port of debarkation, and then when they made a little bit of money they would move, either up to St. Paul's [in the Outer Mission], which was a little higher up, or out to Daly City or something like that."[131] St. Peter's shared many of the district's working-class qualities. As another priest remarked, "[it] was known at all different places as a church that was open to workers and to the poor."[132]

The transformation of St. Peter's from an Irish to a Latino parish was gradual, often illustrating ministerial evolutions in the Catholic Church. John Bourne, who served the parish as deacon, remembered a "big influx of Latinos" beginning around 1946 or 1947, while the European immigrant populations still predominated.[133] In 1950, responding to the increasingly evident need for Spanish-speaking priests at the parish level, the San Francisco Archdiocese assigned the Nicaraguan-born Luis Almendares to St. Peter's as an assistant pastor. As discussed in chapter 2, Almendares served as much of the Bay Area's Latino community as he could, often filling in at Guadalupe Church and serving as the first chaplain of the Federation of Guadalupana. At St. Peter's he not only heard confessions in Spanish and offered the general services of a Spanish-fluent priest, he also instituted a weekly Spanish devotional hour at the church and began the annual commemoration of the feast day of the Virgin of Guadalupe. He also hosted a regular Spanish Holy Hour on a local radio station during which he led prayers, offered a sermon, and publicized cultural events of interest to the Bay Area's Latin American community.[134]

The more general rise of the Latino population throughout the San Francisco Archdiocese did not escape the attention of the local hierarchy. In 1959, the archbishop appointed Father Donald McDonnell chair of a committee to propose bylaws for the Central Council for All Spanish Organizations.[135] McDonnell served as a priest in San Jose, about fifty miles from the city of San Francisco, but still within the nearly 15,000-square-mile radius of the archdiocese. The archdiocese chose McDonnell, a man with a proven commitment to migrant workers in the fields, to evaluate and coordinate its overall efforts with respect to the Spanish-speaking. In 1960, after months of reviewing Catholic service models such as that of the Chicago-based Bishop's Committee for Migrant Workers, his committee crafted foundational documents for what became the archbishop's Council for the Spanish Speaking (CSS).[136] Their stated mission was to create "an overall apostolate to the Spanish-speaking by: 1) Drawing upon the resources of the various diocesan departments with respect to problems of the Spanish-speaking; 2) Sponsoring local and diocesan conferences for the Spanish-speaking; 3) Studying the need for placement of Spanish-speaking priests; 4) Encouraging and assisting Catholic Spanish-speaking lay organizations; 5) Providing for other needs in the apostolate to Spanish-speaking."[137]

The archbishop supported their cause by appointing Father William C. Hughes as chaplain for the Central Council in July 1960. Hughes took on the CSS post in addition to his parish-level duties as assistant pastor at San Francisco's Sacred Heart Church. In an acknowledgment of the growing amount of work involved in coordinating the archdiocese's ministry to the Spanish-speaking, Hughes was released from Sacred Heart the following year. Now given the title of director of the Central Council, Hughes acted as the first general coordinator of Spanish-speaking work in the archdiocese. Reflecting the diversity encompassed by the archdiocese's massive geography, Hughes's appointment also came with the title director of Catholic rural life.[138] In 1962, when the dioceses of Stockton, Santa

Rosa, and Oakland were created from the Archdiocese of San Francisco, the largest share of the rural populations became part of those diocese's concerns.[139] Still, ministering to a rural and migrant population occupied much of Hughes's time. In 1961 he created a CSS initiative called the Catholic Migrant Mission Program (CAMMP). Participating priests ventured out to the fields and held masses in labor camps, performed the sacraments in Spanish, and provided catechismal education for migrant children. Realizing that improvement would require the collaborative efforts of clergy and laity, Hughes also found ways to organize active parishioners to work in unison with the priests. The creation of a Labor Camp Committee, composed of laypeople and priest advisors, coordinated a visitation program to bracero camps, handed out religious articles, and promoted the faith through interpersonal contact.[140]

As the church created new spaces for lay involvement, it also advanced Catholic ministry to the Spanish-speaking. CSS clergy directed most of their time to the fields, exposing the personnel limits of their larger endeavor. In 1962, this led the Central CSS led to create another council just for the city. Run almost entirely by a committee of local Catholic residents, the Catholic Council for the Spanish Speaking (CCSS) operated as a coalition of San Francisco parishes with high numbers of Spanish-speaking parishioners and organizations.[141] Each parish and parish-based group had two representatives on the CCSS, who elected an executive committee. Father Ronald Burke was chaplain of the organization, which, in turn, appointed an executive director to handle administrative duties. In the early years, that role was filled by layman Eduardo Lopez.[142] The CCSS met annually with the archbishop to update him on local concerns and to make recommendations for improvement. Comprised of men and women from the Spanish-speaking Catholic community, the CCSS offered a "bottom-up" perspective on the successes of Catholic ministry. Where the Central CSS concerned itself with the activities of the clergy, the CCSS sought to foster the development of lay-dominated organizations. In one annual report, for example, it surveyed all the city's parishes for organizations and programs run by laity.[143]

The CCSS's drive for a visible lay leadership did not ignore the need for a stronger and more effective clergy. Its leadership consistently advocated for more Spanish-speaking priests and a greater amount of Spanish language services.[144] One report to the archbishop characterized the scene in a strategically urgent tone: "Due to the scarcity of the priests in Latin American countries (a subject that has been of great concern to the Holy Father) a great number of Spanish Speaking who come to the United States have had very little formal religious training, even though their popular traditions have formed a religious sediment that varies in strength and depth from person to person. Although most Latin Americans in San Francisco are baptized Catholics, a rough estimate of the number of Spanish Speaking who attend Mass on Sunday would be 20% of the total population at the very most; those who receive Communion, less than 2%."[145] Within the archdiocese, the shorthand measurement of Catholic health lay in the attendance reports of weekly masses and the numbers of those receiving regular sacraments, like confession and communion. Using this language to its advantage, the CCSS promoted its cause. It even preyed on the wider Catholic fear of "Protestant slippage." "In St. Peter's parish," the CCSS members wrote, "with two Spanish Speaking priests, it has been found that there are 14 Protestant chapels serving the Spanish Speaking in the same area."[146]

These local developments took place within a larger Catholic Church undergoing its own deep transformations. Organized in fulfillment of Pope John XXIII's 1959 call for an ecumenical council, the Second Vatican Council began in 1962 to institute a host of sweeping changes.[147] The council's 1965 close marked a new era in the way the Catholic Church positioned itself with respect to its members and the Christian world. In an attempt to make the liturgy more accessible to laity, Vatican II decreed that the Latin mass and text be translated into modern languages. On ecumenism the council encouraged the reunion of all Christian brethren, rather than the conversion of all Protestants. Above all, it encouraged all Catholics to enter into dialogue with Protestants and the secular world. Additionally, while acknowledging its own guilt in creating the Christian schism, the Vatican also promoted the belief that the church, its sacred texts, and its past leaders were historically conditioned.[148]

In indirect ways, Vatican II advanced changes in the church's position with respect to the twin processes of community and identity formation as it paved the way for a more democratic and participatory institution at the local level. Where the council redefined the institution's relationship to its members and provided for the possibility of a different future, the lives of all Catholics—regardless of nationality, language, or race—could be transformed through the church and its clergy. The council's most sweeping changes on this count came in the document *Lumen Gentium*, which framed the church as the "whole people of God," stressed the fundamental equality of all people, and described "the common priesthood of the faithful." In the words of one historian, the document asserted the church's role "as primarily one of service to the community."[149] Breaking with the image of the church as a hierarchical institution in which "the clergy ruled, the laity obeyed," the decisions of the Second Vatican Council removed any specter of insubordination from the development of a more active and democratic parish structure. While controversy still marred the work of some activist priests and their parishes, those who sought to create a new church had the commitments of Vatican II to support them. As *Lumen Gentium* proclaimed: "The Church encompasses . . . all those who are afflicted by human misery and she recognizes in those who are poor and who suffer, the image of her poor and suffering founder."[150]

These overlapping developments found dynamic expression at St. Peter's parish through a cohort of clergy that largely reflected these ministerial evolutions. Although none was Latino, they would shepherd the parish's ethnic shift throughout the sixties. Leo Uglesic followed Almendares as the second Spanish-speaking priest assigned to St. Peter's. Arriving in 1958, the Yugoslavian-born Uglesic had learned Spanish while working in Argentina. In an attempt to make St. Peter's a more pertinent to the local community, he unsuccessfully lobbied for a weekly Spanish-language mass. Thwarted by the archdiocese "because he was the only Spanish-speaking priest," Uglesic found his cause bolstered by the arrival of Father Jim Casey in 1963.[151] Casey—a San Franciscan by birth—learned Spanish on his own initiative. Inspired by the work of priests serving the migrant populations in California's fields, Casey made an effort to study Spanish during his years of service at St. Patrick's and St. John's Churches, culminating in two summers of study in Mexico.[152] Once at St. Peter's, Casey made an unmatched effort to reach out to the growing community of color he found in the Mission. Together Uglesic and Casey fought successfully for a Spanish mass at St. Peter's beginning in 1964.

In 1965, Father John Petroni replaced Uglesic as assistant pastor. Petroni learned Spanish as part of his education, but before his time at St. Peter's he "had very little relationship with the Spanish speaking."[153] The team of Casey and Petroni stood in stark contrast to St. Peter's head pastor, Father Hennessy, who did not speak Spanish but was well-regarded by the European immigrant community. Casey and Petroni reached out to the Latino newcomers by incorporating their cultural practices into the liturgy of the mass and the regular celebrations of the parish. More important, they sought to "push St. Peter's and its parishioners beyond the confines of the traditional Catholic parish into the community in order to address the community's needs."[154] Their adherence to a more progressive, philosophical, and justice-oriented Catholicism further catalyzed the formation of the Mission's Latino community.

Casey focused most of his attention on serving the community directly. As chaplain of the CCSS, he helped organize local support for the farmworkers' struggle and stood with his parishioners in their community efforts against urban redevelopment.[155] Casey viewed his political work in the context of social justice and Catholic ministry. When the archbishop asked for Casey's advice before allowing a mass to be held for a Mission organization, Casey objected on the grounds that the group "may turn out to be quite a political force" and that the community of Latinos "are very touchy when it comes to the Church and politics." However, the "political" nature of the group came from its failure to support the Mission Area Poverty Program. "Our task has been to try to form our people in charity so that they will go out into the community and be a leaven. Certainly we are willing and anxious to assist in projects for the social and material betterment of the Spanish speaking people, but to canonize the spirit and principle of this organization by offering a public mass for them seems wrong."[156]

Petroni was dedicated to better meeting the spiritual needs of the Latino community by crafting a culturally specific liturgy to, in his words, "speak more to the Spanish speaking people."[157] Recognizing that these changes would be more authentically made with the input of community members, he created a Spanish liturgy committee to oversee the process. Petroni also developed the "Little Parish" program, modeled on the work of Father Leo Mahon of Chicago. Conceived of as an attempt to split "the large, impersonal parish down to small 'neighborhood cells,' where people were able to deal more personally with the issues of religion and with each other," Petroni's program brought the church directly into the homes of the parishioners. Reading scripture, discussing theology and the sacraments, and building bonds of unity with fellow community members, participants in the program sought to raise "people's social consciousness and consciousness of what the Sacraments are, so they would get involved."[158] In this synergy with Casey's more overtly political efforts, Petroni's work helped transform both the church and the community as he and Casey used religion to encourage their parishioners to become more involved in the world around them.

As the Nuestra Señora de Guadalupe parish had done for the generations of Latin Americans before the war, St. Peter's fostered a faith community that transcended nationality, race, and ethnicity. At the same time, it also bore witness to the more fractious influences of ethnic and racial rivalry. Some European-descended parishioners did not readily welcome Latino newcomers. Petroni recalled that between whites and Latinos "it was not a good relationship at all." The Irish and Italian Catholics, in particular, "were uncomfortable with them, and in some cases hostile. In some cases they would look down on the Spanish speaking as being of a lower class. Basically they were very threatened by them."[159] One priest recalled Pastor Timothy Hennessy's telling him of the first time he publically spoke Spanish during a mass by making an announcement. Not being a Spanish speaker himself, "He read it and had practiced what he was supposed to say. And he said he no sooner got back in the house when one of the Irish parishioners called and was furious with him. He said, 'Why did you give into them?' "[160]

The Latino and Latina parishioners who embodied the cultural shift felt the tension as well. Juanita Alvarez remembered feeling anything but welcome. "I felt like they put the Latinos aside. A Mexican woman married to a Peruvian were my only friends, because the white people didn't speak to us. They didn't want us."[161] At times, the cultural conflict found very personal expression. Alvarez recounted one such event when she and an Anglo woman who lived in a downstairs apartment got into a fight over Alvarez's children. Telling the story in her native tongue, Alvarez remembered how the Anglo woman said her children "parecían animales al bajar," that they seemed like lowly animals.[162]

In many ways, language became the symbol of the community's cultural wars. To some whites, the lack of English proficiency in the Latino community rationalized their prejudice. As one European-descent parishioner put it, "They are anxious to hang on to their language and their culture and everything. I think one thing that bothers me is that they never become Americans. Whatever they are, they're always that all their life."[163] For Latinos, the goal of incorporating their language into the liturgy meant the possibility of making St. Peter's their own, of marking it as "theirs." Isaura Michell de Rodríguez helped organize her fellow Spanish-speaking parishioners when she gathered 500 signatures on a petition for a regular Spanish mass. In meetings with Hennessy, she advocated for the services because, in her estimation, "the people were changing over to the Protestant side."[164] Yet, on the personal level, she noted how, after working for the war industries, she felt she was owed at least this much. "I resented work a lot. . . . I gave my blood for the wounded soldiers . . . and here there weren't any [Spanish] religious services."[165]

The beginning of the regular Spanish mass at St. Peter's, in 1964, indicated an institutional commitment to the Mission's newer population. A recognition of the permanence of the Latino population shift, it also fulfilled the combined efforts of the laity like Rodríguez and clergy like Casey. Casey remembered the first mass as a success: "The church was packed. . . . It was just outstanding. The singing was so loud and spirited." By accepting the Spanish language as a marker of the wider Latino community, and integrating it into the church's ministerial duties, the mass helped make St. Peter's into a significant space for the Latino community. In subsequent weeks, Casey remembered, "it became standing-room-only."[166]

Ethnic rivalries among the various segments of the Latino population provided for a consistent parochial challenge, much as they did during the heyday of Guadalupe Church. Mexican, Salvadoran, and Nicaraguan communities often imported their specific forms of nationalist prejudice into the local church. For example, while the celebrations of Latin American religious feast days communicated a positive shift by incorporating Latino cultural commemorations, these same celebrations revealed deep divisions. As one priest described it, "The Nicaraguans had a feast for the Immaculate Conception. They had a triduum [the praying of the rosary over three consecutive nights], December 8–11. The Mexican celebration [of the feast of Our Lady of Guadalupe] was December 12, and they were always fighting about altars. The Nicaraguans would build their altar, and they'd want to take it down. Then the Mexicans would want to use the same altar, and there was quite a bit of rivalry between Our Lady of Guadalupe and the Immaculate Conception."[167] While the Salvadoran celebration of the feast of El Salvador del Mundo and the Guatemalan commemoration of the Black Christ—Nuestro Señor de Esquipulas—did not conflict with other celebrations by date, the proliferation of these national religious events rarely involved the participation of the entire Latino community.[168]

Sometimes rivalries existed within national groups as well. Immigrants from Nicaragua came to San Francisco for many of the same economic reasons as other Latin Americans. Complicating these trends, however, thousands also fled the political repression by the Somoza regime in the fifties and sixties.[169] When an earthquake struck Nicaragua, the San Francisco expatriate community and others mobilized a local relief effort. Father James Flynn, appointed to a citywide committee organizing the relief drive, witnessed firsthand how life-and-death political disputes crossed borders. "They were on all sides of the [political] question," he recalled. "There was an extremely hot and almost violent confrontation among the two major groups, the anti-Somoza crowd and the government crowd, which was led by the consul general. Then there was a fight over who was going to get the money. There was a rumor out that they were going to lynch me or something like that."[170] Such political divisions made attempts to create a more cohesive Latino community all the more challenging.

Local members of the Spanish-speaking community used the church to address these dynamics. The laity-led CCSS, for example, took an active role in local politics, focusing on the collective needs of a poor and working-class immigrant community. The CCSS supported the efforts of antipoverty programs funded by the Economic Opportunity Council (EOC). Working with such groups as Arriba Juntos—funded by the EOC and housed at St. Peter's—they attempted to ameliorate the problem of "unemployability" among the Spanish-speaking. They also struggled to expose and defeat anti-Latino discrimination among local employers, including the U.S. Postal Service, the San Francisco Municipal Transportation Agency, and Pacific Gas and Electric. The CCSS led the lay Catholic drive to support the United Farm Workers in the mid-1960s. And when the issue of community redevelopment came to the Mission District, the CCSS supported the Mission Coalition Organization—the leading community organization on the issue. Many of CCSS members were elected to leadership positions in the coalition.[171]

The CCSS also proved effective in the religious realm. In September 1962 it opened a "Centro Católico," a gathering place in the heart of the Mission where the CCSS could meet, the community could plan activities and organize, and individual community members could find valuable information on social services, jobs, and education. More than 100 people visited the center in its first year.[172] The CCSS sponsored regular religious celebrations such as the feast days of Nuestra Señora de Guadalupe (for Mexicans), El Señor de Esquipulas (for Guatemalans), and El Salvador del Mundo (for Salvadorans), among others. It also sponsored the traditional Christmas commemoration of Las Posadas.[173] Beginning in the mid-1960s, it hosted an annual Latin American Unity Day, an attempt to use Catholic faith to build fellowship and overcome the fierce national rivalries dividing ethnic groups.[174] In the final analysis, Catholic religious practices may have been the most powerful factor in shaping a cohesive Latino Catholicism. John Petroni observed that the "different groups—Mexican, Nicaraguan, Salvadorian, Puerto Rican, and Cuban—tended to stay very much separate from one another." Simply put, "it was just difficult to get them to cooperate." The Spanish mass, however, was a regular exception to this rule. "That was very crowded. The people loved the singing, the Mariachi music, and we tried to use that to build up the religious inspiration of the people."[175] Institutionalized as a part of the Latino community, the weekly Spanish-language mass was both a continuation of what St. Peter's had done for generations and emblematic of something new.

The Yorke Memorial Mass illustrated the point. By 1960, thirty-five years had passed since the death of Peter Yorke, the beloved pastor of St. Peter's and revered member of the local Irish community. Each year, however, a shrinking contingent marked his passing with the Palm Sunday 11:00 A.M. mass, the same slot the Spanish-language mass occupied beginning in 1964. Father Casey remembered the first Yorke service after the change.

> Shortly after we got our Spanish mass started it was time for Father Yorke's celebration. . . . So here we had this huge Spanish-speaking group, about 1,000, and there was this little contingent of about twenty sitting in the first rows. So this little group came to the mass with no music, and I think they tried to sing a few hymns, but they just didn't come through. Finally, at the end of the mass we asked the Spanish-speaking to sing a hymn. They just erupted in song. It was so beautiful, and it convinced the [Yorke celebrants] that maybe they ought to try the 12:15 mass next year. . . . It was a visual sign of what was happening at St. Peter's. The Irish were outnumbered and finally had to face up to the fact that it was a Spanish-speaking [parish].[176]

St. Peter's made the shift to being a Spanish-speaking parish with the adaptability that marked its past. As one historian commented, the genius of St. Peter's "has been its ability to adapt and respond to the rapidly changing ethnic and social composition of the parish. And to make each new parishioner, whether Irish, Italian, Latino, or Filipino, feel at home."[177]

THROUGHOUT THE FIRST HALF of the twentieth century, commercial and manufacturing enterprise continued to position San Francisco as central to U.S. economic designs throughout the Pacific. Stories of Latino community formation in this period vividly demonstrate the human results of these endeavors, as multifaceted projects of economic imperialism facilitated new migratory and resettlement patterns. The extension and maturation of the city's hemispheric networks, connections that moved capital and raw goods from the Spanish-speaking South through the Golden Gate, also moved distinct segments of the Latin American people. The Mexican, Salvadoran, Nicaraguan, and other Latin American migrants who resettled in the Bay Area were a living embodiment of the colonial adage: "We are here because you were there."

Once in the city, Latinas and Latinos engaged a multifaceted process of "homemaking," re-creating the tastes, sounds, and sights of the familiar. Whether in a Mexican restaurant or a Central American newspaper, those new articulations of life in the urban West should be seen for the simple yet important acts they are—active attempts to forge lives of meaning, dignity, and community. As Latinos emerged as new social subjects, men and women with visibility and agency in midcentury San Francisco, they altered the focus and, at times, the purpose of powerful institutions. The cultural remaking of parishes within the San Francisco Archdiocese, as demonstrated in the transformation of St. Peter's into San Pedro, also remade these institutions into sites of Latino Catholicism, a culturally specific spirituality that simultaneously reflected Latina and Latino agency and helped set the context for its ongoing emergence. As new institutions, political events, and movements facilitated cultural dialogues within community spaces, Latino San Franciscans would continue to create and express something uniquely their own.

## CHAPTER FOUR

# All Those Who
# Care about the Mission,
# Stand Up with Me!

*Latino Community Formation and the*

*Mission Coalition Organization*

"We are mainly a Latin American community which is proud of its heritage," proclaimed Ben Martinez, president of the Mission Coalition Organization (MCO), at the alliance's second annual convention in October 1969. Standing before more than 800 community leaders—representing eighty-one local civil rights, labor, church, and community organizations—Martinez publicly recognized Latinos as the dominant racial or ethnic group in the Mission and the foundation of efforts at coalition-building. "But this is also a mixed community," he continued. "And I know that the Samoan, the Black, the Italian, the Irish, the Filipino, the American Indian, the Anglo, and every other group in this community is proud of its heritage." Martinez had already overseen a growth in the membership, programs, and public reputation of his fledgling organization. "It is in our interest," he said, "to recognize the identity each of us has, and then to go from that point to developing a working program that will meet all of our interests."[1]

Beginning in 1967, the largely working-class, heavily immigrant, and decidedly multiracial neighborhood of the Mission District underwent a profound transformation. Incited by the specter of urban redevelopment, and against the backdrop of local movements for racial justice, a multigenerational population of both politically active and previously uninvolved residents came together under the banner of community empowerment.

Once celebrated as the "largest urban popular mobilization in San Francisco's recent history," the MCO united residents in an effort to win jobs, housing, education reform, and the power to implement their collective vision.[2] In the process, they asserted a powerful sense of *cultural citizenship*, "of claiming what is their own, of defending it, and of drawing sustenance and strength from that defense."[3] In the early seventies, when the formal organization began to decline, the Mission was a far more cohesive community than it had been before, and Latinos' sense of collective identity had been fundamentally reshaped.

Designed as a grassroots, multi-issue coalition, the MCO brought together scores of local organizations representing more than 12,000 residents. At its height, the MCO was an institutional force, recognized as the "voice" of the district in political circles and authorized as the local agent of Model Cities—a 1966 federally funded "community development" program mandating "citizen participation." Through an assortment of programs and campaigns, the MCO made lasting and meaningful changes to the infrastructure of everyday life for both contemporary and succeeding generations of local residents. Its legacy—having helped a multiracial and working-class population successfully claim rights and ownership over its neighborhood—extends beyond the programmatic. In the ways it envisioned its collective effort, and integrated and deployed the racial and ethnic diversity of the Mission, the MCO nurtured a collective community identity within the largely Latin American–descent resident population. It re-created the historic community identity of the Mission District, substantively rooting in the neighborhood a hybrid and shifting form of class-based *latinidad*, an identity that continues to the present.

## Immigrants and the Mission

The Mission District has, for most of its history, housed a community marked by cultural adaptation and change. In the early twentieth century, population growth recast it as San Francisco's "entry neighborhood," a "stopping-off place for successive waves of the foreign-born." By midcentury, most considered the district to be the place "where San Francisco was born," a testament to the role of immigrants in the city's history.[4] In these early decades, San Francisco was the West Coast's largest city as well as its city with the largest population of foreign-born. During the apex of early-century immigration—in the years just before the United States devised a racial quota system to control "nondesirables" in 1921 and again in 1924—immigrants made up almost 28 percent of San Francisco's total population. Contrary to second-place Los Angeles, where Mexicans predominated, San Francisco's immigrants came mostly from Italy, Germany, and Ireland.[5] These demographic forces played out in the Mission District, as Irish and Italian immigrants constituted the heart of the neighborhood's working-class diversity. Before the Second World War, "the Mish" had become the multicultural center of a varied European-descent population, with unions, churches, lodges, and social clubs catering to the residents' cultural, economic, and social needs.[6] Geographically and culturally, the Mission was somewhat "cut off from the rest of San Francisco" and nurtured its distinctiveness as "a city within a city."[7]

A generation later, postwar forces solidified the conception of the Mission as an immigrant enclave and altered its residential composition. Most notably, early-century residents began to migrate out of the district, pulled to developments in the suburbs and other newer residential districts in the city. This "flight" of the Mission's traditional population had much to do with the opportunities for class mobility afforded postwar residents. Buoyed by the rising expectation of individual wealth tied to a consumerist impulse, many Mission residents began to see their district as lacking. "The Mission had the climate, but it wasn't the place to raise a family," said one former local. "Nobody wants his kids playing in the street."[8] As the mostly white and working-class residents moved up the economic ladder and out of the Mission, they were replaced by a multiracial assortment of working-class residents who sought out the district for its affordability.

The shift had an accompanying effect on the neighborhood's institutions, like St. Peter's Catholic Church, the district's largest parish church, located on 24th Street in the "heart of the Mission." The boundaries of St. Peter's matched those of the Mission District's core. In the 1958 Parish Report, Father Timothy Hennessy noted that "during the past five years there has been a very large increase in the number of Spanish type families, with a corresponding exodus of families of other national origins."[9] If anything, the observation was understated. The postwar population shift was so severe that by the close of the fifties, over 60 percent of St. Peter's residents had moved into the parish in the previous six years.[10] And that wave of "Spanish type families" continued in the decades to come. By 1965, more than 6,200 Latinos lived within St. Peter's borders, representing 30 percent of the total parish rolls.[11] As a profound wave of resettlement overtook the Mission in the postwar years, these Latino newcomers rooted themselves to the Catholic parish, imbuing it with a sense of their culture, as Irish, German, and Italian "old timers" continued to move away.

Racial/Ethnic Breakdown of South of Market, Mission, and Inner Mission, by Percentage, 1970

|  | South of Market | Mission | Inner Mission | Citywide |
|---|---|---|---|---|
| White | 39 | 49 | 26 | 57 |
| Black | 10 | 2 | 7 | 13 |
| Latin | 33 | 37 | 55 | 14 |
| Chinese | 4 | 2 | 2 | 8 |
| Japanese | — | 1 | — | 2 |
| Filipino | 10 | 6 | 6 | 4 |
| American Indian | 1 | 1 | 1 | 0.5 |
| Other | 3 | 2 | 3 | 1.5 |
| Foreign-born | 51 | 55 | 60 | 45 |
| Spanish-speaking | 28 | 32 | 50 | 12 |

Source: Figures from San Francisco Department of City Planning, "San Francisco 1970: Population by Ethnic Groups" (March 1970).

By 1970, more than 70,000 Latinos made San Francisco their home, comprising almost 10 percent of the city's population.[12] They also began to concentrate in a few neighborhoods. Beginning slowly in the 1930s, and escalating after the war, the largest share of Latinos resided in the Mission District and along the Mission Street corridor. This settlement pattern is the demographic story of the Latinization of the district, where the Spanish-surnamed population doubled from 11 percent in 1950 to 23 percent in 1960, and, again, to 45 percent just ten years later.[13] This transformation made Latinos "the most concentrated of any major racial or ethnic group in San Francisco."[14]

This cultural change further confirmed the Mission's place in the city's immigrant history. To some, it embodied other continuities. Joseph Tinney, who served on the San Francisco Board of Supervisors and whose Irish-immigrant family raised him in the Mission before he moved up and out, saw the indelible traits of the district as a form of cultural tolerance. "People in the Mission aren't inclined to be prejudiced against a foreigner," he thought, "for the simple reason that they or their parents were probably foreigners themselves."[15] Father James Hagan—affectionately known as "Padre Jaime" among Latino parishioners—agreed, as he observed the formation of a new community in the parish pews of St. Peter's. "There were an awful lot of people who lived in the Mission District who liked the idea of living with their neighbors, whether they were Spanish-speaking, English-speaking, or they came from Nicaragua, Guatemala . . . whatever part of the world. They were neighbors." Those who stayed, he reasoned, found community in diversity. "They went along with anybody who came. They preserved and added an awful lot to the neighborhood itself. People talk about the differences between ethnic communities, but I noticed that there were a number of people there who stood for other things besides their own ethnicity. They reached out and got to know the people, and they were all considerate of others."[16] Whether a mixed district of European heritage or one made up of Mexican, Central American, and other peoples of color, the Mission served as a beacon for working-class migrants to the city. The resulting diversity came to distinguish the district as much as its class character. "I can think of people who chose to live there because of the ethnic diversity, not in spite of it," said Hagan.[17]

The cultural differences between Latin America and Europe also promoted less favorable interpretations of the Mission's postwar transformation. More than a few locals viewed the Latinization of the district as part of a broader "decline," demarcating a favorable past from a doubtful future. In the spring of 1962, a five-part series in the *San Francisco Chronicle* revealed the growing dichotomy in the neighborhood between longtime residents and Spanish-speaking newcomers. Articles spanned both topics and emotions, ranging from a nostalgic celebration of "the men who are proud of being Mission boys" to lamentations over an "invasion" led by "the Spanish" and a general "problem of indifference."[18] One merchant viewed the transformation as both a cultural and financial loss. "Twenty-five years ago, I used to sell a ton of potatoes a week. Now I'm lucky if I sell 600 pounds." Another saw the newcomers as threatening traditional ways of doing business practices, saying, "If you don't speak Spanish now, you're dead." For many across the city and within the district, the rise of Latinos was not just a challenge but also part of a more general decline. "The neighborhood is running down something awful," said one resident. No longer able to find the familiar in their hometown, many longtime residents became fearful. One local—described as a "71 year-old barber"—remarked, "Twenty years ago, my wife and I used to stroll around the block after supper, but the streets aren't safe at night anymore."[19]

Beyond the district, the postwar Latinization of the Mission accompanied a more general rise in the impulse to identify and cure urban decay. Ever concerned with their city's postwar future, municipal and business leaders, including some in the Mission, sought to remake and modernize San Francisco. Structural age and the rapid growth pressures of the war had strained many residential districts. As early as 1950, when the Census identified 13,286 dwellings in San Francisco that were "beyond repair" and another 53,145 in need of "immediate work," city planners had begun to cast places like the Mission as the "slums of tomorrow."[20] Though the interests of community groups tended more toward fostering an affordable environment for families than toward creating a profitable landscape for commerce, throughout the fifties they largely agreed with business leaders' assessments of their district. In 1958, Mission Neighborhood Centers, a nonprofit community service center, undertook its own community study to detail local living conditions. The report discussed the profound postwar changes to the Mission, marked by "population growth" and "population shifts" in a "deteriorating neighborhood."[21] While the linkage of these twin phenomena echoed a current of racial prejudice, the 1960 Census only confirmed the severity of conditions in the neighborhood. In a square-mile tract in the heart of the Mission, more than 2,000 units out of 15,000 were classified as "deteriorating." Two hundred and sixty-two homes were listed as "dilapidated."[22] Compounding the sense of change resultant from the new racial composition, the increasing majority of newcomers entered the district as renters rather than homeowners, reflecting limits on the economic progress once promised by the Mission. Local groups estimated that by the mid-1960s only 20 percent of residents owned their own home.[23]

The area's physical decline became an issue of increasing concern in municipal politics. In early 1963, the head of the city's Redevelopment Agency—Justin Herman—proposed the largest redevelopment project in the city's history. With more than 3,000 acres involved, the proposed area under study stretched from Market Street and the South of Market District southward to the Mission and Eureka Valley.[24] The election of Mayor John Shelley in 1964 furthered the cause of redevelopment for the Mission. Shelley was celebrated as a "Mission boy made good," with his own personal history rooted in the neighborhood's immigrant past. Shortly after entering City Hall, he commissioned a research study of the entire city, the results of which echoed previous analyses. The report singled out the Inner Mission as one of two places in the city in need of "major tearing down and rebuilding."[25] It identified one-third of all Mission housing as "substandard," and 23 percent of the units as lacking proper plumbing. Largely ignored in the rebuilding and development processes marking the postconflagration city, 75 percent of the housing stock in the Mission was built prior to 1919. The report described 20 percent of the Mission's housing as "converted to multiple units with structural problems." The Mission found itself plagued with inadequate facilities, including the lack of proper school sites to meet the demands of a growing youth population.[26]

The raw data only darkened the Mission's already tarnished reputation, inside City Hall and beyond. Elected officials and business leaders saw redevelopment as the road to a modern San Francisco. As in major municipalities throughout the nation, this entailed the "eradication of 'blight' . . . [to] increase city tax revenue, revitalize the decaying urban core, and improve the living conditions of the poorest slum dwellers."[27] To prodevelopment constituencies in San Francisco such a vision also included a rapid transit system, the development of retail corridors, and the general replacement of older buildings with new ones. Yet concern over the emerging racial profile of the city also played a role. City planners promoted planned redevelopment as the only strategy to stall "white flight." One report warned that if left unchecked, San Francisco would be almost a third nonwhite by 1978.[28] While clearly some associated decline with the arrival of new migrants to the city, others proactively sought to cure "urban blight" for the newcomers. For example, a representative of the Mission Neighborhood Center recognized the need for improvements to infrastructure and local services as a way to build community anew. The city, he argued, should begin by giving the Latino "residents a feeling of identity as a neighborhood, so they'll want to stay."[29] In the spring of 1966, rather unintentionally, the cause of federally funded "urban renewal" catalyzed just such a transformation.

## Urban Renewal and the Mission

On the surface, the Mission seemed an ideal candidate for investment and structural improvement, if not formal renewal. By the middle of the decade, however, the promise of federal dollars for local building improvements had created a backlash in the city's poor and working-class communities. San Francisco's first renewal project, begun in 1956, focused on the Western Addition. Rather than improving life for the primarily black, working-class residents it dislocated many of them, leaving the area's core surrounded by vacant lots and public housing units and plagued by a rising crime rate. Widely studied as an example of failed urban planning and popularly understood as "urban *removal*," by the 1960s the bureaucratic buzzwords *urban redevelopment* incited fear among the city's communities of color. Not surprisingly then, when rumors of a proposed study by the San Francisco Redevelopment Agency (SFRA) circulated through the Mission, landlords and tenants united in opposition.

In 1966 the SFRA secured funds for a study of the "Mission Street Corridor," the core of the district into which the Bay Area Rapid Transit system (BART) would extend. The planning for the transit system had already caused some concern among local property owners and residents. City leaders celebrated the extension of the rail system as modernity and economic progress, while critics warned local residents to participate actively in the decision-making processes. Early municipal studies had suggested there would be an increase of "moderate rents" in the geography surrounding the stations and the construction of new buildings as high as thirteen stories. Hired planning consultants saw BART as an opportunity to "create a new skyline in the Mission" through additional forms of urban development.[30] Local property and business groups organized their opposition to the SFRA study almost immediately. Led by realtor Mary Hall and self-described "right-wing populist" Jack Bartalini, longtime homeowners' associations coalesced. Groups like the Potrero Hill Boosters, East Mission Improvement Association, and Noe Valley Improvement Club were joined by local merchants in their conservative effort. Fearing the proposed "clearance" of deteriorating properties and the forced relocation of businesses, they sought to defeat redevelopment by labeling it "creeping socialism."[31]

Bartalini and Hall spoke for constituencies with political clout but a diminishing presence in the Mission—white, propertied residents who were becoming numerically eclipsed by a multiracial mix of migrants, most with roots in Latin America. Although few noticed, the "new" Mission had already begun addressing the issues of working-class renters in a neighborhood undergoing structural decline. These Latin American organizational efforts also helped constitute the collective voice of the emerging majority in the struggle against redevelopment. For their constituencies, the prospect of urban renewal was mixed. It meant the possibility of new jobs in construction and business and commercial development but at a potential cost—the SFRA estimated that the "improvement activities" would result in the displacement of "1,900 families and 1,300 single individuals."[32] When they coupled this prospect with the known outcomes of earlier redevelopment plans, many Latinos recognized that their future in the city depended on organizing an effective opposition. Just such a coalition began to emerge when organizations—all in some way committed to Latin American community empowerment—began to craft a unified voice for the Spanish-speaking.

Throughout the sixties, San Francisco witnessed a maturing of the political voice of the Spanish-speaking, with the visible emergence of organizations seeking to represent Latino issues in the larger political system. Building on the city's self-conception as a "frontier for tolerance" that incorporated the racial and ethnic "other," these groups were able to close the gap between a municipal imagination and the everyday lived experiences of the nonwhite.[33] Organizations like the Community Service Organization (CSO), a statewide and grassroots Mexican American group, worked in the Bay Area in the early 1950s. Initially focused on the more than 90,000 Latinos living "in a squalid condition" in Alameda, Contra Costa, and Santa Clara Counties, by the sixties the organization also had a strong voice in San Francisco's Spanish-speaking community.[34] Concerns of the Spanish-speaking, as well as those of native-born Latinos, were further represented by groups like the Mexican American Political Association (MAPA) and the League of Latin American Citizens (LULAC); the Catholic Council for the Spanish Speaking, which wielded influence in this decidedly Catholic town; the Mexican American Unity Council; the Puerto Rican Club of San Francisco; and other cultural, educational, and civic organizations. In the early decade these Latino-focused groups worked on issues ranging from municipal jobs to school desegregation to housing.

Latino representation in the anti-redevelopment campaign benefited from a recent history of coalition-building around "race issues." In 1964, the fair housing campaign inspired a cooperative effort, foreshadowing some of what was to come. The specter of Proposition 14—an attempt to repeal elements of the Rumford Fair Housing Act—united CSO and MAPA in the common cause of voter registration. In the Bay Area alone, according to one MAPA leader, more than 130,000 Latinos registered to vote.[35] Jess Hernandez, the local president of the CSO, and Albert Corona, the local MAPA representative, represented a united front, saying they would "continue to fight any discriminatory practices inflicted upon the Latinos or other ethnic groups." This local, Latino-based coalition against Prop 14 further connected these organizations to various segments of the Catholic Church, which supported the effort, as well as Reverend Roger Granados of El Buen Pastor Presbyterian Church.[36] Granados would later serve as the interim head of the Bay Area War on Poverty Committee and play a supportive role in the creation of the Mission Tenants Union in 1965.[37]

Cognizant of their ethnic and national diversity, as well as their dispersed settlement patterns throughout the region, some Bay Area Latinos had been developing models of organization that crossed the bay. In August 1964, they created the Spanish-Speaking Citizens Foundation, an attempt to bring together Latino leadership from the nine Bay Area counties.[38] Though comprised of many residents of the East Bay, their 1965 leadership conference was held in the city at Mission High School. Initially focused on education, the group played an important role in the initiation of the San Francisco Head Start Program.[39] Even the Bay Area's more ethnically homogenous Latino organizations—such as MAPA, which largely focused on increasing the political power of Mexican Americans—exhibited tendencies toward multiethnic and multiracial coalition. In 1966, for example, the local chapter of MAPA broke ranks with their statewide leadership and endorsed Carlton Goodlett in his campaign for governor. Goodlett was the best-known and most respected African American in San Francisco who, despite his strong reputation as an advocate for civil rights in the city, stood very little chance of winning the gubernatorial contest. MAPA's statewide leadership threatened to censure the chapter for its unilateral decision, accusing it of "diluting the voice of the whole" and breaking ranks.[40] The leadership even went so far as to suspend the San Francisco chapter for its unwillingness to retract its endorsement.[41] This would not be the last time Bay Area Latino groups found themselves at odds with a state Mexican American–focused political organization. When a statewide "Brown Power" conference took place in Sacramento in 1967, two Mexican American organizations from San Francisco—the Spanish Speaking Citizens Foundation and the Spanish Surnamed Political Association—were denied seats on the platform after unknown political differences left them unwilling to participate on the statewide planning committee.[42]

Even with this organizational maturity, collectively translating into increased visibility for Latinos and their issues in municipal politics, authentic local Latino leadership had lagged behind in the eyes of some. As one resident put it, despite the organizational flowering and the numerous people associated with each group, "there was a scarcity of locally-developed leadership among the Hispanos."[43] By the latter part of the decade, this had clearly begun to change. Herman Gallegos was perhaps the most respected Latino voice in the city at the time. Active in community issues, Gallegos was a trained social worker most notably involved with the CSO, and by the middle of the decade he was earning a reputation for his work with Arriba Juntos. Begun in 1965 by Gallegos, Leandro Soto, and James McAlister, the multifaceted group largely worked "to prepare Hispano Americans to enter the job market." In addition to a jobs training program for youth (Horizons Unlimited) and for adults (New Careers), it also established a center for Central and South American immigrants in a spare room at St. Peter's Church.[44] Soto brought his connections to Catholic Charities and work experience with the War on Poverty with him when he became Arriba's first executive director. More than providing a singular, representational voice, the leaders of Arriba Juntos formed a broad and emerging cadre of leadership, along with others in the Mission and beyond. Individually, they were people with deep ties to neighborhood community issues and, at times, overlapping organizational bases. Combined, they helped to set the stage for a Spanish-speaking coalition in local politics.

The War on Poverty played some role in the maturation of local leadership. In the eyes of some, it "led directly" to the anti-redevelopment campaign by nurturing organizational development and a consciousness of community needs.[45] Such analyses echo historians like Robert O. Self, who argue that the "primary arena of significance" for poverty programs is in their ability to articulate "local struggles over fairness, economic opportunity, and power."[46] Initiated as Lyndon Johnson's "all-out assault on poverty," the federal programs comprising the War on Poverty were initially established under the Economic Opportunity Act of 1964. Among the funded programs were the Neighborhood Youth Corps and Job Corps, both related to job training, and the Community Action Program (CAP). Underfunded from the start, and widely controversial among some sectors in the government, CAP "started with a simple, radical idea": to foster change by funding local community efforts "developed, conducted, and administered with the maximum feasible participation of residents of the area and members of groups involved."[47] The program's liberal optimism inspired suspicion from some on the Left. Organizer Saul Alinsky, an early critic of the program, called it "a prize piece of political pornography," finding the model of community liberation from above inherently untenable.[48] Even a flawed model, however, can produce unintended beneficial results. Local community workers like Soto believed that "to the powerless, to the poor, to the ethnic minorities, and to millions of others," War on Poverty programs like CAP provided "their first opportunity in decades to obtain a better life for themselves."[49] Experiences working within these federally funded programs could hone skills in real-world contexts and animate more radical efforts.

The CAP requirement of "maximum feasible participation" sometimes led to conflicts among racially and linguistically distinct constituencies. Poverty work in the Mission often required the cooperation of Mexican American, Native American, and African American community members to secure funds. The Mission District office—headed by Alex Zermeño— brought a multiracial and multiethnic cadre of workers together in the same space. One San Francisco participant described how conflicts could develop "not only between the community and City Hall . . . [but also] between the African American and the Latino in the Mission District." Out of necessity, Zermeño and his staff became adept at solving these conflicts through an internal process of debate. By integrating these constituencies in pursuit of a common cause, the War on Poverty in the Mission helped promote a kind of coalition and a democratic process of decision-making that later came into play in the fight against redevelopment.[50]

Many of these organizational developments fed into the growing number of constituencies that joined property owners in their crusade against redevelopment. Local labor—which theoretically had much to gain from redevelopment—added its support. Union activity and organization ran deep in the neighborhood's history, fostering the sense that the "Mission is a fighting district for the working people."[51] The Mission's most prominent union was the Building and Construction Workers Union, Local 261, whose support came most visibly via Abel Gonzalez, head of the Latino union caucus, the Centro Social Obrero, often called "Los Obreros." Focusing on service issues for Spanish speakers in the union, Los Obreros had made a name for itself through its popular English-language classes and citizenship programs. The support of socially committed clergy proved instrumental to harnessing various forms of material support and establishing legitimacy within mainstream political circles. With forty-nine churches of various faiths and denominations, the Inner Mission had more churches per capita than any other neighborhood in the city—approximately one for every 1,000 people.[52] Over the course of the decade, the city's Catholic Church hierarchy became increasingly concerned with issues of race and civil rights, and it remained a force in neighborhood and citywide politics.[53] St. Peter's Parish—the historic home of the Irish working class now transformed into the church of the Spanish-speaking—already provided space and support to various community efforts. Many of the city's priests, committed to a philosophy of social change, viewed support for the poor as synonymous with their religious ideal of service. Protestant churches, overcome by a progressive "mission mentality," were already involved in local race politics, seeking to improve the material conditions of life in the city's ghettos and barrios. El Buen Pastor Presbyterian Church had been active in Latino advocacy for years. Reverend William R. Grace, director of the Department of Urban Work in the Presbyterian Church, sought social change by implementing the grassroots model for change designed by Saul Alinsky. Grace's assistant, Reverend David Knotts, already worked as a minister in the Mission. Seeking to nurture the ability of local Latinos to foster meaningful change, Grace and Knotts had created the Spanish-Speaking Information Center.[54]

Serving as a counterbalance to the conservative alliance represented by Bartalini and Hall, the Mission's radical Left added another oppositional voice to the diverse mix. Skeptics of government-sponsored "community development" and proponents of mobilizing communities for their own control, members of the Progressive Labor Party worked to create a meaningful movement for change among the district's poor. Led by John Ross, and finding organizational and representational focus in the Mission Tenants Union (MTU), the party's neighborhood influence expanded as it became widely known as a credible advocate for the rights of renters, particularly on the issue of rising rents amid a deteriorating stock of residences. Where City Hall sought redevelopment, the MTU pursued a people-focused set of solutions to "blight." The group's efforts earned it respect: even politically moderate church leaders sent their parishioners to the MTU when experiencing problems with their landlords, despite the MTU's open dedication to a Marxist ideal.[55]

Individually, each constituency and organization represented but a slice of the Mission District. United together, they left few recognizable sectors of the district unrepresented. This unlikely merging of the neighborhood's political and demographic diversity came only with the threat of redevelopment, and the shared perception that municipally determined progress would mean catastrophic loss. The groups formally came together in 1966 as the Mission Council on Redevelopment (MCOR), representing a cross-section of the Bay Area political landscape of the times. Members of the San Francisco chapter of the Student Nonviolent Coordinating Committee (SNCC), themselves veterans of the anti-redevelopment struggles in the Western Addition, attended the founding meeting, as did Presbyterian clergy familiar with the same struggles in South of Market. War on Poverty staff rounded out the group, along with "a representative of the American Indian Center, Mexican-American political leaders, plus some Alinsky-trained priests and ministers who had gone out on a political limb supporting the Delano strike."[56] The homeowners demanded that MCOR unequivocally oppose the SFRA plans. The groups representing nonpropertied interests shared their concerns about redevelopment—equating it with "complete clearance" while telling residents, "Don't trust the Redevelopment Agency"—but they were most interested in creating an authentic representational voice.[57] As they reasoned, residents could not control their neighborhood's future until City Hall saw MCOR as more than an obstructionist movement. To preserve that possibility, they did not oppose urban renewal but instead sought the power of the veto over its local manifestation. Recognizing that goal could only be met if they legitimately represented their neighborhood, MCOR recruited the Catholic "network," Los Obreros, block clubs and tenants' associations, the Protestant churches, various Latino organizations, and the Spanish-speaking staff of the local EOC.[58]

MCOR represented the authentic diversity of the Mission, including poor and middle-class, propertied and renter, Catholic and Protestant, and the multiracial population who called it home. As the only local voice supporting urban renewal, the Mission Renewal Commission—comprised of large local merchants—emerged as MCOR's only "competition." As plans progressed, MCOR demanded that the impact on everyday people be considered as redevelopment came before the Mission and, later, the Board of Supervisors, consistently asking of the advocates: "Where am I in this picture?"[59] In the eyes of SFRA officials like Justin Herman—who seemed to struggle to envision actual community residents as part of his plans—the broad, democratic coalition was a threat. "They don't want the right to take part," he lamented. "They want the right to stop it, the right to do their own planning."[60] Although the homeowners' group refused to formally join because of MCOR's willingness to negotiate, and Los Obreros and other labor groups provided only minimal support, MCOR emerged successful in late 1966. When Mayor Shelley could not accede to an MCOR veto, the group sought to scuttle any chance for redevelopment. In December, faced with the overwhelming opposition of most of the community, the Board of Supervisors squashed renewal in the district.[61] Phil Burton, who represented San Francisco in the U.S. Congress, stated it simply: "The diverse company of progressives and conservatives alike merely points up how widespread the opposition is to disruption of the neighborhood."[62]

Organized as a single-issue coalition, once MCOR effectively defeated the redevelopment process it ceased activity, folding in early 1967. The Mission, however, still confronted the fundamental issues that had inspired the city's redevelopment crusade. Residents continued to face a housing stock in visible and structural disrepair, an inadequate education system, a lack of jobs and job training, and no effective political voice. Local grassroots organizers, in particular those focused on Latinos, sought to sustain the level of activism beyond MCOR. Single-issue and diffuse campaigns garnered some attention and success, notably revealing an emerging new leadership. A young Latina named Elba Tuttle—who had worked in War on Poverty efforts—rose up in the Mission Area Community Action Board (MACABI). Ben Martinez became increasingly known for his work with the Office of Business, Education, and Community Advancement (OBECA), which changed its name to Arriba Juntos (Upward Together) in 1967.[63] Reflecting the growth of Latino labor, Abel Gonzalez and Los Obreros helped secure the election of Mayor Joseph Alioto. Other community members nurtured their political and organizational development in CAP-funded organizations. The lack of a cohesive effort, however, as well as growing conflicts over federal funds, revealed the deep fissures of race, nationality, and generation that remained. Mission activists were learning the same things as working-class communities all over the United States. As Thomas Jackson phrased it: "Overcoming poverty is not simply a matter of political will; it is and has become even more one of political structure."[64]

## The Mission Coalition Organization

Another opportunity presented itself in February 1968, at a Spanish-Speaking Issues Conference sponsored by MACABI. Mayor Joseph Alioto, speaking before the group, suggested he would seek Model Cities funds if a "broad-based group representative of the Mission" so desired.[65] The Model Cities Program—part of the City Demonstration Act of 1966—provided funds for community improvements ranging from structural development to housing, education, employment, and health. Realizing the potential for a more sustained grassroots coalition, Tuttle and Martinez (along with the Presbyterian minister David Knotts) took the lead in organizing the community voice. When the first phase of Model Cities came before the Board of Supervisors in May, the camps had substantially changed. A growing segment of the community advocated for the program, remaining opposed to redevelopment but linking these federal dollars to an opportunity to begin "rehabilitating homes, improving schools, and creating parks." These residents submitted a ten-point plan that would require community control of any funded project by granting a Mission-based coalition veto power. Now, the opposition dwindled to a mere fraction of the MCOR base, amounting to only the San Francisco Committee and the Responsible Merchants and Property Owners. Jack Bartalini and the homeowners said they opposed Model Cities but "agreed with the desires of the Coalition."[66]

By June 1968 a coalition of about twenty-five groups came together to constitute the community voice, calling themselves the Temporary Mission Coalition Organization (TMCO). Several key principles guided the TMCO. First, it strove to be a multi-issue organization. Second, it sought democratic governance within its own structures, such as that of its steering committee (which met weekly), its monthly delegates' council meeting, and its annual convention of member organizations. Third, it remained dedicated to nonviolence, hoping to utilize the full tactical repertoire of the civil rights movement. Finally, its members believed they could succeed only if their coalition was representative and broad-based: any and all identifiable constituencies in the Mission were encouraged to join. That meant making room for organizations with varied membership bases, as well as clear constituencies without active organizational outlets. The TMCO sought to represent the diversity of the Mission, a neighborhood made up of ethnic Mexicans, Central Americans (the combination of Nicaraguans and Salvadorans outnumbered Mexicans), Puerto Ricans, and South Americans, as well as Irish, Italians, Germans, Russians, Filipinos, Native American Indians, Samoans, and African Americans. Organizers began mobilizing support for the TMCO's inaugural convention, carefully strategizing to unify a cosmopolitan neighborhood.[67]

In 1968, the Mission District possessed a kind of community "momentum," one that nurtured a local, democratic, and representative leadership working toward the goal of "maximum cooperation."[68] Organizers of the TMCO harnessed this energy and its component resources toward organizing the first mass meeting of the coalition—a fall convention. The convention would foster their democratic ideal by selecting officials, creating committees, and adopting bylaws, but it could only work if a representative group showed up. They hired Mike Miller—a former SNCC organizer who trained under and maintained connections with Saul Alinsky—as the full-time community organizer to prepare for the convention and foster the coalition's "multi-issue" character. Others played their roles in the effort to expand community involvement. Ben Martinez, the organizing group's leader, sought to incorporate the support of labor, a lukewarm participant in MCOR. Exploiting his close ties to Abel Gonzalez, he recruited Los Obreros into the fold. Elba Tuttle and John McReynolds, with their connections to MACABI, focused on organizing the grassroots constituencies for the convention. The group secured a budget from multiple sources, both nurturing and reflecting the growing base. Local 261—the organizational parent of Los Obreros—provided financial support, as did the United Presbyterian Church. Staff donations also came from the Presbyterians in the assignment of Knotts, as well as from MACABI, which donated the services of Tuttle and McReynolds. Though diverse, the TMCO—which, after the first convention, changed its name to simply the MCO—followed in the footsteps of MCOR by continuing to rely on a broad Latino organizational base.[69]

The efforts of City Hall and Mayor Alioto provided the backdrop for the evolving community coalition-building effort, as municipal advocates of redevelopment incorporated the lessons of their previously failed efforts. Alioto pursued federal renewal dollars in a noticeably different manner than the previous administration, making public and private assurances that any plans by his office would seek to preserve the community and meaningfully integrate the voice of the people. In September 1968, Alioto announced the city's inclusion in the Model Cities program with the designation of a $259,000 planning grant intended for both the Mission and Hunter's Point Districts. His office characterized the move as an opportunity for the two districts "to say what they want done" as part of the process of further negotiation before any project could be physically initiated. The mayor reassured residents of the Mission who might still be concerned about "urban removal." "All this means is that we're going to get a sum of money to plan where we want to put new schools, parks, recreation and medical facilities," he cautioned. "It does not mean any wholesale demolition, particularly in the Mission District. Our emphasis there will be for the rehabilitation of the fine old Victorian homes."[70] In both choice of wording and political maneuvering, the planned actions of City Hall revealed the clout of the fledgling MCO. Building from this position, the coalition got to work expanding its base and assuring a formal seat at the table in the decision-making process that lay ahead.

At the first convention, in October 1968, more than sixty organizations participated, representing an attendance of between 600 and 700. They gathered in the hall of El Centro Social Obrero.[71] The sheer number of participants testified to the organizing skills of the cadre that brought this gathering to fruition, in addition to residents' clear interest in avoiding any dismantling of their human community. Most of the organizations participating in the convention sought control over any Model Cities funds coming to the city, a position assured only if municipal officials recognized the MCO as the district's legitimate representative. Almost immediately, however, the convention also exposed the challenges facing the coalition, as a small group disrupted the meeting. The youth-serving Mission Rebels in Action portrayed themselves as political radicals, though in fact the group was funded by the EOC and, hence, part of the aid bureaucracy in the Mission. Labeling convention leaders "sell-outs," the Rebels took to the stage during the proceedings, seized the microphone, and called the entire gathering a "farce." As the *Chronicle* described it in an article titled "Mission Coalition's Fighting Mad Start," the Rebels then tried to nominate their own platform of leaders. While their tactics upset most members of the audience, the group did manage to stall the agenda.[72]

The convention might have ended in disarray if not for keynote speaker Cesar Chavez. Too ill to attend the meeting in person and confined to a hospital bed, Chavez spoke by telephone to the crowd. His call for collaboration and "love" quieted the room and diffused the confrontation. "The poor have much in common, common dreams and desires of social justice," he said. "The question of goals should not be a problem. The

Ben Martinez, president of the MCO, addresses
an MCO rally in front of City Hall, May 1969. Bancroft Library,
University of California, Berkeley.

question that kills coalitions is the inability to take that first step in the most
common causes, and that is, to determine who is an adversary. . . . La Raza
to me was the whole human race."[73] Promoting a hybrid ethnic and racial
identity infused with class sensibilities, Chavez cautioned against the dis-
abling effects of infighting and inaction.

His plea did not move everyone. Mission Rebels leader Jesse James took
to the microphone once again and proclaimed, "You're being used again
and you don't even know it." Accusing MCO leadership of being an inau-
thentic voice another Rebel declared, "You're speaking about community
and you don't even live here."[74] Sensing a favorable response to Chavez's
words, Herman Gallegos, moderator of the convention, challenged attendees to work in the spirit of cooperation. According to local reports, he
chastised the Rebels, imploring them to remember Chavez's earlier comments. "Love means a lot of people out here want a better place to live and
you're not letting them." In a simple yet moving articulation of common
cause and interrelation, he shouted, "All those who care about the Mission,
stand up with me!"[75] The vast majority of attendees took to their feet, effectively neutralizing the Rebels. Convention organizers and Rebel representatives agreed to a compromise, allowing last-minute nominations from
the floor. The convention proceeded, with the Rebels' slate not faring well.

The majority elected officers, established committees, and ratified bylaws. The decision of an organizational platform was tabled to a later meeting.[76]

Unwilling to support the coalition's majority voice, the Mission Rebels remained in small company. Comprised primarily of black youth, with some Latinos, whites, and Samoans, the Rebels could not envision cooperation beyond their own organizational interests. Their departure demonstrated their stance. Other youth-focused organizations remained, many of which—like Horizons Unlimited, the Real Alternative Program (RAP), and East Mission United Neighborhood Youth Organization (EMUNYO)— worked with "at-risk" youth of color. Other constituency groups disagreed with the MCO vision but remained part of the coalition. Members of the Progressive Labor Party, for example, whose Mission Tenants Union took decidedly radical stances, stayed though they objected to the MCO's use of conciliatory language.[77] The various homeowners associations represented by Bartalini and Hall never agreed with the MCO's stance seeking direct control over federal funds and, hence, never attended the convention. In the eyes of some organizers, these groups simply mistrusted the Latino plurality's attempt to speak for the community.[78]

The convention concluded a month later, in November 1968. There it solidified an organizational structure and hammered out a platform. The tone was moderate, though the Progressive Labor Party's issues of tenants' rights, reducing unemployment, improving police-community relations, and education were included, with the broad support of attendees.[79] Some disagreement arose over the stance on Model Cities, with the convention leadership advocating a position in favor. The thirteen-point platform outlined the coalition's vision of future Model Cities involvement. It included the demand for absolute veto power within the Model Cities program and the right to name two-thirds of the Model Cities Neighborhood Corporation—a twenty-one-member representative body charged with fulfilling the federal requirement for "community participation." Veto power meant the MCO could stop any redevelopment effort it thought would adversely affect its community. The demand for two-thirds control would give the MCO absolute community control over federal funds. As the staff organizer Mike Miller remarked, however, "The lesson of words vs. real power was yet to be observed."[80]

The MCO's founding convention emboldened the hundreds of participants. With twenty-four-year-old president Ben Martinez at the helm, the coalition sought to build on its momentum by organizing the community into a mass movement. That entailed advocating for local control of Model Cities funds. As Martinez framed it, "We don't want the money unless we in the Mission have a major voice in how it will be spent."[81] It also meant meaningfully addressing community needs. Combined, these goals demonstrated the MCO's commitment to self-determination—the community's right to control its destiny—and inspired a grassroots model that gave structure to the "insurgent mood" of the times.[82] It fostered the participation of more than eighty local organizations and nearly 1,000 residents by its second convention. In less than a year, the MCO would become one of the most effective community efforts in the Bay Area, as it improvised solutions to neighborhood needs and mobilized for a head-to-head battle with the Board of Supervisors.

In order to authentically call for self-determination, the MCO had to surmount differences within the Latino-dominant community. The rivalries between groups of different national origins, in particular between the more established ethnic Mexican population and the more recently arrived Salvadoran and Nicaraguan ones, constituted a widespread and longstanding challenge. By the late 1960s, Salvadorans and Nicaraguans collectively represented about 40 percent of Latino residents in the city. Ethnic Mexicans, however, enjoyed greater visibility and power in local politics and in the city's Spanish-speaking cultural milieu. Their presence helped nurture the integration of new migrants from Latin America, whether they came from Mexico, Nicaragua, El Salvador, Guatemala, or Puerto Rico. The high rates of intermarriage among the city's Spanish-speaking populations suggest some level of integration, as the more established Spanish-speaking population "pull[ed] everybody together." Indeed, as one resident saw it, when members of her family came to the city in the early twentieth century, they migrated into a "Mexican America."[83] This dynamic seemed increasingly anachronistic in a Mission District where the MCO tried to foster authentic democracy. To remain true to its vision and address potential weaknesses, the MCO had to create representational space for constituencies whose voice was not already served by a standing community organization. The solution came via the MCO Steering Committee—made up of the president, seven executive vice presidents, and the various committee chairs—which met weekly as it took responsibility for implementing the convention's action plan. To meet the goals of inclusivity and accountability, the delegates created a vice presidential position for each racial and ethnic constituency in the Mission and other identified interest groups, adding a vice presidential position for each of the following groups: Mexicans, Nicaraguans, Salvadorans, businesses, youth, senior citizens, block clubs, Mexican Americans, Central Americans, South Americans, Samoans, Afro-Americans, Anglo-Americans, and Filipino Americans.[84]

To outsiders, this array of constituency groups might have seemed re-dundant. From the perspective of Mike Miller, the MCO's chief organizer, the community had a tacit understanding of how it worked. "The under-standing was that neither the Nicaraguans nor the Salvadorans would go for the Central American position. Either a Guatemalan or a Honduran would get that. But we couldn't, we didn't want to have a Honduran vice president, or a Guatemalan vice president because they were small enough in number that the Salvadorans and Nicaraguans said well if you're going to have a Guatemalan vice president then we want three. . . . And then you were going to have a body of sixty or seventy people."[85] Most significant, by recognizing the diversity of the Mission, *as understood by the residents of the district*, the MCO positioned itself to be more than symbolically col-lective. A blanket assertion of "Latinoness" would ring hollow in a district where the needs of bilingual Mexican Americans differed from those of monolingual Salvadoran immigrants, or African American youth, or Fili-pino families. Though the MCO certainly embodied a kind of *latinismo*, it did not rely on a limiting definition of who belonged. Unlike a traditional barrio identity, rooted in formal and informal segregation, the MCO's *lati-nismo* relied on the integration of multiple voices, needs, and identities. It shared space with non-Latino groups and coalesced in the expression of a common cause.

## Becoming the Community's Voice

Once a representative structure was solidified, the MCO refocused its en-ergies on serving the community's needs. Without tangible results, its representative structure would be meaningless. Functioning like issue-specific grassroots campaigns, the MCO's committees focused on issues like housing, the police, youth, employment, health, and community maintenance.[86] As a coalition of already standing organizations—many of which had experience with these issues—the MCO enjoyed early suc-cess, increasing community support and making membership a source of community pride. Early campaigns sought to create new playgrounds, ban pawn shops on Mission Street, and convert an adult moviehouse into a family theater. In each instance, the MCO sought both cosmetic and sys-temic change, finding creative ways to make its district more responsive to residents' needs. For example, earlier redevelopment in the South of Market area pushed some businesses southward into the Mission. One of those businesses was the adult theater, whose presence in the neigh-borhood would have been unheard of in an earlier generation. After negotiations with the owner failed, the MCO targeted his patrons, picketing the theater entrance and handing out fliers declaring its intention to notify their communities of their patronage. Members followed theatergoers and took down their license numbers. They even had a nun take photos as customers entered, though her camera had no film.[87]

The Housing Committee focused on "absentee landlordism" and deteriorating housing. Involving district residents who enjoyed a high degree of respect among the Latino base—like Father Jim Casey, Elba Tuttle, and Luisa Ezquerro—the committee sought meaningful mechanisms for tenants to secure and protect their rights. It began organizing residents to negotiate with landlords, peacefully, by respectfully informing property owners of the problems tenants faced as well as suggesting solutions. Reflecting both their creative humor and the working-class improvisation of some of their tactics, they invited landlords to the negotiating table by mimicking the process by which a tenant might be evicted—issuing a first, second, and, if needed, third notice, with each succeeding notice communicating a harsher tone. "We made up forms—form number one, two, three—but we gave them big numbers so that people would think 'God, this organization has five hundred forms before this one,' cause this is 501, 502, 503. . . . So you'd get your first notice . . . very polite, 'We would like to meet with you, please call us.' If we don't hear from you within a week, second notice. 'Please call us within three days.' If you don't call us within three days, third notice. 'If we don't hear from you within forty-eight hours, we will take further appropriate action.' It didn't say what the further appropriate action was."[88] When a landlord appeared, the committee tried to work out a solution. If the landlord ignored them, or failed to appear at an agreed time, the MCO traveled to his or her home or business and picketed. Seeing the utility of social coercion, members distributed fliers in these neighborhoods informing neighbors that an abusive, absentee landlord lived among them. These combined tactics produced results; in their second year, the MCO served as the official dispute agent for twenty-three buildings in the Mission. Grievance procedures and maintenance agreements the MCO devised were used. Always willing to support fellow members of the community, it sometimes even helped landlords deal with irresponsible tenants.

The Employment Committee was widely regarded as the MCO's most successful, a status visible in the growth of its membership. In its second year, it developed a youth employment campaign and secured a meeting with a manager at the Wonder Bread and Hostess Bakery. The goal of the committee was to get summer jobs for neighborhood teens. When the

Representatives of the MCO give
Ethel Kennedy a tour of the Mission District, circa 1970.
Courtesy of Spence Limbocker.

meeting was unexpectedly cancelled, a dozen committee members staged a sit-in at the manager's office, forcing him to agree to a new meeting. The committee successfully negotiated about a dozen jobs—each for a third of the summer—and the power to place local youth in the positions. When the members returned to the MCO office, the question arose as to who would get the jobs. Internal committee deliberations stalled until a young woman—Joan del Carlo—silent up to that point, asked, "Why don't we give the jobs to the people who worked to get them?" The principle led to the MCO "Point System," where members earned points through their support of the MCO—by attending meetings, participating in actions, or otherwise supporting the coalition. Then, as jobs came in, they were awarded to the people with the most points, who could take the positions or pass them along. Within weeks, the number of young participants rose to more than 100. By fall, with full-time jobs the committee's primary goal of regular weekly participation ballooned to 300.[89]

The success of its committees propelled a growth in the MCO's membership, adding substance to its claims of representing the community's voice in municipal negotiations for a Model Cities agreement. Its primary objective in this realm was functional control over the Model Cities Neighborhood Corporation, the board responsible for programmatic and financial oversight of federal funds. Whoever controlled the corporation controlled the future of the Mission. Ben Martinez sought to convince City Hall that the MCO was the only representative body that could speak for the diverse community. The standard of "maximum feasible participation" to enable "broad-based community support"—first articulated Title II of the Economic Opportunity Act of 1964—guided the federal evaluation of a successful proposal, and MCO leaders hoped to compel the city to include them. In May 1969, an agreement reached after six months of negotiations with the mayor gave control of the corporation to the MCO, on its own terms. While the MCO sacrificed its demand for veto power, the compromise required the mayor to appoint fourteen of the twenty-one board members from a list provided by the MCO. Additionally, the MCO could create a committee to review proposals for funds, evaluate the work of the corporation, and recall board members it had nominated.[90]

The agreement now required the support of the Board of Supervisors. At the board's Planning and Development Committee, which met on September 16—Mexican Independence Day—the MCO mobilized more than 500 community members to attend. Using the public testimony session to present seventy-five two-minute speeches in support of the agreement with City Hall, the MCO presented an "orderly, disciplined show of strength" that the *San Francisco Examiner* contrasted with the unorganized opposition of no more than 150. Their opponents called the agreement an "unholy alliance" and accused one supervisor of being a "political prostitute."[91] Calling themselves the San Francisco Fairness League, the opponents presented the board's committee with a petition signed by more than 100 locals, most self-identified as "homeowner." The MCO submitted its own petition, but with a stack of more than 2,500 signatures of propertied and nonpropertied alike.[92] The Planning and Development Committee voted to approve the agreement, forwarding the issue to the full board.[93] Maintaining its visible community support throughout the fall in multiple mass rallies, the MCO helped ensure formal approval at the full Board of Supervisors meeting on December 1, 1969. The supervisors voted in favor of the MCO-backed agreement, 7 to 4.[94]

Unfortunately, the U.S. Department of Housing and Urban Development (HUD), which oversaw the program at the federal level, vetoed the agreement as giving too much power to the MCO. After some stalling and political maneuvering, Mayor Alioto and the MCO reopened negotiations on a new agreement that would meet HUD's standards. To enhance its position, the MCO invited the mayor to take a "walking tour" of the district and view, firsthand, the fruits of its labor. As capable in the traditional political arena as they were at the grassroots, the MCO also invited the Board of Supervisors, state assemblymen, and a representative from Governor Ronald Reagan's office. When Alioto canceled, the MCO conducted its tour for the other dignitaries, winning favorable press coverage. The mayor's absence contrasted with the attendance of key Democratic and Republican leaders, including Assemblymen Willie Brown and John Burton, and a representative from the Model Cities Liaison Group controlled by Reagan's office. In remarks to local reporters, that representative—a former "Mission boy" himself—declared: "The governor has heard of radical elements in the coalition, but the people you see aren't that at all."[95] Soon thereafter, Alioto reached an agreement with the MCO that the supervisors ratified, 6 to 5.[96]

## Articulating a Better Community

The second MCO convention came in the midst of the coalition's Model Cities campaign. The celebratory mood reflected the MCO's continuing success, leading Ben Martinez to reflect on the passage of only one year in an internal MCO memo. "I can remember when I first chaired MCO meetings that all the faces were familiar," he wrote. "They were either agency people (EOC, Arriba Juntos, etc.), the middle class Mexican-Americans, and the fulltime 'revolutionaries' (Progressive Labor Party). There was only a scattering of other people in the crowd. This has changed a lot."[97] Among the changes Martinez celebrated were the inclusion of new faces and organizations, as well as the growing strength of the coalition. No longer merely a coalition of existing organizations, the MCO inspired members of the wider community to envision a better neighborhood for themselves and then implement that vision.

Martinez and the MCO leadership remained acutely aware of the interethnic rivalries embedded in the Mission District's Spanish-speaking diversity. They paid consistent attention to assuring that these dynamics would not reemerge as power struggles within the MCO. Still, such tendencies would never fully disappear. In the same memo, Martinez wrote about a local "Central American realtor" who headed an opposition group called the Spanish Speaking Political Institute (SSPI). In the past, Martinez wrote, these opponents could "point to the preponderance of Mexican-American leadership in the MCO and [they] used that with the Central Americans." By the second convention, however, Martinez saw the improvements in the leadership structure as removing "that ammunition." "At the Model Cities hearing," he wrote, "when we turned out 700 people, [the SSPI] turned out no more than 20 Latins, and that is a generous estimate.[98]

The MCO demonstrated its ability to transcend these tensions, in both the structure and the culture of its multiracial and multiethnic coalition. In his speech at the second convention, Martinez emphasized that strength. He described the Mission as "mainly a Latin American community" while acknowledging "the Samoan, the black, the Italian, the Irish, the Filipino, the American Indian, the Anglo, and every other group" that comprised its "mixed community." He then powerfully asserted how this diversity remained bound together in present condition and future aspiration. "We must recognize that it is in our interest to work together. It is in our interest to recognize the identity each of us has, and then to go on from that point to developing a working program that will meet all our interests. The battles waged between ethnic and racial groups only serve the forces outside that exploit us. We cannot fight employers who discriminate if we cannot work together. The divisions between Mexican and Central American must be settled here."[99] That unity and cooperation would be built on the "general principle of self-determination." No matter their past, all would participate in articulating the Mission District's future.

By invoking "self-determination," Martinez suggested the extent to which the nationalist politics of the late sixties also imbued the MCO. Of course, this version did not speak to what some Chicano radicals called the "national question."[100] Conveying the MCO's deep commitment to democracy and community agency, the use of "self-determination" collectively pitted the diverse residents of the Mission in a shared struggle with empire and its effects at the local level. As Martinez noted, "Put another way, we are a community that is seeking a way to shape the decisions affecting our lives. That is the essence of self-determination. It is the opposite of colonialism, which is a system in which someone else says he knows what is best for you and in which he has the power to make you do what he thinks is best for you. We want to decide what is best for us."[101] Hardly a "radical" compared to leaders of, say, the Black Panther Party, Martinez matured politically, and so did his understanding of the Mission. The injustices its residents faced were more than a product of neglect; they were systemic and intentional. The United States had "convinced most of the brown, black and yellow minority people of this country that they are not qualified to participate fully in the benefits of our society," he said. "But now the victim is growing restless."[102]

In practice, self-determination proved more difficult than imagined when practiced through the federal funds of Model Cities. In the ensuing years, the MCO struggled under the bureaucratic weight of its new responsibilities. It maintained control over the Model Cities corporation but engaged in fewer mass actions as a coalition. Most of its attention focused on the distribution of federal funds. As Leandro Soto put it, "the Mission Coalition Organization [lost] opportunities to develop a broad-based CDC [Community Development Corporation] because of community politics— a fight for power which did not exist, and the cooptation of activists by City Hall by putting them on the Model Cities payroll."[103] Control over Model Cities and its federal dollars meant a necessary shift from mass movement to bureaucratic organization, leading some to conclude they had become victims of their own success. As Mike Miller put it, "Even the best people in the Establishment are trapped by its limitations."[104] In this way, the MCO exhibited a familiar pattern within movement circles, as marginal success necessitated a transition "from protest to politics," in the words of Bayard Rustin. As others have noted, these are the encumbrances that come with concessions of power and are "part and parcel of measures to reintegrate the movement into normal political channels and to absorb its leaders into stable institutional roles."[105] Similarly, although the MCO made significant material improvements to the community, and helped foster a collective identity for Mission Latinos, success and institutional obligations distanced some leaders from the neighborhood, in stark contrast to an assortment of grassroots organizations continuing their work in the Mission. Often derided as "poverty pimps," bureaucratic agents were less popular than community organizers.

BY ACHIEVING ITS GOAL of authentically representing the Mission District, and assuming its bureaucratic role within Model Cities, the Mission Coalition Organization initiated its own decline. As a movement organization, however, it was anything but a failure. At its height, the MCO successfully involved more than 12,000 Mission District residents in bettering their community and planning its future. Transforming a fractious community divided by class, generational, and ethnic conflicts, the MCO helped create an environment where all its members could begin to understand their common interests as well as realize the power of their common efforts. This was especially true for the District's emerging Latino majority. The MCO provided a grassroots structure that incorporated the struggles, needs, and hopes of the Spanish-speaking. As it did, the MCO orchestrated their emergence as a visible constituency in the city. No longer thought of as merely a *population,* Latinos became the *community* most associated with the postwar Mission. Buttressed by their demographic predominance, their recognition as a collective entity emerged simultaneously with their organizational work nurturing a community identity.

The sense of cultural citizenship mobilized their movement and animated their expressions of Latino community. This diverse population coalesced within the MCO, not only as a product a common past but also in their articulation of a united future. This is notable, for in an era when Mexican Americans throughout the Southwest came together in multiple forms of political action, usually under the nationalistic rubric of *chicanismo,* the MCO exemplified a predominantly Latin American–descent population uniting under the umbrella of multiracial and multiethnic coalition. Such efforts relied on their ability to express shared identities based on class, race, generation, and national origin, but they also required the recognition of difference. In the case of the MCO, this found organized expression in a hybrid form of *latinidad,* most often under the term *la raza,* a collective identity encompassing difference while suggesting similitude.

While it suffered as a bureaucracy, the MCO achieved lasting victories as a coalition movement. For the first time in the modern history of San Francisco, the interests and needs of the plurality of Latinos in the city found purchase within the municipal power structure. In many ways, they voiced the same interests and needs for tens of thousands more in the city. As Soto put it, "The residents of the Mission District are not any different from the residents living in any other part of San Francisco, or any American town or city. They have aspirations for a better life. They seek self-determination, or more than they now have. They want good schools for their children. They want their families to be able to enjoy a good life. They want good and fair police protection. They want clean streets, good homes at reasonable prices, parks, recreation, jobs, safe streets, good health services, attention from city hall, etc."[106] As locals built a community movement, they also asserted this collective humanity. In so doing, Mission District politics were forever changed.

The political culture of self-determination and collaboration remains today, as does the human dignity that comes with a meaningful, grassroots movement. In the end, as the lead organizer described it, their greatest success may have been achieving "the dignity." Mike Miller recalled one such instance: "When we came out of the phone company meeting—we got an agreement for, I think on an annual basis it was in the hundreds of jobs—and the guy who was the chairman of that negotiating committee was Segundo Lopez. . . . So we're walking out of the front door, I turn and say, 'Segundo, wasn't that fantastic?' And I'm talking about the jobs. He looks at me and says, 'Yeah, Mike, you know that vice president called me Mister Lopez.'"[107] Segundo Lopez was not alone in his newfound sense of pride. In countless other situations, thousands of residents encountered the same transformations within themselves. As they looked toward their future within the city, with increased expectations of the role they could play in shaping their destinies, succeeding generations of Latino residents of San Francisco would also benefit from the work of the MCO.

## CHAPTER FIVE

# ¡Basta Ya!

## Raza *Youth in an Era of Radical Third World Possibility*

"I grew up with a lot of kids who were African American, and Italian, and Maltese, and Latino," recalled Steve Arcelona. The son of a Filipino father and a Puerto Rican mother, Arcelona grew up in the Bayview–Hunter's Point District, in a neighborhood whose diverse population lives largely in public housing or small houses and works at the naval shipyard. "For the most part we were not college-bound kids," he said. "We were going to finish school somehow, but we also knew that once we finished school we could basically go over the hill, apply for a job at the naval shipyard and get one." Despite this perceived track, after graduating from Mission High School, Arcelona followed a group of his friends to City College. After three years he earned an A.A. degree. "Somebody said, 'You know you could really keep going to school and get a B.A. degree.' And I said, 'Really? You can do that?' So that was sort of my counseling to go, [to] keep going into college."[1] He arrived at San Francisco State College in the fall of 1968, a few months before a coalition of students of color effectively shut the campus down in protest. "And I was sitting in one of the classes, with a full class, and the door opened and these fifteen guys walked in and surrounded the classroom and stood there," he remembered. "And I was scared shitless, you know, these were big guys and they were mean looking, and one guy turned to me and said, . . . 'What are you doing here, brother?' I did not have an answer." Those events began a process of identification for the young Arcelona. "And so the rest of my life was sort of understanding, getting a good understanding of what he meant when he said that."[2]

In this era of transformation, while some youth in the city began to ask new questions about themselves, their communities, and the world, others discovered new answers. On May 1, 1969, two well-known police officers in the Mission District confronted a small group of Latino youth who were moving a television set from a car to a house. Neither of the officers wore a uniform, and one carried a gun. Both sides would later dispute the subsequent chain of events while agreeing on this: in the ensuing struggle one of the officers was shot dead. After an extended manhunt for the youth, authorities apprehended six—Tony Martinez, Gary Lescallett, José Rios, Danilo Melendez, Mario Martinez, and Nelson Rodriguez— and charged them with the murder of Officer Joseph Brodnick. They also charged a seventh local, Gio Lopez, though he fled to El Salvador and was not apprehended.[3] Almost instantaneously, politically active youth in the Mission District started an organization to mobilize for "Los Siete"—the seven "brothers" they viewed as "political prisoners." In their effort they articulated a racial and ethnic self-identification steeped in a radical vision of political engagement. "Our strategy," they said, "is . . . not only relating to the needs of the seven brothers but also relating to the needs of the people, in the courts and in the community." They framed their purpose as protection from "the kind of oppression that is being exercised by people being kept poor, brutalized by the police, inadequate medical treatment, and [without] decent jobs and places to live in."[4] Increasingly, their analysis inspired connections beyond the Mission District. In an issue of their movement paper, ¡Basta Ya!, they linked their efforts in the Mission to liberation struggles in Central and South America, as well as Vietnam. "We say that we fight at all levels and in different parts of the world against the same man: the racist capitalist pig who creates oppression and exploits the people, the same man who creates political prisoners."[5]

In the late 1960s and early 1970s San Francisco was home to a host of political movements, including an assortment of efforts led by and for youth and predicated on the desire to create a more just and racially egalitarian world. While these movements marked the urban landscape throughout the United States, the role played by the San Francisco Bay Area is difficult to overestimate. Home to the Black Panthers, the birthplace of high-profile campus radicalism, and the cultural epicenter of the counterculture, the cultural geography of the bay occupies an enduring place in the history of the period. Latinos were a part of this political maturation as well. When members of a broad-based coalition in the Mission District asserted collective ownership over their community, they fostered a cross-ethnic and transnational identity of *latinidad* for themselves and their neighborhood. Latina and Latino youth also participated in the urban-based movement of the United Farm Workers, getting markets from the San Francisco Bay to Europe to boycott table grapes. By the late 1960s, the local and regional ascendancy of more radical political movements provided new avenues for participation in an already vibrant field, further nurturing a generational exploration of the meaning of being Latino in the United States.

Raised in the multiracial spaces of San Francisco's ghettos and barrios, and coming of age in a moment of profound radical potential and cross-fertilization of ideas, Latina and Latino youth searched out new models within which to change their lives and the lives of those around them. Often, their politics reflected what we might call a "Third World sensibility." This gave shape to a host of ideological movements by articulating "an identity and a set of politics that were rooted *within* a particular community, yet simultaneously *opened outwards* to embrace the struggles of others."[6] Third Worldism linked the struggles of blacks, Chicanos and Latinos, Asian Americans, and other nonwhites in the United States to the anticolonial movements of the Third World by "seeing American racism and European colonialism as two sides of the same coin."[7] Armed with a Marxist critique, it animated a multiracial community of activists identified as the "Third World Left."[8] On the ground, however, it also crafted both real and imagined linkages *among* domestic radical (and often nationalist) movements. The myriad forces of U.S. neoimperialism—structures of economic hegemony propelling human as well as resource migration—shaped this possibility by laying the foundation of postwar, multiracial San Francisco. The rise of these movements should be understood, then, as an unintended consequence to the local manifestations of empire—the dislocation and resettlement of the migrant, the systematic harnessing of nonwhite labor, and the residential segregation of the barrio and ghetto. Third Worldism grew from the innumerable daily, multiracial interactions of everyday people in the city. And for the youth who came of age at midcentury, it emerged from the social relations unfolding inside the city's schools and neighborhoods.

Located in radical political culture of the late 1960s and early 1970s, this chapter explores the formation of a multiracial and transnational perspective among segments of Bay Area youth. This perspective informed the movements these youth sought to inspire, in particular ones collapsing the space between the campus and community. As other scholars have cautioned, only a minority of youth of color became activists in this period.[9] Their impact, however, could extend beyond their limited share of the population. In San Francisco, Latina and Latino youth used these movements to improvise an identity critical of traditional power structures expressed as their own version of *latinidad*. In struggles such as the 1968 San Francisco State strike and the Mission District–based para Defender los Siete, they connected themselves to a long tradition of radicalism and internationalism as they fostered new communities of resistance in the city. At decade's end, as they helped transform local institutions of higher education and mobilize the creation of community service centers for their barrio, they also communicated a San Francisco *latinidad* with political meanings beyond the Mission.

## Spatial Segregation and Multiracial Possibility

The emergence of Third Worldism in late-sixties San Francisco is inseparable from the growth of the city's nonwhite population. A product of the multiple migrations both during and after the Second World War, by mid-century, poor and working-class spaces in San Francisco distinguished themselves by their multiracial populations. Called "the second Gold Rush" for the infusion of both financial and human capital propelling these changes, the war brought African American, Latino, and Filipino workers to the city for their labor, though many stayed to reshape the working-class neighborhoods. Demographics hint at the scope of these changes. Between 1940 and 1950 San Francisco saw a 22 percent growth rate in its residential population, an increase of more than 140,000.[10] While "whites" represented the largest share of newcomers, African Americans in the city rose from 0.8 to 5.6 percent of the total population. More generally, the nonwhite population of San Francisco grew by more than 156 percent.[11] In the postwar years, this translated into diverse public housing developments and apartment buildings, as well as multicultural working-class neighborhoods like the Mission, Fillmore, and Bayview Districts.

The frenzied growth of San Francisco during the war years strained more than just its resources and housing stock. Tensions also rose as the Bay Area responded to the new nonwhite population in repressive, if not violent, ways. As Luis Alvarez contends in his study of Los Angeles and New York in these years, "forces borne of the wartime political economy" defined nonwhites' experience "by the denial of their dignity."[12] In April 1943, servicemen in Oakland attacked Chicanos and African Americans in various neighborhoods.[13] Similar abuse could also come at the hands of law enforcers themselves. Sam Rios looked back at the war years as a time of crisis for Latino males, when local police harassed the Mexican American community under the guise of stamping out crime. "During the war . . . the police started to crack down on people they thought were *pachucos*, people who were members of gangs. . . . If any three Mexicans were standing on a corner, a police car would pull over, mess you up. If you wore a ducktail at the time . . . just by your dress they would pick you out."[14] African Americans faced even more frequent abuse and discrimination. In all cases, the local establishment showed itself unwilling to address the growing problem. Carlton Goodlett—a major figure in the history of civil rights in the city and the longtime chair of the local chapter of the NAACP—testified before the Mayor's Commission about the widespread evidence of "police brutality." "We have tried to institute a police course in group relations and like problems," he said, but "the present Chief believes a problem does not exist."[15]

The heightened attention to Mexican American criminality promoted anger and fatalism in the barrios of San Francisco. Rios remembered, "there were maybe twenty, twenty-two guys who were considered *vatos locos*—the strong, *pachuco* type." From an outsider's perspective, "there was no doubt about what they were up to."[16] These young men affiliated with gangs based on where they lived. Rios recalled a gang from the South of Market barrio fighting with another from the Mission District when they accidentally met each other on a city bus. Leaving little doubt as to their understanding of their own social marginalization, the aggressiveness of local *pachucos* sometimes focused itself on more external foes. Theaters, restaurants, and a host of other private and public spaces operated with sometimes explicit, sometimes tacit policies of segregation during the war. Latino and other youth of color recognized certain places to be "off limits" due to racial exclusion. *Pachucos* attacked these policies with the same disregard they held for most rules and customs. "The one thing that they did, collectively they would go into theaters that were segregated. And so the usher would tell them, "You can't sit here, you have to sit over there." How you gonna tell these guys they can't sit wherever the hell they want to? . . . If the usher didn't get out of their way, they'd just knock him down, you know, go wherever they wanted to. They did the same thing in restaurants. They'd go in . . . and they would tell them, 'We don't serve your kind here.' And they'd say, 'Either you serve us or we'll tear up the place.' . . . And they would do it."[17] Their disruptive behavior should not be seen as "detours on the road to political consciousness" but rather, as others have argued, an "essential element" of it.[18] Though bounded by the limits of the period, *pachucos* were adapting and responding to San Francisco's racial norms.

Despite its self-conception as a racially tolerant city, in the course of San Francisco's history intolerance has proven less the exception than the rule. Throughout the 1940s, however, a discourse of "racial liberalism" overtook municipal politics, as it did in most major urban centers. Proponents argued "that American democracy was incomplete so long as Jim Crow laws separated the races in the South and a combination of legal restrictions and common practice kept black people from jobs and neighborhoods in the North."[19] This animated a wartime antifascist debate and, later, a postwar anticommunist one, with racial discrimination becoming linked to a weakening of the U.S. position abroad. In San Francisco, the debate also included more lofty purposes. As one local advocate put it, "It seems to me to be self-evident that if we sincerely believe that discrimination is morally wrong (and I have heard no disagreement on this score) then we have not only the moral right but also the moral obligation, to legislate against it."[20] Operating through groups like the San Francisco Mayor's Committee on Human Relations, the project of racial liberalism harnessed broad municipal participation in a very public, and city-sanctioned, crusade against discrimination.

Perhaps the most significant consequence of these civic efforts was a general lack of tolerance for racism expressed as prejudicial viewpoints. Elected officials and municipal bureaucrats had ample room to vilify and pathologize what they considered to be "racist" views. For example, when the Board of Education conducted a districtwide survey of parents in 1949, a handful of respondents expressed dissatisfaction with "too many colored children" in the schools or the *lack* of legal segregation based on race. When considering these viewpoints in their final report, education officials wrote, "It can only be said that those with such a point of view should not send their children to public schools."[21] The progressivism of such a culture challenged far fewer instances of racial inequality than it sustained. When racism is viewed as individual prejudice—or more often, as a dysfunction afflicting individuals—it frames an inability to understand racial issues in more systemic ways. When the city confronted the escalating rates of African American unemployment after the war, a commission defended the general unwillingness of local employers to hire blacks when it proved unable to locate any specific policies of hiring discrimination. This led one official to conclude it was "not racial discrimination but overall lack of work opportunities which causes overall employment."[22] Similarly, in September 1956, when an African American family discovered a burning cross in their front yard, law enforcement hesitated to label the act as racially motivated without an investigation.[23] Police later reported they "could find no resentment against the family and no strong proponents of racial segregation" in the immediate neighborhood, leading them to believe that the cross-burning was a "juvenile prank."[24] When seven boys later admitted their guilt, authorities quickly proclaimed, "We're satisfied there was no racial animosity involved."[25]

If the postwar years contained a multiracial possibility, this resulted in no small part from the shared material reality of nonwhite San Franciscans, the foundation upon which Third Worldism was built. The commonality of encountering racial and class inequalities framed the context in which a more conscious politicization could occur. In the city, the residential integration of Latinos in multiethnic working-class neighborhoods accelerated the process. When Elba Sanchez immigrated to San Francisco from Mexico in 1960, for example, the eleven-year-old and her family moved to the largely African American Fillmore District. Sanchez remembered, "We were actually one of maybe four Latino families living in that block, everybody else was African American, and there was a Chinese family also that lived on the same street that we did." When she began attending public school as a monolingual Spanish speaker, she seemingly had little in common with her classmates. To them, she was white. "I remember kids would come up to me and would look angry and they would say things to me and, of course, I wouldn't understand what they were saying. For a long time they kept calling me 'Patty, Patty,' and I kept thinking, 'Why are they calling me Patty? That's not my name!' Well it took me a while to realize they were calling me 'White Patty, White Patty.' And I was like, 'Psht! I'm not white! What is wrong with you all? Can't you see I'm not white! And my name is not Patty!' "[26] Adjusting to life in a new country while also acculturating to a nonwhite neighborhood "in the midst of the civil rights struggles," she learned lessons in multiracial possibility. She remembered "seeing cops with hoses, and hosing people down, and dogs going after them, and just being horrified, and . . . identifying with what they were going through. And realizing and that this wasn't just their struggle, that they could easily turn around and come against us at any time."[27]

Manuel Vasquez spent part of his childhood in the Valencia Gardens housing projects, in the heart of the Mission District. There he encountered diversity he had not known before, and it touched his life in important ways. As he recalled, "that was the first time I remember having a number of cross-cultural relationships." While his mother worked at a local bakery, Filipinas and Native American women acted as his caregivers. Providing a moment of nurturing consistency in a young life marked by multiple movements in and out of youth systems, the diversity of the projects intimately connected Vasquez to a cultural world beyond his own. "It was a nice way of being introduced to different foods and different customs, but what I did find was a lot of good care."[28]

When Esperanza Echavarri's family migrated from the San Joaquin Valley to the city, she maintained her ethnic Mexican identity through social interactions among her extended family and their *compadres*, not through life in an external barrio. "It wasn't like I was in a Chicano community or a Latino community," she said. "So those formative years, the way we stayed connected to our culture was through this family and going to these parties and these groupings."[29] Her school environments reflected the racial and ethnic diversity at the base of her cultural formation, a social context she would later label as "very Third World." "It was very diverse in three cultures: Asian; white, Jewish white; and African Americans. And that was it. And very, very few Filipinos, very, very few anything else. And Latinos, very, very little."[30] With a best friend who was Filipina and classmates from nearly every other race and ethnicity, Echavarri came of age in an uneven multiracial context, shaping how she would later relate to others as an adult. "And I didn't see people any differently, because you know that's how I grew up." Remembering the same images of dogs, hoses, and other violence that greeted civil rights advocates in the South, she also described them as fundamental to her political identity. "I just knew there was something wrong with that. Even as a kid you're building this consciousness without realizing that's what it is, but that's what it was during that time."[31]

The structural context of postwar San Francisco nurtured multiracial and multiethnic possibility in both the public and private realms, as witnessed through multiracial unions. As a nexus of U.S. imperialism, San Francisco united many transnational lives within its urban spaces. When Quentin Ele came to San Francisco in the first half of the century, the Philippine-born Chinese-ethnic used the shipping lines of the U.S. military to escape the poverty and violence of his hometown of Tondo, Manila. Earlier, Maria Pacheco's family arrived in the city most directly from Hawai'i, after having migrated along well-established labor networks from their home in Puerto Rico. They settled in the North Beach barrio, with "other Puerto Ricans and Central Americans," and there Maria was born. Quentin and Maria met in a San Francisco dancehall and later married. Their biracial and bicultural children grew up in the Catholic Church—with all of their major sacraments received at Guadalupe Church—and attended schools in both Chinatown and the Mission. Their daughter, Debra, remembered many "mixed kids like me" in her multiracial social world.[32] Other mixed-race couples moved to San Francisco after meeting. Steve Arcelona's father migrated from the Philippines to Seattle in the early century, performing jobs ranging from fieldwork to fishing. His mother migrated from Puerto Rico to New York, where mutual friends connected the two. After a courtship through

A diverse group of Mission youth gather to support local parks. From Stan Creighton, "Park of the Future," 1969. Bancroft Library, University of California, Berkeley.

correspondence, they met face-to-face, married, and settled in San Francisco, where they raised their biracial son.[33]

These intersections suggest the meaning of diversity in the Mission, where the emergent cultural and demographic predominance of Latinos coexisted with other nonwhites in a generally diverse neighborhood. The poet Juan Felipe Herrera, who spent his youth in the district, remembers the neighborhood as a dynamic environment where the "streets were spitting up pure fantasy and magic." Recalling the sights and sounds of a neighborhood where "people are quick-stepping, soul stomping and huffing to exist," he continues:

> Picture a Diego Rivera mural populated with Siquieros children in Gaugin apartment buildings where the clotheslines are hung by Frida Kahlo—purple corduroys, saris, Sonora ranch hats, black shawls, pedalpushers, sawed off levis [*sic*] pants, catholic [*sic*] pleated dresses, khaki trench coats, flowered muslin tank tops, laundry pressed polyester slacks, maroon turbans, Club jackets, Latino/as, Filipinos, Afro-Americans, Cubans, Asians, Irish, Indians, Vietnamese and Whites. You can hear Hindi, Samoan, Black English, Tongan, Chicano/a and Salvadoreño talk, all in a bebop stream of sounds. The local Spanish is elastic, at once polished, bilingual and re-invented with adolescent first generation speech play and Nicaragüense, Salvadoreño, Guatemalteco, Hondureño, Peruano, Brasileiro and Chicano/a rap styles.[34]

Indeed, in Herrera's imagining, the polyethnic character of the district helped nurture its politicization, "a ground where the boundaries between cultures, languages and power create a radical tension, a hot stream of resistance, re-thinking and re-invention."[35]

While significant for building a sense of commonality, the existence of multiracial spaces did not necessarily create multiracial unity. All San Franciscans lived in a context of "differential racialization"—where distinct processes and experiences attached sets of racial meanings to different racial and ethnic groups in a variety of ways.[36] These meanings fundamentally shape all people's lived experiences as, reciprocally, their material experiences substantiate and inform the process of assigning social meanings. People of color often differed in the ways they encountered the city, in the structures that brought them here and distributed them into distinct work and living spaces, as well as in the institutions that gave shape to their daily lives. One longtime African American resident remembered his experience with the unpredictability and multiplicity of racism in San Francisco when he was thrown out of a local bar while his Mexican American friend was served. "Now I done been in there before," he said. "But this time, I'm coming in *after him*. I sit down and order a beer and they start talkin' about they 'don't serve black in here.' "[37]

Similarly, only immigrant San Franciscans needed to fear surveillance and apprehension by the Immigration and Naturalization Service (INS). Other communities of color could even benefit when Latin Americans were targeted for deportation. In 1954, when the INS deported thousands of Mexican nationals from Northern California, many were rounded up in the industrial hub of San Francisco. News accounts reported more than 3,000 jobs opening throughout the region as a result of the raids.[38] And, of course, differences could exist along the familiar lines of ethnic rivalries as well. As one Mission District community worker phrased it: "I'm born Puerto Rican; you're Mexican, and you're *nicaragüense*, and you're Salvadorean, and, you know, 'We're all the same!' Well, no we're not."[39]

## Politicizing Latina and Latino Youth

The 1960s gave youth of color many outlets for expressing their experiences with racial inequality. Some of these political opportunities also crossed the traditional boundaries between and within populations while fostering new alliances. For Latina and Latino youth, this entailed the simultaneous process of connecting with a larger activist community and carving out their own political space apart from the proliferation of movements involving an older generation. The emergence of the United Farm Workers (UFW) movement in 1965 provided both. Cesar Chavez and the UFW maintained a deep connection to the city of San Francisco, because of both its long history as a "union town" and its general support for the grape boycott. Much of that support had originated with Father Donald McDonnell, a priest in the Archdiocese of San Francisco, which at the time measured more than 14,000 square miles and included tens of thousands of migrant farmworkers. McDonnell and a small group of other similarly dedicated priests began strategizing as early as 1949 how they might better serve the needs of Latino parishioners outside of the major cities.[40] The following year they created the Spanish Mission Band to minister "directly to the poor, migrant workers." Dividing among themselves responsibility for the counties of the archdiocese, the priests of the Mission Band had no formal parochial duties but rather served the spiritual needs of the Spanish-speaking poor as they fostered the development of local leaders, provided spaces for cultural expression, offered housing and employment assistance, and created such needed institutions as a credit union.[41] In the 1950s, in his capacity as a Mission Band priest assigned to the San Jose barrio of Sal Si Puedes, McDonnell first met Cesar Chavez. Chavez later said, "My education started when I met Father Donald McDonnell."[42] McDonnell's involvement undoubtedly played a role in the San Francisco Archdiocese's proclamation of support for the UFW in early 1966. Drawing the ire of the Council of California Growers, the church hierarchy declared "that principles of social justice be applied in labor-management relations" while also expressing support for the union's attempt to become the workers' sole bargaining agent. The archdiocese even used its status as a major purchaser of altar wine to pressure Napa producers.[43]

For many young Latinas and Latinos in the city, the UFW made a significant contribution to the formation of their political consciousness and, eventually, to their training. "I was very conscious I was different in terms of being a minority, that I was not part of the kind of dominant culture," Esperanza Echavarri remembered. She understood discrimination but "wasn't political about it." That seemed to change with Cesar Chavez. "He'd be on the news, we really gravitated 'cause he was a *mexicano*, he was from the farm workers . . . and this is my history."[44] Once she finished high school, Echavarri took a job working for the UFW in the city, which gave her an education in grassroots organizing: "We canvassed every street, knocked on every door, picketed every Safeway store, did the trips to Delano to bring the food." These experiences and the skills they developed proved useful when she arrived at San Francisco State, just months before the start of a multiracial student movement called the "Third World Strike." Her work in the UFW also connected her to a larger community of local Latino political activities, mostly based in of the Mission District. "I was unaware that . . . there [were] all these organizations," she said, "but being part of the farm workers was what connected me to that."[45]

As a Spanish-speaking immigrant, Elba Sanchez remained conscious of her identity and culture as distinct from the environment in which she found herself, yet encountering the UFW was a major political turning point in her life. She credited a nun who taught her during her sophomore year with introducing her to the farmworker struggle. She recalled, "My sophomore year was like *whoosh*! The light bulbs went on and I started realizing, 'Holy shit this is . . . we're in the middle of a major crisis here, and I need to know what's going on.'" After attending a presentation by a UFW farmworker, Sanchez began to view the workers' struggle as her own. "I remember being in this high school uniform when I heard all of that and realizing that these were my people . . . this is my struggle too, and feeling very emotional with that kind of consciousness." Sanchez felt so moved that she began participating in the UFW-sponsored marches and pickets in the city, even "sneaking out to do those things because I knew that my parents were so against Chicanos at that time."[46]

African American political struggles in the Bay Area also significantly influenced not only Latino youth movements but also the wider current of Third World politics of which they were a part. The emergence of "Black Power" as an organizing thematic held sway over segments of the youth population in the Mission. No single organization was more important to the Black Power struggle—in the Bay Area and nationwide—than the Black Panther Party for Self-Defense. Founded by Bobby Seale and Huey Newton, the Black Panther Party emerged in a confluence of black migration, campus activism, and poverty politics in Oakland, California.[47] Dismissing nonviolence as an organizational philosophy and drawing "from the tradition of black anticolonialism," the Panthers pointed to a historical legacy of injustice and outright terror as proof of existence of the "Black colony" in the United States.[48] Building on the Community Alert Patrols founded by African Americans in Los Angeles after the 1965 "Watts Riots," the Panthers instituted armed patrols of their Oakland community in order to "curb police mistreatment of blacks."[49] This radical posture in inner city relations spoke volumes about the Panthers' evolving ideology. Concepts like self-defense, self-determination, and community power suddenly became more real with visible embodiments of what those theories could look like in practice.

The Panthers sought to be the vanguard for the black community. As Seale explained, "We tried to establish an organization that would articulate the basic desires and needs of the people and in turn try to organize black people into having some kind of power position. . . . Our politics comes from our hungry stomachs and our crushed heads and the vicious service revolver at a cop's side which is used to tear our flesh, and from the knowledge that black people are drafters to fight in wars, killing other colored people who've never done a damn thing to us."[50] Those material sources of politicization manifested themselves in the Panthers' ten-point platform and program, which spoke to a comprehensive vision "ranging from such mundane but fundamental matters as employment and education to broad issues of freedom and self-determination."[51] Both the content of that vision and its form would inspire a host of Latino groups across the country.

Nationally, Black Power attracted black urban youth with the same frequency it alienated white liberals. In San Francisco, however, it garnered greater mainstream support. For example, local "unrest" led a group of religious leaders to conclude that because the racial crisis was at a "dangerous, deep and all-pervasive" level, black militancy represented a "legitimate, democratic means for black people to obtain their rights."[52] This represented a stark contrast to Martin Luther King Jr., who during a visit to the city in 1967 called Black Power "impractical, ineffective, and immoral" while acknowledging the context of its growth. "The young militants are in the revolutionary spirit. They are concerned about revolutionizing certain values that have been existing in our society that need to be revolutionized.

And I think the other thing that we must see is, as President Kennedy said, 'Those who make peaceful revolution impossible only make violent revolution inevitable.' "[53] King remained a powerful voice in the struggle, yet to a growing number of observers the events of the mid- to late sixties suggested that a "violent revolution" had begun. Between 1964 and 1967, Harlem, Rochester, Philadelphia, Chicago, Watts, and hundreds of cities throughout the nation experienced urban unrest related to race. Often beginning with an instance of police abuse and ending with riots lasting days, the cycle of very visible episodes of racial violence seemed to be building to a threatening new level by the end of the decade, with 163 uprisings occurring in 1967 alone.[54]

On September 27, 1966, San Francisco joined the crisis when an urban disturbance overtook the Bayview–Hunter's Point District and the Mission. The disturbance began when Alvin Johnson—a white police officer in the Potrero Police District—shot and killed an African American teenager named Matthew Johnson.[55] The death of the sixteen-year-old occurred in his home district of Hunter's Point, a primarily African American neighborhood and home to some of the city's poorest residents. According to the police themselves, "word of the incident spread rapidly" and touched off five days of rioting, "which was to be a toilsome experience for the citizens of San Francisco, and one which taxed Law Enforcement Agencies to the utmost."[56] Indeed, with 253 recorded incidents of property damage totaling more than $135,000, and with 457 people arrested (most of them "Negro"), the Hunter's Point District, and the adjoining Bayview and Mission Districts, felt the effects of the rioting in an especially personal fashion.[57]

Viewed as a "Negro disturbance" by both the local media and city government, the unrest highlighted the frustrations of more than just the city's black community, encompassing a cross-section of multiracial districts. The initial confrontations between community members and police began at the scene of the shooting. Matthew Johnson had been shot dead at 2:30 in the afternoon, while running from a police officer after abandoning what law enforcement "suspected" to be a stolen vehicle. Although the evidence would later show that the car had indeed been stolen, local reports noted that the police officer had no way of knowing this since the theft was not reported until five hours after the shooting.[58] Even worse for police control of the matter, the shooting occurred just outside of the local Economic Opportunity Council office, which was patronized by local youth.[59] After a community meeting later that night, the exiting crowd engaged the numerous officers present and, according to police reports, began vandalizing stores "which were not Negro owned."[60] At 7:35 P.M., police made the first riot condition call.

It would not be the last one. The following day, during the noon lunch break at Mission High School, confrontations between youth resulted in riot conditions being called on all floors of the school. The police forced the school to close early and blocked off streets to control the flow of students exiting the building and going home. As the day before, many of these young people confronted the officers and caused damage at local stores.[61] The next day, Mission High closed its doors again when the principal determined that students were "restless." Even the Sears department store on Mission Street closed early, before nightfall, to "protect staff."[62] For the first time since World War II, the entire San Francisco police force was called into duty at once. They were later joined by the National Guard. By the time the unrest subsided on the fifth day, seven youth had been shot by authorities. Coming to terms with the anger and hopelessness in the shadow of the Golden Gate, officials seemed as fearful as confused. "This is like a cancer," said one local. "This is a potentially dangerous thing."[63]

The murder of Matthew Johnson represented a critical moment in the city's race relations. After the shooting and unrest, officers in the Community Relations Unit (CRU)—an office created in the early sixties to improve relations between the police and the community—redoubled their efforts. Just one year later, however, in a very public statement exposing the CRU's inability to create meaningful change within the department, the head of the unit resigned his position, criticizing the department as racist. The resignation further fueled local criticism of law enforcement.[64] Communities of color believed the local government was doing little to improve the police department, and mainstream progressives kept the issue alive. Two years after the riots, an ecumenical group calling itself the San Francisco Conference on Religion, Race, and Social Concerns authored a lengthy research piece that sought to identify and address the problems of the city's nonwhite poor. Focusing on the creation of what it called a "black-brown ghetto," the group labeled police-community relations as one of the most important problems standing in the way of justice. "The police officer is often the only public official whom the ghetto dweller sees daily. He has, therefore, become a symbol of minority hostility towards white society."[65] The conference called for churches and synagogues to lead the push for substantive reforms.

These events also contributed to a rising discontent in the city among some youth of color, grounded in a mistrust of the police and other institutions of power. For those residing in working-class neighborhoods, the San Francisco Police Department (SFPD) often embodied the city's racial inequality. Law enforcement constituted a site of daily interaction with an institution of authority acting in often abusive defense of the state. One Mission District resident who came of age in the period described the interactions between Latino youth and the police as dehumanizing. "It was like, man, you didn't have a chance. You're just nothing, nothing!"[66] As scholars have argued, in general, "police misconduct toward people of color is a cornerstone of the perpetuation of racism and White privilege."[67] If the state is a body designed to serve the interests of the citizenry, in a system infected with the priorities of white supremacy, police are at the frontlines of managing racial inequality. By enforcing the subjugation of people of color and employing "informal modes of terrorism and violence" the system of "law enforcers" is directed toward protecting the interests of a privileged class.[68] Thus, for more than a century, relations between many communities of color and the police have been marred by fear and violence. It is no coincidence, then, that by the late 1960s a host of race-based movements—like the Black Panthers—had made police brutality a fundamental issue in the struggle for racial justice. Accordingly, the persistence of abusive encounters between youth of color and the San Francisco Police Department framed another possibility for youth of color to think in multiracial ways. The reality of police misconduct in communities of color demonstrated lived commonalities between youth of color in municipalities around the nation.

Though no such intellectual developments emerged immediately after the unrest, the context later shaping their expression remained charged. The unrest following Johnson's murder is testament to the pent-up hostility in segments of the population. During the five days, violence spread outside the immediate neighborhood of the shooting, and included students at both Mission High School and Horace Mann Junior High School.[69] Most students at both schools belonged to racial "minorities." Throughout the decade, elements within the school district had sought to better educate youth of color and address issues of segregation and systemic undereducation. As with attempts to enhance the community-relations efforts of law enforcement, these efforts brought little substantive change, locked as they were in the seemingly race-neutral system of the "neighborhood school." The mounting effects of structural inequities in the district had nurtured tensions within student populations, often visible in interracial violence and animosity. As early as 1960, most students surveyed at Mission High School described the cause of social problems as rooted in the presence of one or more racial groups. Some chastised the "Spanish" students, who called themselves "Barts." One said they "act like big shots," while others warned they "gang up" and "drink, are flunkouts, [and] go robbing." Others described the main culprits as the "White Shoes," white students who look "ivy league and clean cut but get suspended for cutting." Still more students identified the troublemakers as being "Negroes" and "colored guys [who] act like kings," who "have to fight," and who "don't know how to act." Even in this context of rising tensions and animosities, manifesting itself as racial violence, a few students also began to express glimpses of a larger perspective. "Some people always look at the wrong side of things and we have suffered from bad publicity because of the actions of the Negro and Latin students," wrote one. "If there is a fight, the newspapers seem to make a big thing out of it; whereas the same and worse things happening in other schools or districts are covered up."[70]

Reflecting the inability of municipal officials to address issues of educational equity and police abuse, the unrest surrounding the murder of Johnson was followed by a greater level of policing of communities of color, part of a longer trend. An early report on Mission High had noted the fundamental connections between student behavior and academic success and relations within the larger educational institution. On issues of "Administrative Control and Discipline," the report concluded: "The atmosphere needs to be kept free of rules and regulations and policing bodies. An encouragement of responsibility and cooperative effort in which faculty and students are seen as working together may reduce the chances of rebellion and resistance. Here it should be kept in mind that the negative attitudes toward all law enforcement agencies in the neighborhood community will defeat any attempt to utilize faculty in such role. The 'friendly, helping policeman' is unknown to these students."[71] Facing complex challenges including gangs, drugs, violence, and truancy, Mission High implemented very different policies and practices over the course of the decade. By the late sixties, San Francisco police worked on school campuses in the form of their Community Relations Unit. Full-time security guards, hired and trained by the district, policed school grounds on a daily basis. And at least one counselor on each campus worked in liaison with the SFPD's Police Narcotics Bureau.[72] When interracial violence flared up at Mission High in the spring of 1968, sending four students to the hospital, the response was to increase police presence.[73]

In the wake of the Johnson shooting, the Mission station of the SFPD created the "Mission Eleven." Comprised of officers in "informal dress" and patrolling in unmarked cars, the group was celebrated by journalists as "the best burglary abatement team in the business." Although based in the

Mission District, the team promoted its efforts in the more affluent Twin Peaks neighborhood, just south. Regularly distributing leaflets to these residents "warning them of the times of greatest burglary threat to homes," the team represented a growing force in the multiracial Mission, where it made the bulk of its arrests. In addition to reducing home burglaries, the Mission Eleven arrested a "prominent Methodist minister" who "made homosexual advances" to two undercover cops while in a Mission steam-room.[74] Among Latino youth in the district, the unit had a bad reputation. They viewed the team members as racist former locals who "resented both the cultural and political changes taking place" in the Mission and repeat-edly abused residents. How the officers viewed their role is impossible to surmise with absolute clarity, but the rubber hose one carried while con-ducting his "duties" is, at the least, suggestive.[75]

Youth of color in the Mission District lived and learned in this amalga-mation of residential segregation, radical political organization, and in-creasing institutional violence. If this confluence of forces and structures offered the possibility of an organized multiracial movement, it might also bring greater interracial dysfunction. The catalyst for a more progressive direction came not only from groups like the Panthers, whose model of self-determination in the face of crisis would prove inspirational, but also from an assortment of local institutional advances in youth services, many promoting self-determination in other forms. Ironically, some of these ef-forts could be fully part of "the establishment," in particular those with roots as Community Action Programs funded by the local War on Poverty office. Agencies like the employment-focused Horizons Unlimited, for ex-ample, directly addressed the issue of poverty and inequitable resources for Mission youth by connecting them to training and jobs in the city. Other groups, like the Mission Rebels, were able to use poverty dollars to expand their effectiveness as well as cultivate a constituency base. Led by Reverend Jesse James, a local African American, and serving a multi-racial grouping of youth while adopting an increasingly radical rhetoric, the Rebels used their radical posture not only to attract youth of color but also to successfully employ various forms of symbolic confrontation (and threats of confrontation) in order to obtain funding.[76] Though differing in tactics, mission, and capacity, Horizons Unlimited and Mission Rebels of-fered youth alternatives to the pessimism and violence of life in the barrio. Along with an assortment of others, they provided a broad range of ser-vices and activity. As important, even within their funding contexts, they provided examples of local people working in organized effort on their own terms.

Many of these advances also emerged from the grassroots and did not envision federal support. The East Mission United Neighborhood Youth Organization (EMUNYO) arose first as an informal "club" of youth of color. Calling themselves the Lucky Alley Gang for the area where they congregated, the multiracial youth involved in the group had already demonstrated their own organizational models before some local agency representatives decided the group needed a meeting space. A man named Jim Queen volunteered to help. Queen had settled in the city after serving in the Marines and found himself working in both Mission youth programs funded by the EOC and the shipping industry at the port. As he told the story, "I hooked up with them, and it was a very interesting group of kids, to begin with—very alive, very dynamic, but a very multicultural group. It was Latinos, . . . blacks, . . . Filipinos, Asians, whites—I mean all of them. It was like a social thing. . . . They were actually doing it. They had actually formed a relationship where they all interacted with each other. It was a fantastic type of thing."[77] A local resident allowed them to use her garage as a club meeting space, on the condition they clean it out and paint it. With paint donated from a local vendor, the youth set up shop. Their initial success demonstrates not only the depth of support in the Mission for alternative forms of service but also the importance there of self-determination. In a community undergoing its own organizational development, led by a Mission Coalition Organization struggling for control of the redevelopment process,[78] youth-focused groups similarly promoted models of leadership rooted in the youth themselves. Stressing responsibility, self-determination, and integrity, the small club first became EMUNYO, with increased funding and support. It later evolved into the Real Alternatives Program (RAP).[79]

## San Francisco State

Harnessing these multiracial possibilities in intentional ways, the student strike at San Francisco State College (SFSC)—known as the Third World Student Strike—reshaped student politics in the city, at both the university and high school levels. A flurry of campus organizing served as the backdrop of the strike, which began in earnest in 1968.[80] A broad-based assortment of racially based student organizations had already taken root on campus. Each had begun formulating agendas that included harnessing the educational resources of the university to serve local community needs. In March 1968, when the campus announced the expiration of two part-time faculty members' contracts, a groundswell of student clubs and organizations describing themselves as "the Third World minority group of students on campus" rose to action. The terminated faculty had advised organizations that engaged in community-based tutoring programs for students of color and agitated for an increase in the "special admissions" rate for minority youth, from 2 percent to 4 percent. The students mobilized in defense of their mentors, one of whom was a Latino named Juan Martinez, as well as in support of the admission changes meant to increase the number of poor students of color.[81] Demonstrating the advanced organizational capacity of the students at San Francisco State, groups of African American, Asian American, and Latino students—in the form of the Mexican American Students Confederation (MASC) and Latin American Students Organization (LASO)—occupied the administration building, securing their demands and contributing to the resignation of the campus president.[82]

The following November, a similar dismissal led the multiracial coalition of students to shut down the college.[83] The initial call for a strike came from African American students organized into the Black Student Union (BSU). A politically active and long-standing organization, the BSU had led the way for other groups in its community-focused and student-run programs, funded by student campus fees, and in the larger struggle to create relevant curricula for San Francisco State students of color. The radicalism of the BSU's multifocused efforts was suggested by the attempt of the California State University's Board of Trustees, in the fall of 1968, to transfer control of student fees away from each campus's student body and to the system chancellor. This move would have gutted the fee-supported community programs. Additionally, the chancellor called for the removal of George Murray—an adjunct member of the English Department and a dedicated member of the BSU and Black Panther Party. On November 6, 1968, the BSU issued a list of ten demands, ranging from the rehiring of Murray and the expansion of "special admission" slots to the creation of a Black Studies Department and the admission, in the fall of 1969, of "all Black students wishing so."[84] After the BSU called for a general campus strike, other organizations representing students of color agreed to join them. Calling themselves the Third World Liberation Front (TWLF), the multiracial union linked African American, Latino, Asian American, and Native American students in common cause. The TWLF issued its own five demands, which included the creation of a College of Ethnic Studies and an expansion in the enrollment of students of color and the hiring of faculty members of color.[85]

Stressing the connection of oppressed peoples throughout the world and the need for communities of color to rely on one another for the success of their political efforts, the TWLF shattered the parochialism of nationalistic movements that only looked inward. The "Third World" identity suggested strong linkages between the historical experiences and present conditions of communities of color. Expansive rather than restrictive, it redefined what it meant to be a person of color in San Francisco, in relation to both the broader community of "third world peoples" and the individual's specific ethnic or racial group.[86] Most important, this vision of multiracial unity was forged in actual practice. As one participant framed it: "Unity and solidarity are more than fronts. They take daily, patient development of alliances. And that takes time."[87] Taking the time to build a genuine multiracial coalition, the shift toward Third World ideology represented a profound evolution in youth politics.

The TWLF relied on the presence of Mexican American and Latina/o student organizations as it fostered their political evolution as "third world activists." As participants in "a loose coalition whose member organizations... still enjoy complete autonomy to do as they saw fit," Latin American-descent students had the freedom to operate both within solidarity structures and independently.[88] For Latinos and Latinas in San Francisco, the TWLF helped create new political bonds out of their own deep multiracial histories. Political formations overcoming the deep-seated rivalries between Chicanos and Latin Americans stood out as the most profound of those bonds. The Latin American Students Organization had participated in the early formation of the multiracial union. Founded as a culturally focused group for native-born Latin American students at San Francisco State, LASO had originally eschewed political issues. By early 1968, the group leaned more toward "social awareness" by uniting with the Latin Tutorial Project, an effort focused on tutoring in the Mission District.[89] When LASO became involved in the TWLF, it helped form a united Latino bloc comprised of itself and groups like the Mexican American Students Confederation. Originally called "El Renacimiento" (the rebirth), MASC emerged under the guidance of a sociology lecturer named Juan Martinez. Dedicated to the idea of community involvement, MASC quickly involved itself in tutoring programs and other community efforts. As its name suggests, Mexican-descent students dominated its membership.[90] Traditionally, the disparate political programs of the two organizations reflected the deeper division between Mexicans and Latin Americans, or between the native-born and immigrants. Within the TWLF, however, MASC and LASO came together under the banner of "Third Worldism."

The San Francisco State strike embodied the leftist political sensibility already alive in segments of San Francisco youth culture. It pursued self-determination in the ways it sought to frame institutional priorities from within a needs assessment of poor and working-class communities of nonwhites, rather than through a state-sanctioned bureaucracy. The demands of both the BSU and the TWLF included changes to admissions priorities and practices, faculty hiring procedures, the processes creating and staffing academic departments and colleges, and procedures relating to curricula development—all domains of one or more segments of the leadership in the legislatively created higher education system. Such demands arose not from hubris but from a deliberate ideological strategy to reshape the locus of power in higher education, a strategy grounded in the organizations' history of creating campus-community partnerships. In part, the TWLF sought to alter not only the university system but also the political consciousness of communities of color. As it described in its "Third World Liberation Front Philosophy and Goals," the group's purpose was "to aid in further developing politically, economically, and culturally the revolutionary Third World consciousness of racist oppressed [*sic*] peoples both on and off campus. As Third World students, as Third World people, as so-called minorities, we are being exploited to the fullest extent in this racist white America, and we are therefore preparing ourselves and our people for a prolonged struggle for freedom from this yoke of oppression."[91] Understanding that their goals required a "prolonged struggle," the participants in the Third World Strike used education as the starting point for a movement they saw as connected to a wider world.

The TWLF and the San Francisco State strike further radicalized a largely optimistic and once reformist generation of community activists. A December 3 protest during the strike met violent repression by police. Known as "Bloody Tuesday," the response of campus authorities shocked many of the students.[92] One recalled it as a study in contrasts. "The horses were there on a sunny afternoon to jam down everybody that attended the rally. And we were literally running to get away from the police and the horses that were coming down on the kids, because they were rallying. And that just struck a chord in me. I said, 'For what?! What is this?' We have a right to protest and yet this kind of repression comes down on us for exercising that [right] about something that's just?" As for this student, powerful lessons could be drawn from confrontations with police violence. "And it instilled in me that anything you want in this country given who we are, we're going to have to fight for it. And we're going to have to put up against some of the structure that's here that won't allow it. I knew in my mind when that happened that that was my turning point."[93] The repression by campus authorities also seemed to inspire deeper support for the students by nonparticipants. Civil rights advocate Carlton Goodlett spearheaded an effort by race-rights organizations, labor, and others in solidarity with the "right of students and faculty to protest" on campus. Calling the strike "the beginning of a long struggle between the Reagan forces, the 'know-nothings' in higher education in California, and the people who believe that higher education has certain prerogatives and certain needs that must be met in a society of social change," this support widened the struggle as it legitimated the students' vision.[94]

Within the Mission District, youth involved in the strike sought the support of the wider Latino community through various means, including the Mission Coalition Organization. As a coalition, the MCO sought to satisfy as many of its member organizations as possible while remaining true to its commitment to democratic decision-making. In practice, this meant "that the groups participating [did] not expect the coalition to fully support their specific interests, particularly if their expression of those interests conflict[ed] with the ideas or interests of other members."[95] The controversy of the strike, coupled with the students' radical stances in their demands and the administration's repressive response, elicited a distinct concern from some in the Mission. The nature of the struggle was off-putting to an older generation as well as to an immigrant population that could be skeptical of students' behavior. When the strikers and their growing cadre of supporters asked the MCO for formal support, they did so by asking for support of their formal demands. In a "hotly debated Delegates Council meeting attended by about two hundred delegates, members, and students," the MCO adopted its own position, supporting the "legitimate interests" of the students while condemning violence.[96] Reflecting the growing chasm between a utopian youth politics and more established political organizations, some segments of the youth movement came to oppose the MCO, viewing its measured stance as a sign of its inherent reformism.[97]

The strike formally ended in March 1969, when a special committee appointed by the new president of the campus, S. I. Hayakawa, reached a settlement with the BSU and the TWLF. The administration's two most significant concessions were the creation of a College of Ethnic Studies and an expansion in the "special admissions" quota system.[98] Without guarantees of how such agreements would be instituted and supported over the coming years, the strike transformed into a more prolonged movement to remake the university by assuring compliance and maximizing the efforts in any new institutions. Dorinda Moreno participated in this subsequent period of the TWLF. Born in Northern California of Mexican and Apache ancestry, Moreno had been a political activist through most of her upbringing in San Francisco and early adulthood in Los Angeles. Returning to San Francisco in the late sixties, she became involved in the Mexican American Political Association (MAPA) and other community organizations in the Mission. Already a mother of two in her early thirties, Moreno was older than the average San Francisco State student activist. As a community organizer, she worked during the strike as part of the broad-based support system for the students. Eventually, she began working more closely with the Latino groups at San Francisco State and helped coordinate their first Educational Opportunity Program (EOP). That involvement would prove life-changing. One of the first students she recruited to attend San Francisco State College was herself.[99]

Her activity at San Francisco State demonstrates the nature of the Northern California movement of Latinas and Latinos in higher education. The conclusion of the strike in the spring of 1969 left this movement more focused and energetic. Working through the EOP, students sought to institutionalize a flow of "Third World" community members into the academy. Latino students took on the added responsibility of working with the faculty in creating the La Raza Studies Program, including developing a curriculum and staffing the classes. At every turn, they tried to institutionalize their philosophy of self-determination and community service. As Moreno put it, "The studies had to be relevant; they had to be community based."[100] To the student activists in La Raza studies, a community focus meant more than rhetoric in the classroom; it meant creating and sustaining links between the university and "real life." For example, in order to reach the community directly, students established a college office in the Mission District. With the goal of transforming their community's consciousness, the Latino and Latina students at San Francisco State also created a movement newspaper to be distributed in the community. Called *El Tecolote*, the paper began as a project in one of the classes in La Raza studies.[101] Physically expanding their movement space beyond the literal borders of the academy, endeavors like these helped bring the movement home.

Reflecting the student movement's aspiration to fundamentally redefine power and privilege, Moreno and others struggled to establish a feminist curriculum as part of La Raza studies. Their first step took place in the early seventies when Moreno helped create a "women's class"[102] in which Chicanas and Latinas could share their experiences as they encountered a revolutionary feminist discourse. Within the masculinist cultural dominance of nationalist movements (including the one in San Francisco), a false dichotomy had been established between racial oppression and gender oppression. Many male activists, threatened by the implications of feminism, argued that racism represented a more insidious foe than sexism and that gender struggles should come a distant second to racial ones.[103] In the eyes of many Latinas and Chicanas, young women whose experiences within movements had taught them the interrelatedness of different forms of oppression, no such conflict existed. The women's class united the two struggles into one, confronting the "sexist racism" in both male-dominated nationalist movements and the larger society.[104] As Moreno understood it, "Sexual equality is inherent in racial equality."[105]

Like other efforts within the city's ever expanding student movement, Chicana and Latina feminist projects also sought to transform the political consciousness of women and men while creating lasting bonds between the community and the college. In fact, in some ways the feminist impulse within the movement created the best examples of the movement's overall community focus. For example, by the early seventies Moreno, while teaching at San Francisco State as well as at junior colleges in Napa and Fremont,[106] began her graduate studies at Stanford. Using those platforms, she created an independent organization for Latina women called Concilio Mujeres. "The group Concilio de Mujeres came out of the woman's class, but it was more than the woman's class. It was the woman's class, together with the community women, together with a roving group of students from various different colleges where I taught." For members of the group, working collaboratively as well as on their particular local environments, "the focus was always to promote the women in their communities."[107] Though initially dependent on the campus, Concilio Mujeres operated in a much larger space. It began to publish its own newsletter featuring poetry and political explorations for a community of Latinas both inside and outside the university. Called *La Razón Feminista*, the newsletter embodied what scholar Maylei Blackwell calls "new sense of creative agency" in the "forms Chicanas invented to 'speak themselves' into poetic and political discourse."[108] A credit to the focus of the women's class, Concilio Mujeres was one of the tangible institutions the movement was able to create, forming a bond between the classroom and the community. In some ways, by institutionalizing itself outside of the academy, the group at least partially isolated itself from the ultimate collapse of radical student politics in the seventies. It thrived under Moreno's leadership until the 1980s.

Such feminist projects could not, however, isolate themselves from "disrespect and ignorance." They often became targets of forms of sexism cruder than the "ideological" debate of racism versus sexism. The women's class frequently came under attack by men. Moreno recounted one example when fellow students—both women and men—conducted staff interviews for the women's class. A man serving on the committee tried to throw off one candidate by asking her to "show her legs." While Moreno recalled that many men supported the cause because they "were very serious and curious as to what would go on" in the women's class, others joined it for less productive reasons. "Some of them would join the class just to heckle, or have a good time, or maybe try to sleep with all the ladies."[109]

Although the movement had its roots in the collaboration of Third World peoples toward a radical agenda, alignment with these causes sometimes resulted in friction. As with the myopic vision of males who felt threatened by the creation of feminist courses, some Latinos attacked organizers who continued to work for multiethnic unity, preferring instead to move in more nationalistic directions. To Third World activists this reflected the disparate levels of education and preparation. "You're ready to do it, other people aren't. They're still tripping over their shoe laces. They're not growing up to meet the demands [of the movement], and so they're not understanding some very basic principles like the women's movement, or aligning with Central America and blacks."[110] The progressive elements within the movement would constantly challenge these limitations, both in theory and ideology and in the slow work of building an educational and community movement.

The Third World Strike at San Francisco State created new progressive identities for youth of Latin American descent. The mass appeal of the movement often proved too much to resist. One former student, a high school teenager during the year of the strike, remembered that all her friends would rush to the college after school each day. "It was the place to just hang out and see what was going on."[111] As the Latina and Latino components of that larger movement institutionalized themselves within the college, the same occurred within the Mission. As one would expect, high school radicalism often had direct ties to the SFSC groups. Many members of the TWLF sought to organize high school students of color and empower them to make changes in their own institutions. Indirectly, the popularity of the movement at SFSC planted the seeds of radical activism in the hearts and minds of many youth. Both forces played roles in the events at Mission High School. Beginning in late January 1969, just over two months into the strike at San Francisco State, students at Mission High launched a ministrike that further involved the Latino community in an identity-building movement.[112] Though the strike at Mission High was brief, its importance lay in the way it demonstrated a student body transformed by identity politics. In the demands they sought, the tactics they chose, and the ideologies they expressed, the students at Mission joined the ever-expanding Latina/o movements of the era.

Mission High provided ideal conditions for this kind of movement to take root. By the late sixties Mission High reflected the kind of diversity that marked the district as a whole. Latinos made up roughly 40 percent of the school's more than 2,000 students. Whites were about 33 percent and blacks about 20 percent, while Chinese, Samoans, Filipinos, and others made up the remaining population.[113] That kind of diversity often caught school systems by surprise. Almost 40 percent of the students at Mission were classified as bilingual, yet few successful programs existed to deal with students who were learning English as a second language. Facing the kinds of challenges present at most inner city schools, Mission High failed to meet the needs of a diverse and undereducated population. Its annual dropout rate was 33 percent, while an average of 400 to 600 students were absent daily.[114]

The influence of the San Francisco State strike proved enough to temporarily refocus the larger pattern of interracial violence at the school. A two-day period of tension between Latino and black students that began on January 22 precipitated the outbreak of what local radicals called the "Mission Rebellion." Police came on campus to break up a fight and make arrests. Rather than continue quarreling among each other, the students united under the banner of their own Black Student Union and began protesting the presence of law enforcement. The following Monday—the week of January 27—the BSU called a student strike, no doubt taking their lead from students at SFSC. Latino students passed out fliers with the following message: "We got ourselves together last week fighting the blacks. Now it's time to fight the real enemy."[115] As the movement at the high school progressed, students devised their own list of demands, including the expulsion of police and end to hall monitoring, the creation of ethnic studies courses, the abolition of laminated ID cards, improvements in the cafeteria, an end to IQ tests, and the hiring of more "Third World" teachers and staff.[116]

## Los Siete de la Raza

The violent response of law enforcement to the strike at San Francisco State College, as well as the sustained culture of police aggression at Mission High and in the community at large, further solidified the belief among some local youth that the police department represented a "colonial force" in their neighborhood.[117] When Los Siete de la Raza were implicated in the shooting death of Officer Joseph Brodnick, one of the Latino youth who rose to their defense described how daily encounters with law enforcement prompted this view of the police. "The last time we were arrested the black and Latino pigs came out while the white pig stayed in the car. . . . So the pigs come out and bully people, in fact when they arrest you in the Mission the first thing they do is kick your ass, then ask you questions. If you try to assert your rights, they'll tell you to keep your mouth shut or they'll break it."[118] The adversarial tensions between youth and the police dripped from the increasingly common terms they used to describe law enforcers—*pigs, pig-punks,* and *maranos.*

For many in the Mission, the events of May 1, 1969, brought these issues of violence to a fever pitch. On the very same morning that protesters gathered around the Federal Building in downtown to demand the release of Black Panther Huey Newton from jail, two plainclothes police officers— the best-known members of the "Mission Eleven"—approached a group of Latino young adults at 433 Alvarado Street in the Mission District and tried to arrest them on suspicion of burglary. In the ensuing altercation, one of the officers was beaten, another was shot to death, and a group of young men fled the scene.

According to the first reports in the press, only three men—Nelson Rodriguez, José Rios, and Mario Martinez—were actually present at the scene of the shooting.[119] The reporting of their identities seemed to confirm what local youth argued almost from the beginning, that the officers "knew each one of the brothers by face."[120] As the media portrayed the three "Latin types" as "young hoodlums" and members of a "gang," police accused them of attacking Officers Paul McGoran and Joseph Brodnick and then shooting Brodnick to death.[121] Within a few days the manhunt expanded to include four more suspects, including one who fled to El Salvador and was never apprehended. When police finally apprehended the six, José Rios told the press their version of events. "It was really the fault of the pig who didn't die," he said. "He was calling us punks and hitting us. . . . The dead pig was beating us too."[122] Under the headline "The Angry Suspect," the newspaper seemingly printed Rios's words for their sensationalist value. But the young activists in the community saw a reflection of their own experience in his account.

The small cadre of Latino youth in the Mission that mobilized support for Los Siete all had direct ties to the Bay Area student movement and significant organizational experience. Donna Amador, Roberto Vargas, Roger Alvarado, and Yolanda Lopez attended the first meeting. Amador and Alvarado had been members of the Brown Berets. More recently, they and

"Serve the People: Free los Siete," 1970, poster for the Comité Para Defender Los Siete de la Raza. Image courtesy of Lincoln Cushing/ Docs Populi.

the others had been involved in the strike at San Francisco State.[123] Many of the accused were also well-known student activists who had been involved in a flourishing student movement at the College of San Mateo.[124] The group named their support effort El Comité para Defender los Siete (most often referred to as, simply, "Los Siete"). In the months ahead, what began as a support vehicle for the seven accused would transform into its own organizational movement "relating to the needs of the people, in the courts and in the community."[125]

Los Siete members traveled throughout the Southwest in an effort to connect with other facets of the Chicano student movement and raise money to support the legal defense of the accused. They met with Bobby Seale and David Hilliard of the Black Panthers, resulting in an important relationship. The Panthers offered the Comité space in their community newspaper, microphone time at all of their local rallies, and the educational support of their organization. The night after the first meeting of the two groups, Seale mentioned the six arrested youth in a television interview. He then came across the bay to meet with their parents. He told them about Huey Newton, "a brother" also imprisoned on "political grounds." The most important visible show of support from the Panthers came in the gift of a lawyer. Although three of the six already had representation,

Seale offered the others the services of Panther lawyer Charles Garry.[126] The relationship between the two organizations had a significance deeper than logistics: it "was the biggest chance [the Panthers] had to unite brown and black people."[127]

The cause of Los Siete de la Raza provided not only an opportunity to defend "seven brothers" but also a perfect rallying point for a broader movement that could address systemic racism and inequality from a radical political perspective. The ideological foundations of the Los Siete movement can be seen in the content of its newspaper, *¡Basta Ya!* (Enough Already!). It began as a four-page mimeographed newsletter detailing the plight of the accused in both English and Spanish.[128] By the end of the summer, using the Panther press for support, *¡Basta Ya!* had become a full-fledged, bilingual effort to educate their community, preaching a revolutionary ideology on a variety of topics. It regularly attacked the media, explaining to readers how "propaganda is fed to the people through corporate controlled television."[129] Most issues of the paper contained a critique of the U.S. presence in Vietnam, supporting the self-determination effort of the (North) Vietnamese while arguing that the war was "only serving the rich" as it used "our brothers."[130] Local coverage included topics like tenants' rights efforts and educational campaigns. Whether at the local or global level, all of the newspaper's contents communicated a radical critique of power as it sought to inform and educate.

*¡Basta Ya!*, like the movement itself, made a special effort to create a sense of solidarity with other radical movements around the country and the world. Stemming from their connection to the Black Panthers, but also to the multiracial strike at San Francisco State, the Comité saw its movement as part of a larger liberation struggle of people of color. Special issues had in-depth coverage of events like the San Francisco State and Mission High walkouts.[131] Other Mission District movements—like the fight led by the Mission Coalition Organization against redevelopment—also received periodic coverage, despite the Los Siete organization's increasing hostility to the MCO approach. Expressing solidarity with movements beyond their immediate community, *¡Basta Ya!* covered the struggles of the Black Panthers in Oakland, the Young Lords Party in New York, the American Indian Movement in the Bay Area, and guerrilla campaigns in Latin America.[132] Reflecting both the group's limited resources and its connection to activist networks, many of the articles in *¡Basta Ya!* were reprinted from other sources, such as the locally printed *Black Panther* and New Mexico's *El Grito*.

Although police violence and Panther support launched Los Siete, its members sought to create a revolutionary struggle in their community and build their own constituency. Roger Alvarado, one of the leaders of the Comité, brought to this work many of the skills he had acquired as a spokesman in the TWLF movement. In one interview, he described the Los Siete movement as one for all the oppressed, not just the accused. "We feel that the whole relationship of this government, society, and system to poor people, particularly brown people, is one of oppression; one in which they are not offered any opportunity to make any kinds of changes so that any poor person who gets arrested is being arrested because of his attempt to survive under the oppression."[133] Radical analyses of this sort were true to the base of support mobilized by Los Siete, but they did not always resonate with the general public of the Mission District. Constituencies within the MCO, for example, had made law enforcement an important issue in their organizing, yet they "would not support blanket indictments of the police."[134] Though the Comité used the underground and radical media to its advantage, and even went directly to the community in a "street organizing" program, the radicalism of Los Siete "preached to the choir" while it alienated many in the uneducated, working-class community. As one member of the Comité said, "people got turned off . . . [by] that theory we were talking." But at the early stages of the movement, excited by an analysis of society that placed their movement in context and empowered by the support of the Black Panthers, members had only radical theory on their minds.[135]

In time, however, the Los Siete movement evolved into something more than an ideological machine. The historical trajectory of Los Siete reflects a consistent maturation process, as members applied the lessons learned from participation in the movement. Committed to becoming a radical, antiestablishment organization that could address community issues, the Comité refocused itself in the summer of 1969 and began searching for ways to "serve the people."[136] Implementing a core principle of the Panther movement—the self-determination of the community—the Los Siete group merged with a breakfast program housed at St. Peter's Catholic Church, in the heart of the Mission District.[137] Originally begun by students affiliated with San Francisco State, the program sought to feed the community's hungry children, in particular those who had fallen through the cracks of the social welfare system. Linked with an institution most could trust, and geared toward a basic need for most Mission families, the Comité hoped its leadership of the breakfast program would legitimate its organization in the minds of community members. Whether or not it did, the program continued to provide a needed service to the community.

The breakfast program at St. Peter's was but the first incarnation of the Comité's community service model. After its popularity resulted in a daily attendance of more than 150 children, the Comité expanded it to create another program housed at St. John's in the North Mission.[138] Along the same lines as its attempt to feed the hungry, the Comité also sought to care for the sick by establishing a free medical clinic. By the fall, the storefront office on Mission Street that it used as a base became something of a community service center. From it, Los Siete members recruited volunteers to provide draft counseling and oversaw an ambulance pool for the sick and elderly. Utilizing the knowledge base of many of the organizers, they also created a college recruitment center in their office. And after a neighborhood man named Vicente Gutierrez died suspiciously while in police custody, the Comité created a community law clinic. Formed with the aid of some progressive lawyers, La Raza Legal Defense provided legal advice and representation to residents filing suits against the city. When it finally opened its office in early summer 1970, La Raza Legal Defense had a pool of about thirty lawyers dedicated to issues ranging from police brutality, to drug busts, to immigration troubles.[139]

For many young Latino activists coming of political age, the movements at San Francisco State and in the Mission led them to reconceptualize their vision of self and community. Much of this took the form of internationalist ways of thinking, what local youth referred to as Third World. As one scholar notes, "Third World was also more than *descriptive*—such as the contemporary notion of 'people of color'—it was *prescriptive*, reflecting a certain racial and class politics . . . rooted in a specific social praxis."[140] These youth activists forged that praxis through coalition and solidarity. In the multiracial and multiethnic Mission, this generation of activists had distinct advantages in this arena. Indicative of the long history of San Francisco's Latino population, the seven young men accused of killing Brodnick were Salvadoran, Nicaraguan, and Honduran. The organization behind them exemplified the same Central American diversity, as well as including Chicana and Chicano activists from the neighborhood. When they explored alliances for support, they visited the key organizational efforts behind the Chicano student movement. Reflecting their solidarity with these efforts, their newspaper *¡Basta Ya!* listed its address in the masthead as "P.O. Box 12217, San Francisco, Califas, Aztlán."[141]

In a southwestern sea of Chicano nationalist organizations, Latina and Latino youth in San Francisco explored the movement through an assertion of a more inclusive *raza* or "brown" identity. In the first issue of *¡Basta Ya!*, Roger Alvarado authored a piece articulating his community's support for the seven accused as well as what he and other Bay Area Latinos viewed as the emerging *raza* movement. "We have lived as a conquered people, struggling in the mouth of the lion," he wrote. "We like to think of ourselves as individuals accepting our situation individually and letting the rest of La Raza get along as it can. We have forgotten and ignored so much of what was once La Raza, the communal living, the spirit and character of los pueblos, in favor of this middle-class thing called individuality."[142] Typical of the early phases of both the Los Siete and San Francisco State movements, activists envisioned a communal movement for the liberation of "Raza people." In step with the Chicano nationalism that was expressed in El Plan de Aztlán, these San Francisco Latino and Latina movements helped expand the notion of *chicanismo* through their mere participation in the wider Chicano movement, or *el movimiento*.

In some ways San Francisco's Latino movement also represented a particular vanguard within the Chicano movement by dealing with some of its limitations and articulating possible answers. As the Chicano movement evolved, the term *Chicano* became ever more fixed as a marker for Mexican American youth with a specific set of political commitments. Concurrently, San Francisco activists sought to avoid the movement's linguistic and ideological weaknesses. When the Comité made an effort in the fall of 1969 to be less ideological and more pragmatic in its focus, it dropped the "Aztlán" masthead of ¡Basta Ya! and replaced it with "A Mission Community Paper."[143] Of course this change was more cosmetic than ideological. The organization remained committed to the principles of self-determination and community empowerment; it simply sought better strategies to implement these philosophies in the community. At San Francisco State, the formulation of the TWLF's Latino contingent required dealing with the tensions between "Chicano students" (ethnic Mexicans) and "Latino students" (ethnic Latin Americans). The movement itself helped create bonds that transcended differences in terminology. As activists institutionalized the movement in classes and programs, they reflected Chicano principles while remaining conscious of these principles' rhetorical limitations. They named their academic program "La Raza Studies," though in content and form it mirrored what Chicano activists outlined in "El Plan de Santa Barbara," a movement document that called for the creation of Chicano studies programs.[144] These activists saw the movement as a collection of highly regionalized movements that spoke to local concerns while exhibiting shared principles and beliefs. With that in mind, their task became organizing their own community as part of a larger struggle of liberation for all oppressed peoples.

YOUTH MOVEMENTS OFTEN HAVE a reduced life span in the already unpredictable world of radical politics. The young are stereotyped as being the most easily moved to passionate action and, simultaneously, to something new. Indeed, when movements rely on student populations they run the risk of declining when those students move on, as unavoidably they must. That life span is threatened in other ways when the newness of the movement—the degree to which it has distinguished itself from mainstream political responses—places it in a position threatening to societal traditions and norms. By most accounts, radical youth movements rarely possess the wherewithal to become the lasting revolutions implied in their utopian visions. In the late sixties and early seventies, San Francisco's youth of color participated in the political developments indicative of their times. Latinos and Latinas created their own incarnations of that phenomenon as they strove to create a society reflecting their vision of justice. While many of their goals may have never materialized, something lasting did remain: a particular racial and ethnic identity that recast what it meant to be *raza* in the Mission District, in San Francisco, and in the world.

The meanings infused into Latina/Latino identity by these movements altered institutions. San Francisco State saw the creation of permanent programs, like La Raza Studies. The Mission witnessed the creation of health centers like Instituto Familiar de la Raza and legal clinics like Raza Legal Center, institutions whose sole goal became the betterment of community life. These organizations emerged out of a growing sense of *latinidad*, one that incorporated *chicanismo* but expanded to include Latin American diversity and multiracial realities. United under "a recognition of our common humanity in the face of the brutal inhumanity which has oppressed us," and nurturing of "a passionate sense of our dignity as a people and the courage which unity provides us,"[145] they simultaneously articulated a practical vision of "Third World" San Francisco. Ultimately, the single most enduring institution these movements built was a lasting sense of community predicated on this identity. In contrast to the present day, when gentrification is the dominant force in the Mission, fostering community stories marked by "loss, erasure, emotion, and death" and "endings,"[146] the battles of the late sixties and early seventies are ones of empowerment, hope, and community cohesion, both analyzed then and remembered since as the beginning of La Misión.

# Speaking Latino

## *San Francisco in an Era of Latino Evictions*

"These are also our working families, caregivers, maintenance workers, cooks, servers, day laborers," proclaimed Guadalupe Arreola, "people that literally build San Francisco, that literally make San Francisco what it is."[1] Speaking before the San Francisco Board of Supervisors in July 2007, Arreola—a representative of St. Peter's Housing Committee—was part of an overflow crowd of neighborhood residents, housing advocates, and antigentrification activists. This multiracial assortment from the Mission and other working-class eastern neighborhoods in the city voiced their shared opposition to a development proposal making its way through the city's bureaucracy. As communicated in more than four hours of public testimony, they sought to derail the construction of a new four-story building with plans to provide sixty units of "owner-occupied residential units," as well as four ground-floor retail spaces that would become home to the fourth Walgreens in the neighborhood. In the words of one advocate, they gathered to "defend and nurture the Mission community."[2]

At the start of the twenty-first century, the Mission District of San Francisco finds itself in the midst of a battle over the occupation and usage of its space. Years of economic prosperity in the region unleashed a flood of new migration and settlement unlike any seen before. The flow of newcomers that began with the establishment of new "dot-com" businesses in the greater Silicon Valley has scarcely ebbed with the tech industry's more recent decline. Largely white, young, and professional, these newest Mission residents herald a new force on the landscape. Drawn to the district by the affordability of the city's largest barrio, these twenty-first-century migrants brought with them their own visions of what a community is and should look like. The onetime home of affordable housing and Latin

American culture is also home to new upscale lofts and businesses catering to a wealthier clientele.

On the surface, the present struggle is about housing. While all parties involved agree there is a profound need for more affordable housing in the city, the contention lies in whether or not developments like the one opposed in the summer of 2007—fully compliant with the city's requirements for affordability—embody the ethical foundations undergirding such regulations. After all, even at reduced prices, the majority of community residents could not dream of buying one of the new units. Beneath the surface, however, this is a struggle about much more than housing. The Latino community of San Francisco today is struggling for survival. As Arreola put it, the "people that clean San Francisco, feed San Francisco, . . . are always at risk of not being able to live in San Francisco."[3]

The struggle now playing out in the city stretches back a century and a half, to when Latin American migrants first sought a place of visibility and community in the city. Forces of "economic progress" facilitated their movements in that time, fostering the rise of a business class of transnational migrants as well as a population of displaced and dislocated laborers. It also has roots in the twentieth century, when Latin American migrants first rose to prominence in San Francisco's historically working-class Mission District. Drawn to the neighborhood for its immigrant character, affordability, and proximity to local industry, Latinos culturally transformed it to reflect their presence and meet their needs. The struggle today is heavily informed by the successes of these past generations. It feeds on a legacy of panethnic unity and cooperation as harnessed by the church. It is shaped by earlier efforts to engage in a multifaceted process of homemaking, re-creating the familiar on a new landscape. Quite directly, it benefits from the grassroots multiracial coalition of the late sixties and early seventies, a group that took control of the Mission's immediate future as it derailed civic efforts at "urban renewal." The present struggle is imbued with more than thirty years of community formation, of expressions of "cultural citizenship," of movements of solidarity. In the host of nonprofits and new coalitions that lead this movement, the historical legacy of Latino San Francisco is clear.

The Mission District that Latinos and other working-class constituencies seek to protect emerged in the wake of the stories contained in this book, as locals successfully institutionalized their postwar movements in lasting ways. The creation of service agencies like La Raza Centro Legal, Mission Neighborhood Health Center, and Dolores Street Community Services all signal the transformations from mass movements for self-determination to its actual realization. At the same time, in the businesses that line Mission Avenue, the churches standing on numerous corners, and the annual celebrations of community life, the remaining level of Latino cultural ownership of the Mission is a continuing testament to the long-standing and evolving quest for lives of dignity and meaning.

Historically, struggles over Latino displacement have as much to do with the solidification of global processes as they do with local urban concerns. In fact, the local context is largely framed by these broader processes. San Francisco, like many U.S. cities, is an urban core built via the machinations of U.S. neoimperialism—of networks of commerce, production, and capital forging the foundation of U.S. hemispheric hegemony. For a century, these forces structured the flow of capital and goods through this "Pacific metropolis" as they nurtured an on-the-ground material reality marked by commerce, industrial production, and finance. As goods and capital flowed, so too did labor, that indispensable element of economic production. In ways definitive for Latino community formation, these economic networks linked the port of San Francisco to specific localities throughout Latin America, facilitating the movement of people from one part of the hemisphere to another, and framing the birth of a Latino population in this city. Displacement became a feature of life for them as thousands left their homelands for the Golden Gate. Beginning as early as the conclusion of World War II, San Francisco witnessed another pattern in U.S. urban history—deindustrialization. As industrial forces shifted to overseas labor and production markets, San Francisco re-created itself as a "postindustrial corporate center," a home for global "commerce, finance, and administration."[4] These transformations disproportionately affected working-class communities in the city, as low-wage, service-economy jobs replaced stable, often union-wage industrial jobs. At the same time, the interest in developing land to attract both finance and a population with disposable income, along with renewed public support to wipe out "urban blight," meant once neglected geographic spaces became the targets of developers and municipal officials alike.

In this nexus of forces lies the heart of Latin American experiences in San Francisco. Framed by a simultaneous inclusion and exclusion, their story is an iconic one, marked by diverse processes of "becoming American." As Spanish-speaking immigrant groups experienced San Francisco, however, they negotiated the dynamics of place, community, and belonging in unique ways. Theirs is also a story of multiple identities, of marginalization and adaptation, and of becoming "Latino." Far from an identity molded by the priorities of market discourse and advertising dollars, this is a panethnicity forged out of necessity, circumstance, experience, and struggle.

The rise of a San Francisco Latino community and identity is also a product of people in the gaps.[5] Immigrants came to a new city and created a sense of the familiar as they defined their space, created institutions, and nurtured community. What they created did not perfectly mirror what they had known in their previous homelands. U.S. society at all levels also played roles in assigning meaning to these people and places they inhabited. This society, however, did not create a mirror of itself either. Like a third space, the vision of a people that arose—their communal identity—is based on other terms. First, it evolves from the sum of these varied agencies, those of the immigrant groups and the majority society in which they settle. Even further, as the manifestations of a community's identity, the ways Latinos defined their spaces reciprocated to redefine them. In that dynamic process is created the third space that is the Latino community of San Francisco. Neither here nor there, it is something new and something dynamic.

Author and cultural icon Ken Kesey offered a more accessible way of conceiving this phenomenon. He once responded to the assertion that he was a bridge between the beatniks and the hippies. "To be the bridge from the Beatniks to the hippies shows that we don't exist in either world," he said. "We lie in the cracks between them. We think of ourselves as crackers."[6] While the humor in Kesey's comments is obvious, the complexity of the idea is more subdued. If we listen closely, however, I think we can find that third space within them. As this is a history of the difference, the unique, and the unfamiliar within the breadth of established Chicano and Latino histories, it is also a story of the cracks, the "space between."[7] The spaces where we are neither "here" nor "there" are the realms in which most of us—whether as individuals or groups—find ourselves. It suggests some sense of movement and process—a going from and a going to. The cracks are also flexible and unfixed. As a fissure in what we know, it becomes something we must understand as we find our ways out of them, outside of them, beyond them.

Whether we situate this history in the cracks, a third space, or assign it to the threshold of the liminal, the same idea can be present. In any case, it is necessary to acknowledge that people shape their identities in the conscious and unconscious choices they make, the strategies they employ for survival, and efforts they take to create better lives for themselves. Taken as a whole, this story of Latino San Francisco can speak to *the* story of U.S. history. For we have too long ignored the cracks and the fissures it possesses.

The histories of Latinos and Latinas in San Francisco remind us that there is something more there, something familiar and something new.

In voicing their present-day commitment to community, Latinos in San Francisco participate with others in building panethnic, multiracial identities through organized effort. In their struggle against the market forces of gentrification, this identity is simultaneously about the protection of the working class, the protection of their immigrant neighborhood, and the protection of the Latino geographies of this city. Voicing this sensibility in 2000, one local resident responded to a developer's claim that even he—as a Latino—could not get the community's approval to build. "If [he] had 'spoken Latino,' he would have made this project better-suited to a neighborhood that can't afford what he's offering."[8] "Speaking Latino" in the twenty-first century means voicing the concerns of the majority of the community about protecting its future while respecting its past.

# Notes

## ABBREVIATIONS

AASF   Archives of the Archdiocese of San Francisco, St. Patrick Seminary, Menlo Park, California

BANC   Bancroft Library, University of California, Berkeley, California

CHS   California Historical Society, North Baker Library, San Francisco, California

MMA   Mike Miller personal archives, San Francisco, California

SFPL   San Francisco History Center, San Francisco Public Library, San Francisco, California

## INTRODUCTION

1. Sponsored by Rep. Jim Sensenbrenner (R-WI), The Border Protection, Anti-terrorism, and Illegal Immigration Control Act of 2005 (H.R. 4437) passed the House of Representatives on December 16, 2005. Public pressure prevented it from reaching a vote in the Senate.

2. Pia Sarkar, "Humanizing the Debate, Day Laborers More Concerned with Work than Politics," *San Francisco Chronicle*, May 19, 2006.

3. "Supervisors to Vote in S.F. as 'Sanctuary,'" *San Francisco Chronicle*, December 7, 1985. The measure also included immigrants from Haiti.

4. "Sanctuary Folly," *San Francisco Chronicle*, December 11, 1985.

5. "Supervisors to Vote in S.F."

6. For the sake of simplicity, I use the term "Latino" when referring to all people of Latin American descent residing in the United States. "Latin American" and "ethnic Latin American" are used irrespective of residency. I employ "Latina" and "Latino" in some late twentieth-century discussions when I feel it is necessary to emphasize distinct political projects informing a gendered identity. I recognize that the terms "Central America" and "Central American" have been used inconsistently in the historical record, variously including or excluding Mexico/Mexicans. They are used here to exclude Mexico/Mexicans, following the practice in most censuses and other government documents.

7. Wirt, 107.

8. Browning, xxxiii.

9. Jameson and Miyoshi, xii.

10. Joseph, 5.

11. Schoultz, xv.

12. Gilbert G. González (2004), 154.

13. Pastor, 17. See also Juan González; González and Fernandez; Gilbert G. González (2006); and Whalen and Vásquez-Hernández.

14. See Laó-Montes and Dávila; De Genova and Ramos-Zayas; and Ricourt and Danta.

15. De Genova and Ramos-Zayas, 209.

16. Dávila, 178.

17. Torres-Saillant, 435. For other examinations of the limits and possibilities of Latino panethnicity, see Valdivia and Garcia; Mize and Peña Delgado; Dávila; and Oboler.

18. Padilla, 6, 164–65.

19. Ibid., 3.

20. De Genova and Ramos-Zayas, 20.

21. Espiritu (1992), 161.

22. The recent work provides dynamic examples and new understandings of the historical roles played by Catholicism in Latino community formation. See Matovina (2005); Badillo; and Treviño.

23. Anderson, 6.

24. Lipsitz, 12.

25. For a general summary of these figures, see Pew Hispanic Center (March 24, 2011).

26. Pew Hispanic Center (May 26, 2011), 1–4.

27. Potoc; Sean D. Hamill, "Mexican's Death Bares a Town's Ethnic Tensions," *New York Times*, August 5, 2008.

28. An Act Amending Title 15, Chapter 1, Article 1, Arizona Revised Statutes, by Adding Sections 15-111 and 15-112; Amending Section 15-848, Arizona Revised Statutes; Relating to School Curriculum, House Bill 2281, passed April 29, 2010, House of Representatives, Forty-ninth Legislature, Arizona.

29. Department of Homeland Security.

30. Amnesty International, 6–12.

31. Others have studied segments of this population in great detail and to powerful end. Cordova is the first scholarly source on the community. I am indebted to Cordova's inquiry, framed with the intimate knowledge of the local and a deft sense of the larger questions requiring further academic attention. Godfrey (1988) focuses on Latinos among other segments of the population. Mission poets Juan Felipe Herrera (1998) and Alejandro Murguía (2002) have both offered their exceptionally rich accounts of community life in the late twentieth century. Menjívar is an anthropological study of Salvadoran migration to the city in the late twentieth century. A stunning examination of the queer Latino community at the end of the twentieth century can be found in Roque-Ramírez.

32. Community studies of San Francisco are too voluminous to note here, though a much smaller body of work reconstructs the social history of the city's racial and sexual minorities. A few of consequence are Daniels; Broussard; Yung; Shah; and Boyd.

33. For a sophisticated demonstration, see Perales.

34. Portelli, 99.

35. Massey, 2, 3.

36. Ibid., 4.

37. Sonia Nazario, "Enrique's Journey: The Boy Left Behind," *Los Angeles Times*, September 29, 2002.

### CHAPTER 1

1. *El Comercio* (Lima), April 10, 1849, reprinted in Hernández Cornejo, 2:142.

2. *Alta California*, August 2, 1849. The reprinted trial transcript confirmed Latin Americans and one German as the victims.

3. The formal charges included a conspiracy charge "to commit riot, rape, and murder, and divers [*sic*] other crimes and outrages against the peace of the people of this territory." Ibid.

4. Ibid.

5. Bancroft, 5:570.

6. Johnson, 26.

7. Berglund, 9.

8. See Pitt, esp. chaps. 14 and 15.

9. Mariano Guadalupe Vallejo, letter to Mexican Ministry of War, 1841, in Tays, 56.

10. Lotchin, 3.

11. McWilliams, 26.

12. Bancroft, 3:700.

13. Dana, 244.

14. Foucrier, 30–37.

15. "Report of the Secretary of State to the Congress of Mexico," July 2, 1938, in U.S. House of Representatives, *H.R. Doc. 351*, 313.

16. Bancroft, 3:711.

17. Smalley, 593–603.

18. Goodman, 73.

19. S. W. Kearny, "Proclamation to the People of California," *California Star*, March 20, 1847.

20. Ibid.

21. Ibid.

22. S. W. Kearny, "Decree of Gov. Kearny, *California Star*, March 27, 1847.

23. "Public Notice," *California Star*, August 28, 1847. For a description of the mechanisms promoting land transfer, see Hornbeck, 343–448.

24. "Statistics of San Francisco," *California Star*, August 29, 1847.

25. Ibid.

26. Ibid.

27. Ibid.

28. George M. Dallas, "Movement of the Age," *California Star*, November 27, 1847.

29. Bancroft, 5:570.

30. Ibid., 571. Regular advertisements and shipping announcements in the *Daily Alta California* provide further testament to the importance of these economic networks.

31. Bancroft, 5:570.

32. Ashbury, 8.

33. Monaghan, 7.

34. James K. Polk, president of the United States of America, "Fourth Annual Message," December 5, 1848.

35. McWilliams, 66; Lotchin, 37.

36. U.S. Bureau of the Census (1853), 972. These numbers do not include San Francisco, whose 1850 data was lost to fire. Accordingly, the figure is likely higher.

37. "Population and Industry of California, by the State Census for the Year 1852," in ibid., 982.

38. Benemann, 35.

39. McWilliams, 69; U.S. Bureau of the Census (1864), 23.

40. Hernández Cornejo, 1:18.

41. Standart, 335.

42. Ibid., 334.

43. Tinker Salas (1997), 80.

44. Ibid., 24.

45. Standart, 338.

46. Tinker Salas (1997), 80.

47. Standart, 338–39.

48. Taylor, 84–85.

49. Tinker Salas (1997), 53, 55.

50. Both the Antonio Uruchurtu contract (dated February 12, 1849) and the Juan Camou contract (dated February 13, 1849) are reprinted in Galaz, 207.

51. Monaghan, 16.

52. Ibid., 17.

53. Johnson, 65.

54. Nasatir, 61.

55. Ibid., 106–7.

56. Hernández Cornejo, 1:37.

57. Monaghan, 55; Johnson, 66.

58. McWilliams, 40.

59. Ibid., 66.

60. *La Aurora* (Cajamarca, Peru), November 18, 1848.

61. Hernández Cornejo, 1:53.

62. Monaghan, 73.

63. Benemann, 1.

64. Nelson Kingsley, "A Journal of a Voyage at Sea in the Bark *Anna Reynolds* from New Haven to San Francisco," BANC; pages are hand numbered by the author.

65. Ibid., 61.

66. Ibid.

67. Ibid., 64.

68. Ibid., 60.

69. Davis, 59.

70. Kingsley, 63.

71. John McCracken, "Letters of John McCracken, 1849–1853; Dealing with His Journey around the Horn in the Ship *Balance*, and His Life in San Francisco. With Four Early San Francisco Lithographs," unpublished ms., BANC.

72. Davis, 7–8.

73. Ibid., 11.

74. Abel R. Biggs, "A Voyage from the City of New York to the City of San Francisco, California on the Barque *Keoka*, James McGuire, Master," handwritten journal, 1849, BANC.

75. Jacob D. B. Stillman, journal, reprinted in Ramírez, 138.

76. Letter from John Lacourt, M.D., to Gov. Riley of California, Concepción, Chile, March 24, 1849, Archives of California unbound documents, 1846–50, H. H. Bancroft Collection, BANC.

77. Hernández Cornejo, 1:69.

78. Ibid., 72.

79. Both letters reprinted in ibid., 88, 89.

80. Letter dated February 1849, reprinted in ibid., 90–91.

81. Letter dated June 8, 1849, reprinted in ibid., 115.

82. Hernández Cornejo, 1:72.

83. Pierce, 60.

84. Pérez Rosales, 10.

85. Monaghan, 161; see also Pérez Rosales, 70–72. The *Alta California* regularly lamented the persecution of Latin Americans in the mines and reported their departures with measured alarm. See *Alta California*, August 26, 1850.

86. Pérez Rosales, 67.

87. Pitt, 55–56; and Monaghan, 114.

88. Pitt, 55–56.

89. Ibid., 135.

90. Almaguer, 4.

91. Ngai, 54.

92. Almaguer, 7–16.

93. Bancroft, 5:649.

94. "Town Council" and "Election Return," *Alta California*, January 18, 1849.

95. *Alta California*, January 25, 1849.

96. Bancroft, 5:652n.

97. Barry and Patten, 27–28.

98. J. K. Osgood, letter to George Strange, August 20, 1849, BANC.

99. Takaki (1993), 11.

100. Kingsley, 196.

101. Carothers, "Early Days in California: Memoirs of Dr. J. H. Carothers," typescript, 1907, BANC.

102. Fisher, 48.

103. de Massey, 153.

104. Robert Smith Lammot, letter to his father, December 15, 1849, as quoted in Benemann, 11.

105. Soulé, Gihon, and Nisbet, 257–58.

106. Ibid., 258.

107. Pérez Rosales, 68.

108. Pitt, 53.

109. Pérez Rosales, 85.

110. Hernández Cornejo, 2:131.

111. Theodore Kimball, "San Francisco and Elsewhere," journal, 1849, BANC.

112. Ramón Jil Navarro, quoted in Beilharz and López, 103.

113. Ibid., 104.

114. Hernández Cornejo, 1:72; Pitt, 195.

115. *Alta California*, August 2, 1849; February 14, 1851.

116. Johnson, 105–6.

117. Hernández Cornejo, 1:70.

118. Camarillo (1996), 60.

119. Pérez Rosales, 6.

120. Bancroft, 6:232.

121. Ibid.

122. Ibid.

123. Ashbury, 33.

124. *Alta California*, February 14, 1851.

125. Muscatine, 107.

126. Johnson, 119.

127. Ibid., 120.

128. Hernández Cornejo, 1:130.

129. Taylor, 102.

130. Ibid., 102–3.

131. Soulé, Gihon, and Nisbet, 243–44.

132. Holliday, 301; Soulé, Gihon, and Nisbet, 244–45.

133. Ashbury, 40.

134. Muscatine, 264; *Alta California*, August 2, 1849.

135. *Alta California*, August 2, 1849.

136. Ibid.; Ashbury, 17.

137. *Alta California*, June 28, 1849.

138. *Alta California*, August 2, 1849.

139. Her named is also printed as "Alvalez."

140. *Alta California*, August 2, 1849.

141. Ibid.

142. Ibid.

143. Ibid.

144. *Senate Journal*, First Session (1850), 493, in Heizer and Almquist, 145.

145. Ibid.

146. Bancroft, 6:240.

147. Ibid., 241.

148. Heizer and Almquist, 127.

149. *Alta California*, January 30, 1852.

150. *Alta California*, February 3, 1852.

151. *El Mercurio*, January 14, 1852, reprinted in Hernández Cornejo, 2:237–39.

152. Kimball. See entries for Manuel Felix, Florencio Gomes, and Charles Ballas.

153. *LeCount & Strong's San Francisco City Directory*, 228; *A. W. Morgan & Co.'s San Francisco Directory*, listing for Roman Catholic Church on Vallejo.

154. Starr and Orsi, 6.

## CHAPTER 2

1. "Los españoles e hispano-americanos de San Francisco, reunidos en junta, convinieron en expedir la siguiente," circular letter, August 2, 1871, distributed via pamphlet in *Lo que puede y necesita la raza española en San Francisco* (San Francisco: Cosmopolitana, 1871), BANC.

2. Matovina (2001), 13.

3. For a discussion of "ethno-Catholicism" as a Mexican countercultural stance, see Treviño, 4–5.

4. Smith, 6.

5. Di Leonardo, 133.

6. Kemble, 331–33.

7. "Population, as Native and Foreign-Born, by Counties: 1880 and 1870" (Table VIII), in U.S. Bureau of the Census (1883), 428; "Statistics of Place of Birth," ibid., 471.

8. "Foreign-Born Population of Fifty Principal Cities, Distributed, According to Place of Birth, among the Various Foreign Countries: 1880" (Table XVI), ibid., 538–41. Mexicans accounted for 1,438 of the total foreign-born, with South Americans numbering 456.

9. "Population, by Race, Sex, and Nativity" (Table V), ibid., 382.

10. "Native Population of Fifty Principal Cities, Distributed According to States and Territories of Birth: 1880" (Table XV), ibid., 536–37.

11. Ramón Jil Navarro, quoted in Beilharz and López, 109.

12. The term originates in Curtin.

13. *La Voz de Méjico*, May 24, 1862.

14. *La República*, August 5, 1882; *La Voz de Chile*, January 31, 1868.

15. *El Cronista*, August 2, 1884.

16. *El Tecolote*, May 4, 1876.

17. Tinker Salas (2007), 627.

18. Gilbert G. González (2004), 17.

19. E. A. M., "Carta de Mazatlán," printed in *La República*, August 5, 1882.

20. F. Elias, "Carta de Tejachipe," printed in ibid.

21. Publisher's notice, *El Cronista*, August 2, 1884.

22. *La Voz de Méjico*, March 29, 1862.

23. Ibid., June 7, 1862.

24. *La Bandera Mexicana*, November 1862.

25. Hayes-Bautista, 9.

26. *La Voz de Méjico*, January 17, 1863.

27. Monroy, 63.

28. Robert Ryan Miller, 12.

29. Tinker Salas (2007), 627–28.

30. Ibid., 630–31.

31. Hipólita Orendain de Medina, correspondence and miscellany, 1852–1922, CHS.

32. Rosaura Soto, Sonora, Mexico, letter to Hipólita Orendain de Medina, San Francisco, February 19, 1867, Orendain de Medina papers.

33. Gómez, 2.

34. See Camarillo (1996), chap. 5; and Chávez-García, chap. 6.

35. "The Mexicans Must Go," *San Francisco Chronicle*, April 29, 1878.

36. Takaki (1989), 87.

37. Ashbury, 143.

38. "Contra los chinos," *El Cronista*, October 25, 1884.

39. Gyory, 257.

40. Rast, 34.

41. Dulce Bolado Davis, family history, typescript, 1952, 9–11, CHS.

42. Ibid., 15.

43. Ibid., 14.

44. Ibid., 16.

45. Tinker Salas (2007), 633, 637.

46. Ashbury, 105, 115.

47. Sandos, 3.

48. Lotchin, 120.

49. De Massey, 37.

50. Circular letter, 1.

51. Ibid., 2.

52. See Sánchez; Gilbert G. González (1999); and Monroy.

53. Sánchez, 109.

54. Circular letter, 2.

55. Ibid., 2.

56. Issel and Cherny, 62.

57. Burns (n.d.), 2.

58. Ethnington, 324.

59. Gutiérrez, 29.

60. Circular letter, 3.

61. Ibid., 4–5.

62. Ibid., 2.

63. McGuinness, 192–93.

64. Stephen J. Pitti, 60.

65. Circular letter, 5–6.

66. Ibid.

67. L. M. de la Sierra, "Brief History of the Parish of Our Lady of Guadalupe," in *La Azucena: Recuerdo de la Dedicación del Nuevo Templo de Ntra. Sra. de Guadalupe en San Francisco de California* 4, nos. 4, 5, and 6 (April, May, and June 1912): 29, Our Lady of Guadalupe file, no. 38, AASF.

68. It fulfilled this role for the *city* of San Francisco, not the entire San Francisco Archdiocese. It is significant to note that the latter encompassed a much larger geography than merely San Francisco proper. From 1860 to 1962, the Archdiocese of San Francisco covered a territory of 14,654 square miles. It included the counties of Alameda, Contra Costa, Lake, Marin, Mendocino, Napa, San Francisco, San Joaquin, San Mateo, Santa Clara, Sonoma, and Stanislaus, although county lines and archdiocese boundaries did not correspond precisely. In 1860 part of an even larger territory was cut off and became the Archdiocese of Sacramento. In 1962, the Santa Rosa, Stockton, and Oakland Dioceses were also created out of the San Francisco territory.

69. De la Sierra, "Brief History."

70. Badillo, 125.

71. Moisés Sandoval, 131.

72. Wind and Lewis, 1–3.

73. For some details of the Latin Quarter, see Issel and Cherny, 73. López, 33–38, provides one estimate of the Latino share of the area.

74. Lee Miller, 137; Robert H. Wilson, "San Francisco's Foreign Colonies: No. 3—Spanish-Mexican," *San Francisco Examiner*, December 2, 1923.

75. Boyd, 49.

76. Petition to Archbishop John J. Mitty requesting the reassignment of Father Francisco Villanueva, from various parishioners of Our Lady of Guadalupe Church, n.d., Guadalupe Church file, AASF. A letter begins the first page of signatures. While only the date "September" is legible, the content of the letter deals with the recognition of the appointment of Father Charles Murphy as administrator of the parish and the accompanying reassignment of Father Villanueva. Since the transfer of Father Rosendo Villanueva took place in 1949, it is a reasonable assumption that the petition dates from that year. While not all of the signatures are legible, at least 345 are identifiable. Of these, nearly 300 list an

address in the immediate Broadway and Mason region, in the close-by South of Market area, and in the areas just west of the church.

77. "U.S. Census of Religious Bodies: 1936," Department of Commerce, Bureau of the Census, filed by Right Reverend A. M. Santandreu, Our Lady of Guadalupe, 1895–1967, Correspondence file, AASF. The report distinguishes the 6,000 members of the parish as 2,300 males and 3,700 females, with more than 60 percent under thirteen years of age. As all the figures are in exact hundreds, it is unlikely that this is a "scientific" statistical report. Yet, even accounting for miscalculations, when compared to the official Census figures for "Spanish surname" whites (between 6,000 and 8,000 for the period in question) this suggests a high level of parish membership. See U.S. Bureau of the Census (1932 and 1943). Of course, these numbers must be considered within the massive deportation drives of the 1930s, which resulted in a fluctuating population as well as a motivation to hide one's presence altogether.

78. Bishop, 329.

79. For early twentieth-century examples, see *La Crónica* and *Hispano América*.

80. *La Azucena*, rear advertising sections.

81. Ibid.

82. Described in George Hodel and Emilia Hodel, "Spain," *San Francisco Chronicle*, April 17, 1932.

83. Sánchez, 108.

84. "Will Celebrate Day of Mexican Independence," *San Francisco Call*, September 2, 1900; "Mexico's Sons Will Celebrate Day of Freedom," *San Francisco Call*, September 14, 1900; "Mexico's Natal Day Will be Celebrated by Local Colony," *San Francisco Call*, September 16, 1900.

85. "Trouble Brewing in Mexican Colony," *San Francisco Call*, August 18, 1901.

86. "Both Factions Still at War," *San Francisco Call*, September 2, 1901; "Independence of Mexico," *San Francisco Call*, September 13, 1901.

87. "Mexicans to Hold Celebration," *San Francisco Call*, April 12, 1902.

88. Gina Marie Pitti, 5. I thank Jeffrey M. Burns at the AASF for access to this essay.

89. Ibid., 4. Italics in original.

90. Ibid., 2–3. Most of the seventeen existed in the San Jose area, which had a significant Mexican population.

91. Ibid., 7.

92. Ibid., 8. See also Treviño, 66.

93. Gina Marie Pitti, 13–20. Even though women made up a majority of the membership, and performed almost all of the organizational work for the associations, they were rarely president of the society.

94. Tomasi, 117.

95. "Chileans Celebrate Their Independence," *San Francisco Call*, September 9, 1904.

96. "Central American 100th Anniversary Celebrated Here," *San Francisco Chronicle*, September 16, 1921.

97. For the reflection of these sentiments among public health officials leading up to the early twentieth century, see the *Report of the Health Officer of the City and County of San Francisco* (San Francisco, various dates). Located in Special Collections, Honnold/Mudd Library, Claremont, CA. Reports for the years 1874, 1893, and 1897 reflect the growing concern with these areas of the city as sites of "filth."

98. Fradkin, 294–96.

99. *La Crónica*, October 9, 1915.

100. Godfrey (1988), 140.

101. Petition to Archbishop John J. Mitty requesting the reassignment of Father Francisco Villanueva, from various parishioners of Our Lady of Guadalupe Church. As noted earlier, more than 345 people signed the petition.

102. Letter from Reverend Charles J. Murphy to Reverend Leo T. Maher, June 18, 1951, Our Lady of Guadalupe, 1895–1967, Correspondence file, AASF.

103. See letter from F. S. Rondero to Archbishop John J. Mitty, May 30, 1952, ibid.

104. Letter from Martina Lopez Castilo and H. Gomez to J. J. Mitty, archbishop of San Francisco, July 28, 1953, ibid.

105. Parish Historical Report, 1950, Our Lady of Guadalupe Historical file, AASF. The report reads: "Many Spanish speaking people moving away partly [due to the] construction of Broadway tunnel. Tunnel construction reduced attendance at church services."

106. Letter from Guadalupe Mena and Christina Laralina to J. J. Mitty, archbishop of San Francisco, 26 August 1956, Our Lady of Guadalupe, 1895–1967, Correspondence file, AASF.

107. *The Monitor*, July 26, 1957.

108. Parish Historical Report, 1946, Our Lady of Guadalupe Historical file, AASF.

109. Ibid., 1960.

110. Various personal correspondence, 1970–198?, "Old Timers" file, Guadalupe Church, AASF.

CHAPTER 3

1. Elba Sanchez, interview by author, June 26, 2007, San Francisco, digital recording.

2. Espiritu (2003), 2.

3. Badillo, xix.

4. Brady Austin, "Californians Opening the Empire of the Southwest," *San Francisco Chronicle*, September 23, 1906.

5. Gilbert G. González (2004), 17. The phrase comes from William Rosecrans, U.S. minister to and major investor in Mexico.

6. Grandin, 3.

7. Ibid., 27.

8. Ibid., 3.

9. Gilbert G. González (2006), 1.

10. Odell, 300, 310.

11. San Francisco Foreign Traders, *Convention Souvenir Booklet and Advance List of Foreign Trade Firms of San Francisco Bay* (San Francisco: F. F. G. Harper, 1926), 9, SFPL.

12. San Francisco Bay Terminals Company, *Port San Francisco: The Past Justifies It, the Present Needs It, the Future Demands It* (San Francisco: 1926), SFPL.

13. Ibid.

14. San Francisco Chamber of Commerce, *San Francisco, the Financial, Commercial & Industrial Metropolis of the Pacific Coast: Official Records, Statistics, and Encyclopedia* (San Francisco: H. S. Crocker, 1915), 22–23, SFPL.

15. Ibid., 22.

16. Ibid., 99.

17. *The Progressive Port of San Francisco*, Board of State Harbor Commissioners promotional magazine, n.d., 10, SFPL; Godfrey (1988), 140.

18. Green Coffee Association of the San Francisco Chamber of Commerce, *Remarkable Growth of San Francisco as a Coffee Receiving Port and America's Foreign Coffee Trading* (San Francisco, December 17, 1919), 3, SFPL.

19. "American's Foreign Coffee Trading," copied from *New York Journal of Commerce and Commercial Bulletin*, and reprinted in Green Coffee Association, *Remarkable Growth*, 7.

20. Green Coffee Association, *Remarkable Growth*, 3–4.

21. San Francisco Chamber of Commerce, *San Francisco, the Financial, Commercial & Industrial Metropolis*, 35–36.

22. Ibid., 61.

23. Don Manuel Alfaro, "El regreso de la comisión de la Cámara de Comercio," *Centro América*, March 3, 1921.

24. "Campaign to Advertise San Francisco," *Centro América*, December 20, 1921.

25. "Guatemala to Have Hospital for Americans and English Aided by Friendly Republic," *San Francisco Chronicle*, March 19, 1921.

26. "Native Californian Receives High Honors," *San Francisco Chronicle*, October 12, 1905.

27. Sánchez, 21.

28. Gilbert G. González (2004), 107–8.

29. Meyer and Sherman, 467.

30. Sánchez, 24.

31. Meyer and Sherman, 450.

32. Interview with Richard Q. Camplis, in Francisco Camplis. My thanks to Francisco Camplis for a copy of his video production as well as its use for my own work.

33. Governor C. C. Young's Mexican Fact-Finding Committee.

34. Sanchez interview.

35. Alfonso Fabila, *El problema de la emigración de obreros y campesinos mexicanos* (Mexico City: Gráficos de la Nación, 1929), 24–27, in Balderrama and Rodríguez, 28–30.

36. Interview with Sam Rios, by author, July 2, 2002, Sacramento, CA, tape recording.

37. Rios interview.

38. Ibid.

39. Whalen, 8.

40. Medina, 84–95; "Threats and Force Put 66 Porto Ricans on Rio, but Fifty Others Escape," *San Francisco Examiner*, December 15, 1900.

41. *Hispano América*, June 10, 1917.

42. *La Crónica*, December 11, 1915.

43. George Hodel and Emilia Hodel, "Spain," *San Francisco Chronicle*, April 17, 1932.

44. "San Francisco Revives Colorful Days of the Dons," *San Francisco Chronicle*, October 2, 1921.

45. *San Francisco Chronicle*, April 17, 1932

46. U.S. Bureau of the Census (1924), 39–40.

47. Robert H. Wilson, "San Francisco's Foreign Colonies: No. 3—Spanish-Mexican," *San Francisco Examiner*, December 2, 1923.

48. Ibid.

49. *La Azucena*, rear advertising sections.

50. Advertisement, *El Imparcial*, February 1, 1935.

51. López, 33–38.

52. Godfrey (1988), 140.

53. *El Imparcial*, August 13, 1938.

54. Ibid., February 1, 1935.

55. See the "California School of Beauty Culture" advertisement, ibid.

56. Interview with Joe Rocha, in Camplis.

57. Ibid. Translation by author.

58. John A. Robinson, papers pertaining to the U.S. Immigration Service, San Francisco, 1906–36, CHS.

59. Journals, n.d., Robinson papers, CHS.

60. For example, the October 15, 1938, edition.

61. "Spanish Folk Have Ball at Palace Hotel," *San Francisco Chronicle*, December 18, 1922.

62. See *Centro América*, July 9, 1921.

63. *Gráfico Internacional*, February 1937.

64. "Azteca Club of Women Holds First Reception," *San Francisco Chronicle*, June 30, 1912.

65. *La Crónica*, July 7, 1915.

66. *Polk's Crocker-Langley San Francisco City Directory*, 1859.

67. "Club to Celebrate Mexico Independence," *San Francisco Chronicle*, September 15, 1921.

68. "Woman Takes Gun to Court; Is Disarmed," *San Francisco Chronicle*, March 9, 1917.

69. "Celebración patriótica mexicana, conmemorando el 127o. aniversario de la independencia de México" (San Francisco: Sociedad Mutualista Mexicana Chapultepec and Club Azteca de Señoras, 1937), folder 2, "Events Concerning Mexicans," BANC.

70. *Hispano América*, January 20, 1918.

71. *Hispano América*, July 17, 1918, and August 24, 1918.

72. *Imparcial*, August 20, 1938.

73. "Actitud del Comité Unionista Centroamericano de San Francisco," *Centro América*, April 9, 1921.

74. *Centro América*, July 9, 1921.

75. Monroy, 62.

76. *Semanario Imparcial*, October 15, 1938.

77. For historical accounts of the roots, process, and effects of the labor systems affecting Mexican migrant workers, see Hernández (2010); and Gilbert G. González (2006).

78. Rosskam, 56.

79. Starr, 67.

80. Kerr (1939), 75.

81. Mullins, 8.

82. Sánchez, 19.

83. Frank J. Palomares, "Preliminary Report, January 1919," California Commission of Immigration and Housing, Department of Industrial Relations, Division of Immigration and Housing Records, 1912–39, folder 24, BANC.

84. Dorinda Moreno, interview with author, March 6, 2002, Concord, CA.

85. Ibid.

86. Echavarri interview.

87. Nash, 67–68.

88. Rios interview. In a city that still functioned with a high degree of social segregation, the housing at Hunter's Point may have created some of the first large-scale diverse communities.

89. Godfrey (1988), 140.

90. Martin del Campo, interview with Marilyn P. Davis, n.d., San Francisco, in Davis, 272–74, 276.

91. Figures compiled by International Institute, 1961, quoted in Stirling, 14. Out of a total of 2,481 immigrants to the city, coming from the six Central American nations of El Salvador, Nicaragua, Mexico, Costa Rica, Guatemala, Panama, and Honduras, 834 were Salvadoran.

92. Galeano, 112.

93. Ibid., 124–25.

94. Stirling, 4–5.

95. Ibid., 6. A majority of the interview subjects who form the sample of this study arrived in San Francisco by air.

96. Ibid., 7.

97. Ibid., 6.

98. Strong cultural rivalries exist between Nicaraguans and Mexicans, a reflection of which may possibly be observed in this tale of migration. See below.

99. U.S. Census charts for 1960, in Stirling, 1.

100. Files of Ayuda Católica para Emigrantes Puertorriqueños, Puerto Rican Migrants file, AASF.

101. Ibid. It should be noted that nine respondents failed to answer the question.

102. Ibid.

103. Godfrey (1988), 148.

104. Ibid., 140.

105. Rios interview.

106. Moreno interview.

107. U.S. Bureau of the Census (1973).

108. *Directory of Large Manufacturers, 1967–68*, San Francisco. For the purposes of discussion, the data in the directory was compiled by author. A spreadsheet was made listing all 98 of the manufacturers that listed 500 or more employees. Included were their addresses, principle industry, and head executive.

109. Josephine Petrini interview, in Camplis. Slaughterhouses were located primarily along 3rd Avenue in the part of town known as "Butchertown." In addition to Latinos, African Americans represented a major component of their labor force. See Tomás F. Sandoval.

110. *Directory of Large Manufacturers*.

111. San Francisco Conference on Religion, Race, and Social Concerns, 9.

112. Ibid., 9.

113. Rios interview.

114. Echavarri interview.

115. Petrini interview, in Camplis.

116. Moreno interview.

117. Rios interview.

118. Sanchez interview.

119. Interview with Helen Lara Cea, by author, October 10, 2001, Berkeley, CA.

120. *Polk's San Francisco City Directory*, 1689. This is further suggested in the community's collective memory.

121. Lara Cea interview.

122. Echavarri interview.

123. Schallert, 48. The quoted data is the sum of the individual parish totals of Spanish-surnamed parishioners.

124. Ibid., 49. The sixteen parishes, from least (10.1%) to highest (30%), were St. Patrick, Epiphany, St. Phillip, Corpus Christi, Visitación, St. Elizabeth, St. James, St. Paul, St. John, Mission Dolores, St. Teresa, St. Joseph, St. Kevin, St. Anthony, St. Charles, and St. Peter.

125. Ibid., 48, 661.

126. Burns (1994), 399.

127. Ibid.

128. Ibid., 412.

129. For an explanation of anticlericalism rooted to this class hostility, see Sánchez, 165.

130. Lynn Ludlow and Mireya Navarro, "The Mission: Poor Streets, Proud Streets," *San Francisco Examiner*, October 20, 1981, 6. Noted in Burns (1994), 399.

131. Interview with Monsignor James Flynn by Jeffrey Burns, January 30, 1989, 14, transcript, St. Peter's file, AASF.

132. Burns (1994), 435.

133. Interview with Deacon John Bourne by Jeffrey Burns, April 6, 1989, 1, transcript, St. Peter's file, AASF.

134. Interview with Isaura Michell de Rodríguez by Jeffrey Burns, July 17, 1989, 2, transcript, ibid.; Gina Marie Pitti, 2–3; Burns (1994), 416.

135. Letter from Right Reverend Leo T. Maher, chancellor secretary of the archdiocese, to Reverend Donald C. McDonnell, San Jose, October 15, 1959, Catholic Council for the Spanish Speaking file, 1959–67, AASF.

136. Their model was heavily informed by the work of Robert E. Lucey, whose Bishop's Committee for the Spanish Speaking provided the first national model of service.

137. Proposed Articles of Constitution for Archbishop's Committee for the Spanish Speaking, March 1960, Catholic Council for the Spanish Speaking file, 1959–67, AASF.

138. General report submitted to Joseph T. McGucken, archbishop of San Francisco, by Reverend William C. Hughes, Central Council for the Spanish Speaking, March 29, 1962, 1, ibid.

139. Dolan and Hinojosa, 221.

140. General report submitted to McGucken by Hughes, 4.

141. "Brief History of the Catholic Council for the Spanish Speaking," in "Scholarship Drive for Spanish Surname Seniors: A Project Proposal Submitted to the Joint Planning Council by the Catholic Council for the Spanish Speaking," 1972, Appendix, Archdiocesan Council for the Spanish Speaking file, 1968–76, AASF. The council as a whole was comprised of forty-three members.

142. Interview with Father Jim Casey by Jeffrey Burns, March 20, 1989, 3, transcript, St. Peter's file, AASF.

143. Report of the Catholic Council for the Spanish Speaking, May 1966, submitted by Eduardo Lopez to Archbishop Joseph T. McGucken, 7–10, Catholic Council for the Spanish Speaking file, 1959–67, AASF.

144. Burns (1994), 428.

145. Report of the Catholic Council for the Spanish Speaking, April 1965, submitted by Eduardo Lopez to Archbishop Joseph T. McGucken, 1–2, Catholic Council for the Spanish Speaking file, 1959–67, AASF.

146. Ibid.

147. Bokenkotter, 365. The three sessions of Vatican II began before and continued after the death of Pope John XXIII, the pontiff whose vision led to their occurrence. The first session lasted from October 11 to December 8, 1962; the new pope, Paul VI, opened the second session (September 29 to December 4, 1963); the third session took place between September 14 and November 21, 1964; and the fourth and final session began on September 14 and ended on December 8, 1965.

148. Ibid., 365–67.

149. Ibid., 365.

150. From *Lumen Gentium,* translated by Father Colman O'Neill, in Flannery, 358.

151. Casey interview, 2.

152. Ibid.

153. Interview with John Petroni by Jeffrey Burns, June 12, 1989, 1, transcript, St. Peter's file, AASF.

154. Burns (1994), 422.

155. See chapter 4.

156. Letter from Reverend James Casey, CCSS, to Joseph T. McGucken, archbishop of San Francisco, February 28, 1966, Catholic Council for the Spanish Speaking file, 1959–67, AASF.

157. Petroni interview, 1.

158. Casey interview, 5.

159. Petroni interview, 6.

160. Flynn interview, 1.

161. Interview with Juanita Alvarez by Jeffrey Burns, July 10, 1989, 10, transcript, St. Peter's file, AASF.

162. Ibid.

163. Bourne interview, 21.

164. Rodríguez interview, 2.

165. Ibid., 1.

166. Casey interview, 2–3.

167. Ibid., 4.

168. In 1970 a Peruvian celebration of El Señor de los Milagros—the Lord of the Miracles—was also included in the list of St. Peter's events. See letter from Roger Hernandez, CCSS, to Reverend Joseph T. McGucken, archbishop of San Francisco, October 19, 1970, Archdiocesan Council for the Spanish Speaking file, 1968–76, AASF.

169. LeFeber, 160–64.

170. Flynn interview, 14.

171. Report of the CCSS, April 1965, 3; Report of the CCSS, May 1966, 11–12; Burns (1994), 428. For a more specific discussion of the connection between the St. Peter's and Arriba Juntos, see below. For a more detailed account of the Mission Coalition Organization, and the role of organized religion in it, see chapter 4.

172. Letter from CCSS to Monsignor Bowe, 2.

173. Letter from Roger Hernandez, CCSS, to Archbishop Joseph T. McGucken, December 20, 1967, Catholic Council for the Spanish Speaking file, 1959–67, AASF.

174. Burns (1994), 428. More on the Latin American Unity Day below.

175. Petroni interview, 7.

176. Casey interview, 3.

177. Burns (1994), 396.

## CHAPTER 4

1. Ben Martinez, "The State of the Community," Second Annual Convention of the MCO, typescript, October 18, 1969, MMA.

2. Castells, 106.

3. Flores and Benmayor, 13.

4. David Braaten, "Close Up of the Mission," *San Francisco Chronicle*, April 4, 1962, and "Signs of a Renaissance in the Mission," *San Francisco Chronicle*, May 4, 1962.

5. U.S. Bureau of the Census (1924), 39–40.

6. David Braaten, "A New 'Citified' District," *San Francisco Chronicle*, May 3, 1962.

7. Braaten, "Close Up of the Mission."

8. Braaten, "Signs of a Renaissance."

9. Parish Historical Report, 1958, St. Peter's file, AASF.

10. Burns (1994), 416.

11. Schallert, 48–49. St. Peter's 6,267 is substantial when compared to the second most populous Latino parish, Mission Dolores, with 2,999.

12. U.S. Bureau of the Census (1973), 435. The prevailing consensus is that "Hispanics" were undercounted in the 1970s Census, in particular the undocumented immigrant segments of their population. The official figures record 69,633 "Persons of Spanish origin or descent" and another 3,667 "Persons of Puerto Rican birth or parentage."

13. Godfrey (1988), 113.

14. Godfrey (2004), 81.

15. David Braaten, "A Place of Many Voices," *San Francisco Chronicle*, May 1, 1962.

16. Interview with Father James Hagan by Jeffrey Burns, July 5, 1989, 3, transcript, St. Peter's file, AASF.

17. Ibid., 3.

18. Braaten, "Place of Many Voices," "Signs of a Renaissance," and "Slow Decay—and the Problem of Indifference," *San Francisco Chronicle*, May 5, 1962.

19. Braaten, "Place of Many Voices" and "Signs of a Renaissance."

20. Jack Burby, "City Making Slums a Good Investment," *San Francisco Chronicle*, October 6, 1958.

21. Mission Neighborhood Centers Inc., *A Self-Portrait of the Greater Mission District in Southeastern San Francisco* (San Francisco, 1960), 3-6, Mission Neighborhood Centers Collection, BANC.

22. Braaten, "Signs of a Renaissance."

23. Mike Miller (1981), 3.

24. "New Renewal Plan for Big S.F. Area," *San Francisco Chronicle*, January 25, 1963.

25. Dean St. Dennis, "Vast Plan for Overhauling San Francisco," *San Francisco Chronicle*, November 4, 1965.

26. Report of the Mission District Renewal Commission, cover letter to the Honorable John F. Shelley, February 8, 1966, MMA.

27. Sugrue (1996), 49.

28. St. Dennis, "Vast Plan."

29. Irving Kriegsfeld, quoted in Braaten, "Slow Decay."

30. "How Transit Plan Could Transform the Mission," *San Francisco Chronicle*, February 25, 1966.

31. Mike Miller (1974), 11.

32. San Francisco Department of Planning, San Francisco Redevelopment Agency, *A Survey and Planning Application for the Mission Street Survey Area* (May 1966); File 148-66-3, Archives of the San Francisco Board of Supervisors, San Bruno, CA.

33. Earl Raab, interview by Eleanor K. Glaser, 1996, transcript prepared as "Executive of the San Francisco Community Relations Council, 1951-1987; Advocate of Minority Rights and Democratic Pluralism," Regional Oral History Office, Berkeley, CA, BANC.

34. "Bay Area Mexicans Live amid Squalor," *San Francisco Chronicle*, May 4, 1953.

35. "Mexican Group Hails Church for Prop. 14 Fight," *San Francisco Chronicle*, October 4, 1964.

36. "Mexican-American Rally on Housing," *San Francisco Chronicle*, June 27, 1964.

37. "Mission District Tenants Unite," *San Francisco Chronicle*, June 4, 1965. Granados was one of two speakers at the groups' founding conference.

38. "Spanish-Speaking Citizens Group for Bay Area," *San Francisco Chronicle*, August 16, 1964.

39. "Velasquez Heads Latin Foundation," *San Francisco Chronicle*, February 5, 1967.

40. "Mexican-American Alliance in Row over Goodlett," *San Francisco Chronicle*, April 17, 1966.

41. "A Roundup of Political Activity," *San Francisco Chronicle*, May 6, 1966.

42. Sydney Kossen, "'Brown Power' Told to Master Anglo Politics," *San Francisco Chronicle*, March 19, 1967.

43. Soto, 83.

44. Mike Miller (1974), 11; Arriba Juntos, *Annual Report, 2005-2006*, 2006.

45. Eduardo Sandoval, interview with author, August 15, 2007, South San Francisco, digital recording.

46. Self, *American Babylon*, 179.

47. Sugrue (2008), 365, 367.

48. Alinsky, 41-47.

49. Soto, 1.

50. Eduardo Sandoval interview.

51. Soto, 85.

52. Braaten, "Close Up of the Mission."

53. "'Racial Wound Must Be Healed,'" *San Francisco Chronicle*, August 25, 1963.

54. "Mexican-American Rally on Housing"; Soto, 86.

55. "Mission District Tenants Unite"; Mike Miller (1974), 10-11.

56. Sharon Gold, "The Story of a Fight against Redevelopment in the Mission District of San Francisco," report of the Mission Council on Redevelopment, 1966, 2, MMA.

57. Ibid.

58. Mike Miller (1974), 15; "Standoff on Renewal of Inner Mission," *San Francisco Chronicle*, October 7, 1966; Gold, "Story of a Fight," 3.

59. Mike Miller (1974), 15.

60. "Standoff on Renewal."

61. San Francisco Board of Supervisors, *Journal of Proceedings* 61, no. 53 (December 19, 1966): 951.

62. "Protest of Mission Redevelopment Plan," *San Francisco Chronicle*, December 17, 1966.

63. Mike Miller (1974), 24.

64. Jackson, 412.

65. Mike Miller (1974), 25.

66. "Mission Debate on Model City," *San Francisco Chronicle*, May 10, 1968.

67. "A Brief History of the Mission Coalition Organization," paper written for distribution within the Mission, July 9, 1970, 1, MMA.

68. Soto, 35.

69. Mike Miller interview (2001).

70. "S.F. Will Get 'Model Cities' Planning Funds," *San Francisco Chronicle*, September 6, 1968.

71. "Brief History of the Mission Coalition," 3.

72. Some derided the group as "poverty pimps." Jim Queen, interview with author, July 25, 2007, San Francisco, digital recording.

73. "Cesar Chavez Habla: His Speech to the Coalition Convention," *La Nueva Misión* 2, no. 10 (November 1968): 7.

74. "Mission Coalition's Fighting Mad Start," *San Francisco Chronicle*, October 5, 1968.

75. Ibid.

76. Mike Miller interview (2001).

77. Mike Miller (1974), 31.

78. "Brief History of the Mission Coalition," 3.

79. Support was not unanimous, however. Latino realtors, for example, did not agree with the MTU's protenant stance.

80. Mike Miller (1974), 33.

81. "Mission Group's Tough Demands," *San Francisco Chronicle*, November 4, 1968.

82. Fernandez, 255.

83. Helen Lara Cea, interview with author, October 4, 2001, San Francisco.

84. "Brief History of the Mission Coalition," 2. The formal list grew over time, including both Italians and Irish who did not identify with the term *Anglo*.

85. Mike Miller interview (2000).

86. Ibid.

87. Ibid.

88. Ibid.

89. Ibid.

90. Scott Blakey, "Mission Plan Clears One Hurdle," *San Francisco Chronicle*, May 10, 1969.

91. Russ Cone, "Stormy Hearing on Mission Model Cities," *San Francisco Examiner*, September 17, 1969.

92. Petitions of the San Francisco Fairness League and the Mission Coalition Organization, respectively, located in File 401-69-1, archives of the San Francisco Board of Supervisors.

93. Blakey, "Mission Plan."

94. Resolutions 838-69 and 377-68, in San Francisco Board of Supervisors, *Journal of Proceedings* 64, no. 48 (December 1, 1969): 974.

95. Joel Tlumak, "MCO Impresses Top Reagan Aide," *San Francisco Examiner*, July 19, 1970.

96. Mike Miller (1981), 6.

97. Ben Martinez, memo to Lou White, November 24, 1969, MMA.

98. Ibid.

99. Ben Martinez, "The State of the Community," Second Annual Convention of the MCO, typescript, October 18, 1969, MMA.

100. Pulido, 177.

101. Ben Martinez, "My People: The Mission District," text of the remarks of Ben Martinez to the Twenty-Third Annual Democratic Club of San Francisco Meeting, 10, MMA.

102. Ibid.

103. Soto, 8-9.

104. Mike Miller (2009), 261-62.

105. Piven and Cloward, 32.

106. Soto, 81.

107. Mike Miller interview (2001).

## CHAPTER 5

1. Steve Arcelona, interview with author, July 26, 2007, San Francisco, digital recording.

2. Ibid.

3. "Policeman Shot to Death in S.F.," *San Francisco Chronicle*, May 2, 1969; "Youths Kill an S.F. Policeman—Wild Siege at Shooting Scene," *San Francisco Chronicle*, May 2, 1969; "Los Siete de la Raza," *Good Times*, August 7, 1969; Heins, 141-43.

4. "Los Siete de la Raza," *Good Times*.

5. *¡Basta Ya¡*, May 16, 1971.

6. Ferreira (2011), 31.

7. Ward, 134.

8. Pulido, 59-60.

9. Ibid., 59.

10. U.S. Bureau of the Census (1973), 20.

11. U.S. Bureau of the Census (1943), 542; U.S. Bureau of the Census (1953), 7.

12. Luis Alvarez, 19.

13. Acuña, 256.

14. Interview with Sam Rios, by author, July 2, 2002, Sacramento, CA, tape recording. Rios is careful not to conflate "*pachuco*" with "zoot suiter" in the cultural sense, instead mirroring the term's usage in the parlance and research of the time. See Delgado and Griffith.

15. Goodlett testimony, in San Francisco Mayor's Committee on Human Relations, 5.

16. Rios interview.

17. Rios interview.

18. Kelley (1989), 163.

19. Self, "Negro Leadership," 98.

20. Statement by Alvin I. Fine, in San Francisco Mayor's Committee on Human Relations, 57-58.

21. "Parental Evaluations of the S.F. Public Schools," San Francisco Unified School District Archives, box 78, folder 17, SFPL.

22. San Francisco Mayor's Committee on Human Relations, 49.

23. "Cross Burns at Home of S.F. Negro," *San Francisco Chronicle*, September 27, 1956.

24. "S.F. Cross-Burning Believed Juvenile Prank," *San Francisco Chronicle*, September 28, 1956.

25. "7 Boys Admit S.F. Fiery Cross 'Prank,'" *San Francisco Chronicle*, September 29, 1956.

26. Elba Sanchez, interview by author, June 26, 2007, San Francisco, digital recording.

27. Sanchez interview.

28. Manuel Vasquez, interview by author, August 17, 2007, Oakland, CA, digital recording.

29. Esperanza Echavarri, interview with author, October 1, 2007, digital recording.

30. Ibid.

31. Ibid.

32. Debra Varner, interview with author, July 30, 2007, San Francisco, digital recording.

33. Arcelona interview.

34. Herrera (1991), 179, 181.

35. Ibid., 181.

36. Pulido, 24.

37. Omer Mixon, interview by author, August 3, 1995, San Francisco, tape recording.

38. "600 Wetbacks Seized in City, Valley Raids," *San Francisco Chronicle*, June 14, 1954; "10,368 Returned to Mexico in Wetback Roundup," *San Francisco Chronicle*, July 8, 1954.

39. Arcelona interview.

40. Notes on the Preliminary Priest's Conference on Problems of the Spanish-Speaking of the Archdiocese of San Francisco, January 5, 1949, Missionary Apostolate file, 1948–60, Donald McDonnell Papers, box 2, AASF.

41. Dolan and Hinojosa, 216.

42. Levy, 89.

43. "Growers Hit Church for Union Stand," *San Francisco Chronicle*, June 11, 1966.

44. Echavarri interview.

45. Ibid.

46. Sanchez interview.

47. Murch, 334–41.

48. Sugrue (2008), 342–43.

49. Allen, 82.

50. Ibid., 83.

51. Ibid., 87.

52. Maitland Zane, "Shocking Race Report on S.F.," *San Francisco Chronicle*, April 26, 1968.

53. Martin Luther King Jr., remarks to press, August 10, 1967, KPIX News, San Francisco, available at https://diva.sfsu.edu/collections/sfbatv/bundles/190083.

54. Sugrue (2008), 325.

55. San Francisco Police Department.

56. Ibid., ii.

57. Ibid., iii, 79–80. The arrests are only broken down into the two categories "White" and "Negro," thereby making it impossible to calculate how many of those arrests were of Latinos or Latinas.

58. "A Suspicion—and Chaos Followed," *San Francisco Chronicle*, September 29, 1966.

59. San Francisco Police Department, 4–7; Hippler.

60. San Francisco Police Department, 7.

61. Ibid., 12–13.

62. "Mission High Closes Doors" and "Sears on Mission Shuts Early 'to Protect Staff,' " *San Francisco Chronicle*, September 29, 1966.

63. "Uneasy Calm after Long Day of Violence," *San Francisco Chronicle*, September 29, 1966.

64. Alvin A. Rosenfeld, "The Friendly Fuzz," *The Nation*, April 21, 1969; Mary Ellen Leary, "San Francisco: The Trouble with Troubleshooting," *Atlantic Monthly*, March 1969.

65. San Francisco Conference on Religion, Race, and Social Concerns, 1.

66. Roger Alvarado, quoted in Ferreira (2011), 33.

67. Nelson, 15.

68. Kelley (2000), 27.

69. San Francisco Police Department, 13.

70. "Status Ranking of High School," 2–3, and "Social Reputation Study Socially Destructive Groups in the School Population," 1–6, in *Student Life Study Mission High School*, report completed by selected members of the faculty under the direction of Marie Fielder, January 1960, San Francisco Unified School District Archival Collection, box 53, folder 5, SFPL.

71. *Student Life Study Mission High School*, 68.

72. Jones and Norberg, 20.

73. "Trouble at Mission High," *San Francisco Chronicle*, April 18, 1968; "More Cops for Mission High," *San Francisco Chronicle*, April 19, 1968.

74. "The End of a Crack Team," *San Francisco Chronicle*, May 2, 1969.

75. Heins, 65–68; Ferreira (2002), 34.

76. Arriba Juntos, *Annual Report, 2005–2006*, 2006; Mike Miller (2009), 73.

77. Jim Queen, interview with author, July 25, 2007, San Francisco, digital recording.

78. See chapter 4.

79. Queen interview.

80. Leahy, 16–20.

81. "Two at S.F. State Claim Racial Firing," *San Francisco Chronicle*, March 6, 1968; Lance Gilmore, "California Colleges Open Up for Minorities," *San Francisco Chronicle*, August 5, 1968.

82. "No Teaching Duties, 'Idle' S.F. State Militant," *San Francisco Chronicle*, September 9, 1968.

83. See Barlow and Shapiro.

84. Leahy, 21–22; "Demands and Explanations," list of the BSU demands, November 1969, available at SF State College Strike Collection, https://diva.sfsu.edu/collections/strike/bundles/187909.

85. Leahy, 29.

86. See Umemoto, which shows that Asian American groups, as they participated in the strike and co-led the TWLF, also underwent transformations in their political identities.

87. Interview with Dorinda Moreno, by author, March 6, 2002, Concord, CA, tape recording.

88. Barlow and Shapiro, 159.

89. Ibid., 157.

90. Ibid.; Umemoto, 20.

91. Umemoto, 20.

92. Barlow and Shapiro, 258–65.

93. Echavarri interview.

94. Dr. Carlton Goodlett, press conference, c. 1968, San Francisco. Footage from KPIX News, available from https://diva.sfsu.edu/collections/sfbatv/bundles/187307.

95. Mike Miller (2009), 88.

96. Ibid., 87–88.

97. Heins, 83.

98. Leahy, 27.

99. Moreno interview.

100. Ibid.

101. Ibid.

102. Ibid.

103. Garcia, 1–16.

104. Anna Nieto Gomez, "La Feminista," *Encuentro Femenil* 1, no. 2 (1974), in García, 87.

105. Dorinda Moreno, "Concilio Mujeres: A Thesis Paper," San Francisco, n.d. Courtesy of Dorinda Moreno. Maylei Blackwell argues that Chicana feminism "functioned as a parallel counter public within the movement as Chicana activists multiplied the subjects enlisted in the Chicano Movement's project of liberation."

106. In Napa, she taught at Napa Junior College, which became Napa Valley College; in Fremont, she taught at Ohlone College.

107. Moreno interview. Concilio Mujeres published its own newspaper, *La Razón Mestiza*, and served as a force in Northern California Chicana/o and Latina/o politics. At the community level, it remained active until the 1980s.

108. Blackwell, 155. She also argues that this is the foundation of a "Chicana counterpublic." See ibid., chap. 4.

109. Moreno interview.

110. Ibid.

111. Interview with Helen Lara Cea, October 2, 2001, Berkeley, CA.

112. Jones and Norberg, 20.

113. Ibid.

114. Heins, 26–27.

115. Jones and Norberg, 20.

116. Ibid.

117. "Los Siete de la Raza," *Good Times.*

118. Ibid.

119. "Youths Kill an S.F. Policeman." That the initial reports listed only three of the seven worked to the advantage of the defendants at trial.

120. "Los Siete de la Raza," *Good Times.*

121. "Youths Kill an S.F. Policeman" and "Huge Search for Killers of Policeman," *San Francisco Chronicle*, May 3, 1969.

122. "The Angry Suspect," *San Francisco Chronicle*, May 8, 1969.

123. Ferreira (2011), 32–33; Heins, 52.

124. "Los Siete de la Raza," *¡Basta Ya!*, August 16, 1969; Heins, 87–104.

125. "Los Siete de la Raza," *Good Times.*

126. Heins, 161; Ferreira (2011), 35.

127. Heins, 162.

128. *¡Basta Ya!*, July 17, 1969.

129. "Television Is Not Free," *¡Basta Ya!*, August 16, 1969.

130. "To All Brown Brothers in Nam," *¡Basta Ya!*, September 20, 1969.

131. *¡Basta Ya!*, September 20, 1969.

132. See advertisement, *¡Basta Ya!*, September 20, 1969, 2; "Young Lords Liberate Church," *¡Basta Ya!*, August 16, 1969, 7; "Pigs Vamp on Red Brothers," *¡Basta Ya!*, September 6, 1969, 3; and "Latin American Struggles," *¡Basta Ya!*, September 20, 1969, 8.

133. "Los Siete de la Raza," *Good Times*.

134. Mike Miller (2009), 171–72.

135. Heins, 162.

136. Ibid., 163.

137. Interview with Father James Hagan by Jeffrey Burns, July 5, 1989, 18, transcript, St. Peter's file, AASF.

138. "La Raza Feeds Her Children," *¡Basta Ya!*, September 6, 1969, 4; Hagan interview, 18; Heins, 163.

139. Heins, 159–69, 191–201; Ferreira (2011), 37–38.

140. Ferreira (2011), 39.

141. *¡Basta Ya!*, various editions.

142. *¡Basta Ya!*, July 17, 1969.

143. Heins, 170.

144. Muñoz, 191–202.

145. "Third World," *¡Basta Ya!*, July 1969.

146. Mirabal, 9.

### EPILOGUE

1. Gabriela Arreola, St. Peter's Housing Committee, public testimony, San Francisco Board of Supervisors, July 17, 2007, San Francisco.

2. Jill Shenker, La Raza Centro Legal, public testimony, San Francisco Board of Supervisors, July 17, 2007, San Francisco.

3. Arreola testimony.

4. Godfrey (1997), 316.

5. My thinking here is derived from Pérez, xv.

6. "Altered State: A Counterculture Legend, Writer Ken Kesey's Life Is a Little More Subdued These Days," *Albany (NY) Times Union*, April 29, 2001.

7. Espiritu (1992), 10.

8. Luis Granados, quoted in John M. Glionns, "Dot-Com Boom Makes S.F. a War Zone," *Los Angeles Times*, October 3, 2000.

# References

## ARCHIVES AND COLLECTIONS

Archives of the Archdiocese of San Francisco, St. Patrick Seminary, Menlo Park, CA
Archives of the San Francisco Board of Supervisors, San Bruno, CA
Bancroft Library, University of California, Berkeley, CA
California Historical Society, North Baker Library, San Francisco, CA
Mike Miller personal archives, San Francisco, CA
North Baker Research Library, California Historical Society, San Francisco, CA
San Francisco History Center, San Francisco Public Library, San Francisco, CA

## INTERVIEWS

Alvarez, Juanita. Interview by Jeffrey Burns. Transcript, July 10, 1989.
Arcelona, Steve. Interview with author. Digital recording, July 26, 2007. San Francisco, CA.
Bourne, John. Interview by Jeffrey Burns. Transcript, April 6, 1989.
Casey, Jim. Interview by Jeffrey Burns. Transcript, March 20, 1989.
Cea, Helen Lara. Interview by author. Digital recording, October 4 and 10, 2001. San Francisco, CA.
Echavarri, Esperanza. Interview by author. Digital recording, October 1, 2007. San Francisco, CA.
Flynn, James. Interview by Jeffrey Burns. Transcript, January 30, 1989.
Hagan, James. Interview by Jeffrey Burns. Transcript, July 5, 1989.
Miller, Mike. Interviews by author. Digital recording, October 4, 2000, and January 12, 2001. San Francisco, CA.
Moreno, Dorinda. Interview by author. Digital recording, March 6, 2002. Concord, CA.
Petroni, John. Interview by Jeffrey Burns. Transcript, June 12, 1989.
Queen, Jim. Interview by author. Digital recording, July 25, 2007. San Francisco, CA.
Rios, Sam. Interview by author. Digital recording, July 2, 2002. Sacramento, CA.
Sanchez, Elba. Interview by author. Digital recording, July 25, 2007. San Francisco, CA.
Sandoval, Eduardo. Interview by author. Digital recording, August 15, 2007. South San Francisco, CA.
Varner, Debra. Interview by author. Digital recording, July 30, 2007. San Francisco, CA.
Vasquez, Manuel. Interview by author. Digital recording, August 17, 2007. San Francisco, CA.

## NEWSPAPERS AND MAGAZINES

The Alta California
Atlantic Monthly
La Azucena
La Bandera Mexicana
¡Basta Ya!
The California Star
Centro América
La Crónica

El Cronista
Good Times
Guadalajara
El Imparcial
The Monitor
  (San Francisco)
The Nation
La Nueva Misión

La República
San Francisco Call
San Francisco Chronicle
San Francisco Examiner
El Tecolote
La Voz de Chile
La Voz de Méjico

## FEDERAL, STATE, AND MUNICIPAL PUBLICATIONS

Department of Homeland Security. *Annual Report.* Washington, DC: Office of
Immigration Statistics, August 2010.

Governor C. C. Young's Mexican Fact-Finding Committee. *Mexicans in California.* San
Francisco: California State Printing Office, 1930.

San Francisco Board of Supervisors. *Journal of Proceedings* 61, no. 53. San Francisco:
Government Printing Office, 1966.

———. *Journal of Proceedings* 64, no. 48. San Francisco: Government Printing Office,
1969.

———. Transcript of public testimony, July 17, 2007, San Francisco.

San Francisco Conference on Religion, Race, and Social Concerns. *San Francisco, a City
in Crisis: A Report to the Churches and Synagogues.* San Francisco, 1968.

San Francisco Department of Health. *Report of the Health Officer of the City and County
of San Francisco.* San Francisco: Department of Health.

San Francisco Mayor's Committee on Human Relations. *Report.* San Francisco, 1949. BANC.

San Francisco Police Department. *128 Hours: A Report of the Civil Disturbance in the City
and County of San Francisco, 1966.* San Francisco: San Francisco Police Department,
1966.

Stirling, James. "Nicaraguans in San Francisco: A Pilot Study." San Francisco: San
Francisco Human Rights Commission, 1964.

U.S. Bureau of the Census. *The Seventh Census of the United States: 1850.* Washington,
DC: Government Printing Office, 1853.

———. *Population of the United States in 1860.* Washington, DC: Government Printing
Office, 1864.

———. *Statistics of the Population of the United States at the Tenth Census, June 1, 1880.*
Washington, DC: Government Printing Office, 1883.

———. *Fourteenth Census of the United States: State Compendium, California.*
Washington, DC: Government Printing Office, 1924.

———. *Fifteenth Census of the United States—1930—Population,* vol. 3, pt. 1, sec. 3.
Washington, DC: Government Printing Office, 1932.

———. *Sixteenth Census of the United States—1940—Population,* vol. 2, pt. 1, sec. 6.
Washington, DC: Government Printing Office, 1943.

———. *Census of the Population: 1950,* vol. 3, pt. 4, sec. 4. Washington, DC: Government
Printing Office, 1953.

———. *1970 Census of Population,* vol. 1, pt. 6. Washington, DC: Government Printing
Office, 1973.

U.S. House of Representatives. *H.R. Doc. 351.* 25th Congress, 2nd Session. Washington, DC, 1838.

## BOOKS

Acuña, Rodolfo. *Occupied America: A History of Chicanos,* 3rd ed. New York: Harper & Row, 1988.

Alarcón, Norma, et al., eds. *Chicana Critical Issues.* Berkeley, CA: Third Woman, 1993.

Allen, Robert L. *Black Awakening in Capitalist America.* Trenton, NJ: African World, 1990.

Almaguer, Tomás. *Racial Fault Lines: The Historical Origins of White Supremacy in California.* Berkeley: University of California Press, 1994.

Alvarez, Luis. *The Power of the Zoot: Youth Culture and Resistance during World War II.* Berkeley: University of California Press, 2008.

Anderson, Benedict. *Imagined Communities: Reflections on the Origin and Spread of Nationalism.* New York: Verso, 1983.

Ashbury, Herbert. *The Barbary Coast: An Informal History of the San Francisco Underworld.* New York: Alfred A. Knopf, 1933.

*A. W. Morgan & Co.'s San Francisco Directory.* San Francisco, 1852.

Badillo, David A. *Latinos and the New Immigrant Church.* Baltimore: Johns Hopkins University Press, 2006.

Balderrama, Francisco E., and Raymond Rodríguez, eds. *Decade of Betrayal: Mexican Repatriation in the 1930s.* Albuquerque: University of New Mexico Press, 2006.

Bancroft, Hubert Howe. *History of California,* vols. 3, 5, and 6. San Francisco: History Company, 1886.

Barlow, William, and Peter Shapiro. *An End to Silence: The San Francisco State College Student Movement in the 60's.* New York: Bobbs-Merrill, 1971.

Barry, T. A., and B. A. Patten. *Men and Memories of San Francisco, in the "Spring of '50."* San Francisco: A. L. Bancroft, 1873.

Becker, Howard S. *Culture and Civility in San Francisco.* New Brunswick, NJ: Transaction, 1971.

Beilharz, Edwin A., and Carlos U. López, eds. and trans. *We Were 49ers! Chilean Accounts of the California Gold Rush.* Pasadena, CA: Ward Ritchie, 1976.

Benemann, William, ed. *A Year of Mud and Gold: San Francisco in Letters and Diaries, 1849–1850.* Lincoln: University of Nebraska Press, 1999.

Berglund, Barbara. *Making San Francisco American: Cultural Frontiers in the Urban West, 1846–1906.* Lawrence: University of Kansas Press, 2007.

Bishop, William Henry. *Old Mexico and Her Lost Provinces.* New York: Harper & Brothers, Franklin Square, 1883.

Blackwell, Maylei. *¡Chicana Power! Contested Histories of Feminism in the Chicano Movement.* Austin: University of Texas Press, 2011.

Bokenkotter, Thomas. *A Concise History of the Catholic Church.* Rev. and expanded ed. New York: Image, Doubleday, 1990.

Boyd, Nan Alamilla. *Wide Open Town: A History of Queer San Francisco to 1965.* Berkeley: University of California Press, 2003.

Broussard, Albert S. *Black San Francisco: The Struggle for Racial Equality in the West, 1900–1954.* Lawrence: University of Kansas Press, 1993.

Browning, Peter, ed. *The Discovery of San Francisco Bay: The Portolá Expedition of 1769–1770*. Lafayette, CA: Great West, 1992.

Burns, Jeffrey M. *San Francisco: A History of the Archdiocese of San Francisco*. Vol. 2, *1885–1945*. Strasbourg, France: Du Signe, n.d.

Camarillo, Albert. *Chicanos in California: A History of Mexican Americans in California*. San Francisco: Boyd & Fraser, 1984.

———. *Chicanos in a Changing Society: From Mexican Pueblos to American Barrios in Santa Barbara and Southern California, 1848–1930*. Cambridge: Harvard University Press, 1996.

Castells, Manuel. *The City and the Grassroots: A Cross-Cultural Theory of Urban Social Movements*. Berkeley: University of California Press, 1983.

Chávez-García, Miroslava. *Negotiating Conquest: Gender and Power in California, 1770s to 1880s*. Tucson: University of Arizona Press, 2004.

Curtin, Philip D. *Cross-Cultural Trade in World History*. Cambridge: Cambridge University Press, 1984.

Dana, Richard Henry, Jr. *Two Years before the Mast: A Personal Narrative of Life at Sea*. New York: Modern Library, 2001.

Daniels, Douglas H. *Pioneer Urbanites: A Social and Cultural History of Black San Francisco*. Philadelphia: Temple University Press, 1980.

Dávila, Arlene. *Latinos, Inc.: The Marketing and Making of a People*. Berkeley: University of California Press, 2001.

Davis, Marilyn P. *Mexican Voices/American Dreams: An Oral History of Mexican Migration to the United States*. New York: Henry Holt, 1990.

De Genova, Nicholas, and Ana Y. Ramos-Zayas. *Latino Crossings: Mexicans, Puerto Ricans, and the Politics of Race and Citizenship*. New York: Routledge, 2003.

de la Torre, Adela, and Beatriz Pesquera, eds. *Building with Our Hands: New Directions in Chicana Studies*. Berkeley: University of California Press, 1993.

Delgado, Manuel Ruben. *The Last Chicano: A Mexican American Experience*. Bloomington, IN: Author House, 2009.

de Massey, Ernest. *A Frenchman in the Gold Rush: The Journal of Ernest de Massey, Argonaut of 1849*. Translated by Marguerite Eyer Wilbur. San Francisco: California Historical Society, 1927.

di Leonardo, Micaela. *The Varieties of Ethnic Experience: Kinship, Class, and Gender among California Italian-Americans*. Ithaca, NY: Cornell University Press, 1984.

Dolan, Jay P., and Gilberto Hinojosa, eds. *Mexican Americans and the Catholic Church, 1900–1965*. Notre Dame, IN: University of Notre Dame Press, 1994.

Douglass, John. *The California Idea and American Higher Education. 1860 to the 1960 Master Plan*. Stanford, CA: Stanford University Press, 2000.

Elbaum, Max. *Revolution in the Air: Sixties Radicals Turn to Lenin, Mao and Che*. New York: Verso, 2002.

Espiritu, Yen Le. *Asian American Panethnicity*. Philadelphia: Temple University Press, 1992.

———. *Home Bound: Filipino American Lives across Cultures, Communities, and Countries*. Berkeley: University of California Press, 2003.

Ethnington, Philip J. *The Public City: The Political Construction of Urban Life in San Francisco, 1850–1900*. Berkeley: University of California Press, 2001.

Fisher, Walter M. *The Californians*. London: MacMillan, 1876.

Flannery, Austin, ed. *Vatican Council II: The Conciliar and Post-Conciliar Documents*. Rev. ed. Northport, NY: Costello, 1987.

Flores, William V., and Rina Benmayor, eds. *Latino Cultural Citizenship: Claiming Identity, Space, and Rights*. Boston: Beacon, 1997.

Fradkin, Philip L. *The Great Earthquake and Firestorms of 1906: How San Francisco Nearly Destroyed Itself*. Berkeley: University of California Press, 2005.

Galaz, Fernando A. *Dejaron huella en el Hermosillo de ayer y hoy: Crónicas de Hermosillo de 1700 a 1967*. Hermosillo, Mexico: Published by author, 1971.

Galeano, Eduardo. *Open Veins of Latin America: Five Centuries of the Pillage of a Continent*. Translated by Cedric Belfrage. New York: Monthly Review Press, 1972.

Garcia, Alma M. *Chicana Feminist Thought: The Basic Historical Writings*. New York: Routledge, 1997.

Godfrey, Brian J. *Neighborhoods in Transition: The Making of San Francisco's Ethnic and Nonconformist Communities*. Berkeley: University of California Press, 1988.

Gómez, Laura E. *Manifest Destinies: The Making of the Mexican American Race*. New York: New York University Press, 2007.

Gómez Quiñones, Juan. *Chicano Politics: Reality and Promise, 1940–1990*. Albuquerque: University of New Mexico Press, 1990.

González, Gilbert G. *Mexican Consuls and Labor Organizing: Imperial Politics in the American Southwest*. Austin: University of Texas Press, 1999.

———. *Culture of Empire: American Writers, Mexico, and Mexican Immigrants, 1880–1930*. Austin: University of Texas Press, 2004.

———. *Guest Workers or Colonized Labor? Mexican Labor Migration to the United States*. Boulder, CO: Paradigm, 2006.

González, Gilbert G., and Raul A. Fernandez, eds. *A Century of Chicano History: Empire, Nations, and Migration*. New York: Routledge, 2003.

Gonzalez, Juan. *Harvest of Empire: A History of Latinos in America*. New York: Penguin, 2000.

Grandin, Greg. *Empire's Workshop: Latin America, the United States, and the Rise of the New Imperialism*. New York: Metropolitan, 2006.

Griffith, Beatrice. *American Me*. New York: Houghton Mifflin, 1948.

Gutiérrez, David G. *Walls and Mirrors: Mexican Americans, Mexican Immigrants, and the Politics of Ethnicity*. Berkeley: University of California Press, 1995.

Gyory, Andrew. *Closing the Gate: Race, Politics, and the Chinese Exclusion Act*. Chapel Hill: University of North Carolina Press, 1998.

Heins, Marjorie. *Strictly Ghetto Property: The Story of Los Siete de la Raza*. Berkeley, CA: Ramparts, 1972.

Heizer, Robert F., and Alan J. Almquist. *The Other Californians: Prejudice and Discrimination under Spain, Mexico, and the United States to 1920*. Berkeley: University of California Press, 1977.

Hernández, Kelly Lytle. *Migra! A History of the U.S. Border Patrol*. Berkeley: University of California Press, 2010.

Hernández Cornejo, Roberto. *Los chilenos en San Francisco de California (Recuerdos históricos de la emigración por los descubrimientos del oro, iniciada en 1848)*. Vols. 1 and 2. Valparaíso, Chile: San Rafael, 1930.

Holliday, J. S. *The World Rushed In: The California Gold Rush Experience.* New York: Simon and Schuster, 1981.

Issel, William, and Robert W. Cherny. *San Francisco, 1865–1931: Politics, Power, and Urban Development.* Berkeley: University of California Press, 1986.

Jameson, Fredric, and Masao Miyoshi, eds. *The Cultures of Globalization.* Durham, NC: Duke University Press, 1998.

Johnson, Susan Lee. *Roaring Camp: The Social World of the California Gold Rush.* New York: W. W. Norton, 2000.

Katz, Michael B., ed. *The "Underclass" Debate: Views from History.* Princeton, NJ: Princeton University Press, 1993.

Kelley, Robin D. G. *Race Rebels: Culture, Politics, and the Black Working Class.* New York: Free Press, 1996 [1994].

Kerner, Otto, et al. *Report of the National Advisory Commission on Civil Disorders.* New York: E. P. Dutton, 1968.

Kerr, Clark. *The Gold and the Blue: A Personal Memoir of the University of California, 1949–1967.* Berkeley: University of California Press, 2001.

Kimball, Charles. *The San Francisco City Directory.* San Francisco, 1850.

Laó-Montes, Agustín, and Arlene Dávila. *Mambo Montage: The Latinization of New York.* New York: Columbia University Press, 2001.

*LeCount & Strong's San Francisco City Directory for 1854.* San Francisco, 1854.

LeFeber, Walter. *Inevitable Revolutions: The United States in Central America.* New York: W. W. Norton, 1983.

Levy, Jacques E. *Cesar Chavez: Autobiography of La Causa.* Minneapolis: University of Minnesota Press, 2007 [1975].

Lipsitz, George. *American Studies in a Moment of Danger.* Minneapolis: University of Minnesota Press, 2001.

Lotchin, Roger W. *San Francisco, 1846–1856: From Hamlet to City.* Chicago: University of Illinois Press, 1997.

Maciel, David R., and Isidro D. Ortiz, eds. *Chicanas/Chicanos at the Crossroads: Social, Economic, and Political Change.* Tucson: University of Arizona Press, 1996.

Massey, Doreen. *Space, Place, and Gender.* Minneapolis: University of Minnesota Press, 1994.

Matovina, Timothy. *Guadalupe and Her Faithful: Latino Catholics in San Antonio, from Colonial Origins to the Present.* Baltimore: Johns Hopkins University Press, 2005.

Matovina, Timothy, and Gerald E. Poyo, eds. *¡Presente! U.S. Latino Catholics from Colonial Origins to the Present.* Maryknoll, NY: Orbis, 2000.

Mazón, Mauricio. *The Zoot-Suit Riots: The Psychology of Symbolic Annihilation.* Austin: University of Texas Press, 1984.

McGuinness, Aims. *Path of Empire: Panama and the California Gold Rush.* Ithaca, NY: Cornell University Press, 2008.

McWilliams, Carey. *California: The Great Exception.* Berkeley: University of California Press, 1999.

Menjívar, Cecilia. *Fragmented Ties: Salvadoran Immigrant Networks in America.* Berkeley: University of California Press, 2000.

Meyer, Michael C., and William L. Sherman. *The Course of Mexican History*, 5th ed. New York: Oxford University Press, 1995.

Miller, Mike. *An Organizer's Tale*. San Francisco: Michael J. Miller, 1974.

———. *A Community Organizer's Tale: People and Power in San Francisco*. Berkeley, CA: Heyday, 2009.

Miller, Robert Ryan. "Arms across the Border: United States Aid to Juárez during the French Intervention in Mexico." *Transactions of the American Philosophical Society*, vol. 63, pt. 6. Philadelphia: American Philosophical Society, 1973.

Mize, Ronald L., and Grace Peña Delgado. *Latino Immigrants in the United States*. Cambridge, UK: Polity, 2012.

Monaghan, Jays. *Chile, Peru, and the California Gold Rush of 1849*. Berkeley: University of California Press, 1973.

Monroy, Douglas. *Rebirth: Mexican Los Angeles from the Great Migration to the Great Depression*. Berkeley: University of California Press, 1999.

Mullins, William H. *The Depression and the Urban West Coast, 1929–1933: Los Angeles, San Francisco, Seattle, and Portland*. Bloomington: University of Indiana Press, 1991.

Muñoz, Carlos, Jr. *Youth, Identity, and Power: The Chicano Movement*. New York: Verso, 1989.

Murguía, Alejandro. *The Medicine of Memory: A Mexica Clan in California*. Austin: University of Texas Press, 2002.

Muscatine, Doris. *Old San Francisco: The Biography of a City from Early Days to the Earthquake*. New York: G. P. Putnam's Sons, 1975.

Nash, Gerald D. *The American West Transformed: The Impact of the Second World War*. Lincoln: University of Nebraska Press, 1985.

Ngai, Mae M. *Impossible Subjects: Illegal Aliens and the Making of Modern America*. Princeton, NJ: Princeton University Press, 2004.

Oboler, Suzanne. *Ethnic Labels, Latino Lives: Identity and the Politics of (Re)Presentation in the United States*. Minneapolis: University of Minnesota Press, 1995.

Padilla, Felix. *Latino Ethnic Consciousness: The Case of Mexican Americans and Puerto Ricans in Chicago*. Notre Dame, IN: University of Notre Dame Press, 1985.

Perales, Monica. *Smeltertown: Making and Remembering a Southwest Border Community*. Chapel Hill: University of North Carolina Press, 2010.

Pérez, Emma. *The Decolonial Imaginary: Writing Chicanas into History*. Bloomington: University of Indiana Press, 1999.

Pérez Rosales, Vicente. *California Adventure*. Translated by Edwin S. Morby and Arturo Torres-Rioseco. San Francisco: California Book Club, 1947.

Pierce, Hiram Dwight. *A Forty-niner Speaks; A Chronological Record of the Observations and Experiences of a New Yorker and His Adventures in Various Mining Localities in California, His Return Trip across Nicaragua, Including Several Descriptions of the Changes in San Francisco and Other Mining Centers from March 1849 to January 1851*. Sacramento: Sarah Wisewall Meyer, 1930.

Pitt, Leonard. *The Decline of the Californios: A Social History of the Spanish-Speaking Californians, 1846–1890*. Berkeley: University of California Press, 1998.

Pitti, Stephen J. *The Devil in Silicon Valley: Northern California, Race, and Mexican Americans*. Princeton, NJ: Princeton University Press, 2003.

Piven, Frances Fox, and Richard A. Cloward. *Poor People's Movements: Why They Succeed, How They Fail*. New York: Vintage, 1979.

*Polk's Crocker-Langley San Francisco City Directory*. San Francisco: R. L. Polk, 1930.

*Polk's San Francisco City Directory.* San Francisco: R. L. Polk, 1957.

Pulido, Laura. *Black, Brown, Yellow and Left: Radical Activism in Los Angeles.* Berkeley: University of California Press, 2006.

Ramírez, Salvador A., ed. *From New York to San Francisco via Cape Horn in 1849: The Gold Rush Voyage of the Ship "Pacific."* Carlsbad, CA: Tentacled, 1985.

Ricourt, Milagros, and Ruby Danta. *Hispanas de Queens: Latino Panethnicity in a New York City Neighborhood.* Ithaca, NY: Cornell University Press, 2003.

Roque-Ramírez, Horacio. *Queer Latino San Francisco: An Oral History, 1960s–1990s.* New York: Palgrave MacMillan, 2013.

Rosskam, Edwin. *San Francisco: West Coast Metropolis.* New York: Alliance, 1939.

Sandos, James A. *Converting California: Indians and Franciscans in the Missions.* New Haven: Yale University Press, 2004.

Sánchez, George J. *Becoming Mexican American: Ethnicity, Culture and Identity in Chicano Los Angeles.* New York: Oxford University Press, 1993.

Schallert, Eugene. *The Catholic Parishes: A Statistical Study of the Catholic Parishes of the City of San Francisco, 1960–65.* San Francisco: University of San Francisco, 1965.

Schoultz, Lars. *Beneath the United States: A History of U.S. Policy toward Latin America.* Cambridge: Harvard University Press, 1998.

Self, Robert O. *American Babylon: Race and the Struggle for Postwar Oakland.* Princeton, NJ: Princeton University Press, 2003.

Shah, Nayan. *Contagious Divides: Epidemics and Race in San Francisco's Chinatown.* Berkeley: University of California Press, 2001.

Smith, Robert Courtney. *Mexican New York: Transnational Lives of New Immigrants.* Berkeley: University of California Press, 2006.

Soulé, Frank, John H. Gihon, and James Nisbet. *The Annals of San Francisco.* Berkeley, CA: Berkeley Hills, 1999.

Starr, Kevin. *Endangered Dreams: The Great Depression in California.* New York: Oxford University Press, 1996.

Starr, Kevin, and Richard J. Orsi, eds. *Rooted in Barbarous Soil: People, Culture, and Community in Gold Rush California.* Berkeley: University of California Press, 2000.

Sugrue, Thomas J. *The Origins of the Urban Crisis: Race and Inequality in Postwar Detroit.* Princeton, NJ: Princeton University Press, 1996.

———. *Sweet Land of Liberty: The Forgotten Struggle for Civil Rights in the North.* New York: Random House, 2008.

Takaki, Ronald. *Strangers from a Different Shore: A History of Asian Americans.* New York: Penguin, 1989.

———. *A Different Mirror: A History of Multicultural America.* New York: Little, Brown and Company, 1993.

Taylor, Bayard. *El Dorado, or Adventures in the Path of Empire.* New York: G. P. Putnam's Sons, 1884.

Tinker Salas, Miguel. *In the Shadow of the Eagles: Sonora and the Transformation of the Border during the Porfiriato.* Berkeley: University of California Press, 1997.

Tomasi, Silvano M. *Piety and Power: The Role of the Italian Parishes in the New York Metropolitan Area, 1880–1930.* New York: Center for Migration Studies, 1975.

Treviño, Roberto R. *The Church in the Barrio: Mexican American Ethno-Catholicism in Houston.* Chapel Hill: University of North Carolina Press, 2006.

Valdivia, Angharad N., and Matt Garcia, eds. *Mapping Latina/o Studies: An Interdisciplinary Reader*. New York: Peter Lang, 2012.

Vigil, Ernesto B. *The Crusade for Justice: Chicano Militancy and the Government's War on Dissent*. Madison: University of Wisconsin Press, 1999.

Whalen, Carmen Teresa, and Víctor Vásquez-Hernández, eds. *The Puerto Rican Diaspora: Historical Perspectives*. Philadelphia: Temple University Press, 2005.

Wind, James P., and James W. Lewis, eds. *American Congregations*. Vol. 1, *Portraits of Twelve Religious Communities*. Chicago: University of Chicago Press, 1994.

Yung, Judy. Unbound Feet: A Social History of Chinese Women in San Francisco. Berkeley: University of California Press, 1995.

## ARTICLES, REPORTS, AND CHAPTERS

Alinsky, Saul D. "The War on Poverty—Political Pornography." *Journal of Social Issues* 21, no. 1 (1965): 41–47.

Amnesty International. *Jailed without Justice: Immigration Detention in the U.S.* March 2009.

Burns, Jeffrey M. "Qué es esto? The Transformation of St. Peter's Parish in the Mission, San Francisco, 1913-1990." In *American Congregations*, vol. 1, *Portraits of Twelve Religious Communities*, edited by James P. Wind and James W. Lewis. Chicago: University of Chicago Press, 1994: 396-463.

Cordova, Carlos B. "The Mission District: The Ethnic Diversity of the Latin American Enclave in San Francisco, Calif." *Journal of Raza Studies* 2, no. 1 (Summer/Fall 1989): 21–32.

Fernandez, Johanna. "Between Social Service Reform and Revolutionary Politics: The Young Lords, Late Sixties Radicalism, and Community Organizing in New York City." In *Freedom North: Black Freedom Struggles outside the South, 1940–1980*, edited by Jeanne F. Theoharis and Komozi Woodward. New York: Palgrave Macmillan, 2003: 255–86.

Ferreira, Jason M. " 'Within the Soul of a Human Rainbow': Los Siete, Black Panthers, and Third Worldism in San Francisco." In *Ten Years That Shook the City: San Francisco, 1968–1978*, edited by Chris Carlsson (with Lisa Ruth Elliott). San Francisco: City Lights Foundation Books, 2011: 30–47.

Foucrier, Annick. "Adventures on the California Coast: French Whalers from 1825 to 1848." *The Californians* (1990): 30–37.

Godfrey, Brian J. "Urban Development and Redevelopment in San Francisco." *Geographic Review* 87, no. 3 (July 1997): 309–33.

———. "Barrio under Siege: Latino Sense of Place in San Francisco, California." In *Hispanic Spaces, Latino Places: Community and Cultural Diversity in Contemporary America*, edited by Daniel D. Arreola. Austin: University of Texas Press, 2004: 79–102.

Goodman, John B., III. "The 1849 Gold Rush Fleet: The Magnolia." *Southern California Quarterly* 67, no. 1 (1985): 71–87.

Hayes-Bautista, David E., et al. "Empowerment, Expansion, and Engagement: *Las Juntas Patrióticas* in California, 1848–1869." *California History* 85, no. 1 (2007): 4–23.

Herrera, Juan Felipe. "Mission Street Manifesto: Circa 1959–1982 (Raza Writing in the Mission District-San Francisco)." *Guadalupe Review*, no. 1 (October 1991): 178–82.

———. "Riffs on Mission District Writers." In *Reclaiming San Francisco: History, Politics, Culture*, edited by James Brook, Chris Carlsson, and Nancy J. Peters. San Francisco: City Lights, 1998: 231–45.

Hippler, Arthur E. "The Game of Black and White at Hunter's Point." In *Culture and Civility in San Francisco*, edited by Howard S. Becker. New Brunswick, NJ: Transaction, 1971: 53–75.

Hornbeck, David. "The Patenting of California's Private Land Claims." *Geographical Review* 69, no. 4 (1979): 343–448.

Jackson, Thomas F. "The State, the Movement, and the Urban Poor: The War on Poverty and Political Mobilization in the 1960s." In *The "Underclass" Debate: Views from History*, edited by Michael B. Katz. Princeton, NJ: Princeton University Press, 1993: 403–39.

Jones, Jeff, and Doug Norberg. "Mission Rebellion." *The Movement* 5, no. 2 (1969): 20.

Joseph, Gilbert M. "Close Encounters: Towards a New Cultural History of U.S.-Latin American Relations." In *Close Encounters with Empire: Writing the Cultural History of U.S.-Latin American Relations*, edited by Gilbert M. Joseph, Catherine C. Legrand, and Ricardo D. Salvatorre. Durham, NC: Duke University Press, 1998: 3–46.

Kelley, Robin D. G. "The Riddle of the Zoot: Malcolm Little and Black Cultural Politics during World War II." In *Generations of Youth: Youth Cultures and History in Twentieth Century America*, edited by Joe Austin and Michael Nevin Willard. New York: New York University Press, 1989: 136–56.

———. "'Slangin' Rocks . . . Palestinian Style': Dispatches from the Occupied Zones of North America." In *Police Brutality: An Anthology*, edited by Jill Nelson. New York: W. W. Norton, 2000: 21–59.

Kemble, John Haskell. "The Transpacific Railroads, 1869–1915." *Pacific Historical Review* 18, no. 3 (1949): 331–43.

Leahy, Margaret. "On Strike! We're Gonna Shut It Down: The 1968–69 San Francisco State Strike." In *Ten Years That Shook the City: San Francisco, 1968–1978*, edited by Chris Carlsson (with Lisa Ruth Elliott). San Francisco: City Lights Foundation Books, 2011: 15–29.

Matovina, Timothy. "Hispanic Faith and Theology." *Journal of Family Ministry* 15, no. 3 (Fall 2001): 13–15.

Medina, Nitza C. "Rebellion in the Bay: California's First Puerto Ricans." *Centro: Journal of the Center of Puerto Rican Studies* 13 (Spring 2001): 84–95.

Mirabal, Nancy Raquel. "Geographies of Displacement: Latina/os, Oral History, and the Politics of Gentrification in San Francisco's Mission District." *Public Historian* 31, no. 2 (May 2009): 7–31.

Murch, Donna, "The Campus and the Street: Race, Migration, and the Origins of the Black Panther Party in Oakland, CA." *Souls* 9, no. 4 (2007): 333–45.

Murguía, Alejandro. "Poetry and Solidarity in the Mission District." In *Ten Years That Shook the City: San Francisco, 1968–1978*, edited by Chris Carlsson. San Francisco: City Lights, 2011: 61–70.

Nasatir, Abraham P. "Chileans in California during the Gold Rush Period and the Establishment of the Chilean Consulate." *California Historical Quarterly* 53 (Spring 1974): 52–70.

Odell, Kerry A. "The Integration of Regional and Interregional Capital Markets: Evidence from the Pacific Coast, 1883–1913." *Journal of Economic History* 49, no. 2 (June 1989): 297–310.

Pastor, Manuel, Jr. "Interdependence, Inequality, and Identity: Linking Latinos and Latin Americans." In *Borderless Borders: U.S. Latinos, Latin Americans, and the Paradox of Interdependence*, edited by Frank Bonilla, Edwin Meléndez, Rebecca Morales, and María de los Angeles Torres. Philadelphia: Temple University Press, 1998: 17–34.

Pew Hispanic Center. *Census 2010: Fifty Million Latinos, Hispanics Account for More than Half of Nation's Growth in Past Decade.* Washington, DC, March 24, 2011.

———. *U.S. Hispanic Country-of-Origin Counts for Nation, Top 30 Metropolitan Areas.* Washington, DC, May 26, 2011.

Portelli, Alessandro. "The Peculiarities of Oral History." *History Workshop Journal* 12, no. 1 (Autumn 1981): 96–107.

Potoc, Mark. "Anti-Latino Hate Crimes Rise for Fourth Year in a Row." Hatewatch, Southern Poverty Law Center blog, October 29, 2008. http://www.splcenter.org/blog/2008/10/29/anti-latino-hate-crimes-rise-for-fourth-year/ (November 14, 2008).

Rast, Raymond W. "The Cultural Politics of Tourism in San Francisco's Chinatown, 1882–1917." *Pacific Historical Review* 76 (February 2007): 29–60.

Sandoval, Moisés. "The Organization of a Hispanic Church." In *Hispanic Catholic Culture in the U.S.: Issues and Concerns*, edited by Jay P. Dolan and Allan Figueroa Deck, S.J. Notre Dame, IN: University of Notre Dame Press, 1994: 131–65.

Self, Robert O. " 'Negro Leadership and Negro Money': African American Political Organizing in Oakland before the Panthers." In *Freedom North: Black Freedom Struggles outside the South, 1940–1980*, edited by Jeanne F. Theoharis and Komozi Woodward. New York: Palgrave Macmillan, 2003.

Smalley, Brian H. "Some Aspects of the Maine to San Francisco Trade, 1849–1852." *Journal of the West* 6 (1967): 593–603.

Standart, Sister M. Colette. "The Sonoran Migration to California, 1848–1856: A Study in Prejudice." *Southern California Quarterly* 58 (Fall 1976): 333–57.

Tays, George. "Mariano Guadalupe Vallejo and Sonoma: A Biography and a History." *California Historical Society Quarterly* 17, no. 1 (1938): 50–73.

Tinker Salas, Miguel. "Sexo, poder y lágrimas: Valores personales y conducta social en el México fronterizo a finales del siglo XIX." In *Historia, nación y región*, edited by Verónica Oikión Solano. Mexico City: Colegio de Michoacán, 2007: 617–49.

Torres-Saillant, Silvio. "Problematic Paradigms: Racial Diversity and Corporate Identity in the Latino Community." In *Latinos: Remaking America*, edited by Marcelo M. Suárez-Orozco and Mariela M. Páez. Berkeley: University of California Press, 2002: 435–56.

Umemoto, Karen. " 'On Strike!' San Francisco State College Strike, 1968–1969: The Role of Asian American Students." *Amerasia* 15, no. 1 (1989): 3–41.

Ward, Stephen. "The Third World Women's Alliance: Black Feminist Radicalism and Black Power Politics." In *The Black Power Movement: Rethinking the Civil Rights–Black Power Era*, edited by Peniel E. Joseph. New York: Routledge, 2006: 119–44.

Whalen, Carmen Teresa. "Colonialism, Citizenship, and the Making of the Puerto Rican Diaspora: An Introduction." In *The Puerto Rican Diaspora: Historical Perspectives*, edited by Carmen Teresa Whalen and Víctor Vásquez-Hernández. Philadelphia: Temple University Press, 2005.

Wirt, Fredrick M. "The Politics of Hyperpluralism." In *Culture and Civility in San Francisco*, edited by Howard S. Becker. New Brunswick, NJ: Transaction, 1971: 101–12.


## DISSERTATIONS, THESES, AND UNPUBLISHED MATERIALS

Ferreira, Jason Michael. "All Power to the People: A Comparative History of Third World Radicalism in San Francisco, 1968–1977." Ph.D. diss., University of California, 2002.

Kerr, Clark. "Productive Enterprises of the Unemployed, 1931–1938." Ph.D. diss., University of California, 1939.

Lee Miller, Lana. "Among Those Not Counted: Mexicans and Their Health in San Francisco, 1915–1930." Ph.D. diss., University of California, San Francisco, 1994.

López, Richard V. "Worlds Apart: Gender and Labor in the Chicano Community of San Francisco, 1880–1900." M.A. thesis, Stanford University, 1989.

Miller, Mike. "The Mission Coalition Organization and the Model Cities Program." San Francisco: Organize Training Center, 1981.

Moreno, Dorinda. "Concilio Mujeres: A Thesis Paper." San Francisco, n.d. Courtesy of Dorinda Moreno.

Pitti, Gina Marie. "The Sociedades Guadalupanas in the San Francisco Archdiocese." Unpublished manuscript. Stanford University, 2000.

Sandoval, Tomás F. "A Community History of the Hunter's Point–Bayview District, San Francisco, California." Unpublished manuscript. San Francisco, 1995.

Soto, Leandro P. "Community Economic Development: More than Hope for the Poor." Typescript. San Francisco, 1979.


## FILMS

Camplis, Francisco X., producer. *Unmined Treasures: San Francisco's Mexican Presence, 1920–1950*. Motion picture. San Francisco: Sunrisa Productions, 2000.

Goodlett, Carlton. Press conference, c. 1968, San Francisco. Footage from KPIX News. https://diva.sfsu.edu/collections/sfbatv/bundles/187307.

King, Martin Luther, Jr. Remarks in San Francisco, August 10, 1967. KPIX News, San Francisco. https://diva.sfsu.edu/collections/sfbatv/bundles/190083.

Stein, Peter L., producer. *The Mission*. Motion picture. San Francisco: KQED, 1994.

# Index

Coalitions, 99, 115, 126, 130, 133–41, 143,
145–46, 149, 171, 180, 184; broad-based,
1, 133, 150; building of, 119, 127, 134; of
Catholic parishes, 109; Latino-based,
127; Mission-based, 133; multiethnic
and multiracial, 128, 144, 146, 168–69,
184; multi-issue, 120, 134; single-issue,
132; Spanish-speaking, 129
Coffee: in Brazil, 88; in Central America,
88; companies, 94; in El Salvador, 101;
importation, 88; industry, 88; markets,
89; monoculture, 101; shipping lines, 3
Colima, Mexico, 56
Collective memory, 10, 202 (n. 120)
College of San Mateo, 177
Colombia, 88, 103
*Colonia, la*, 51
Colonialism, 63; Spanish, 27
Colorado, 8
Columbus Avenue, 71
*Comercio del Valparaíso, El*, 32
Comité para Defender los Siete, El, 152,
177–81
Comité Unionista de San Francisco, El, 98
Commercial development, 17, 126
Commercial enterprise, 18
Commonality, 49, 70; daily life as, 66;
expression of, 38; inequalities as, 155;
sense of, 158; transcendent forms of, 5
Common cause, 2, 39, 127, 129, 136, 139, 168
Community Action Programs (CAP), 129,
166
Community Alert Patrols, 161
Community formation, 13, 84; Catholics
and, 7, 74, 190 (n. 22); Latinos and, 6,
116, 184–85, 190 (n. 22)
Community history, 7, 10
Community Relations Unit (CRU), 163, 165
Community service: centers, 124, 152, 180;
model, 179; philosophy, 172
Community Service Organization (CSO),
127
Community studies, 190 (n. 32)
Concepción, Chile, 30, 40
Concilio Mujeres, 173, 210 (n. 107)
Coney, A. K., 73

Confession, 69, 108, 110
Connecticut, 30
Consulates, 65, 68; Central American,
67; Latin American, 49, 58, 64–65,
68; Mexican, 58, 65, 73, 75, 98; South
American, 67
Consuls, 58, 114; French, 41; Latin
American, 66; Mexican, 98; U.S., 34
Contra Costa County, 127, 196 (n. 68)
Cordova, Carlos B., 190 (n. 31)
Corona, Albert, 127
*Corrida*, 100
Cosio, Señor R., 72
Cosmopolitanism, 10, 22
Costa Rica, 75, 88, 201 (n. 91)
Council for the Spanish Speaking (CSS),
108–9
Council of California Growers, 159
Counterculture: cultural epicenter of, 150
Criminality, 66; attention to Mexican
American, 153; tales of Mexican, 102
*Cronista, El*, 55, 57
Crystal Palace Barber Shop and Beauty
Parlor, 94
Cuba, 55, 87, 103
Cultural studies, 7

*Daily Alta California*, 47, 191 (n. 30), 193
(n. 85)
Dallas, George M., 22
Dana, Richard Henry, 19
Dancing saloons, 42
Debts, 45, 57, 66
De Genova, Nicholas, 5
Deindustrialization, 185
Del Campo, Martin, 101
Del Carlo, Joan, 141
Democracy, 20, 138, 144
Democratic Party, 56
Department of Homeland Security, 9
Department of Housing and Urban
Development (HUD), 142
Department of Urban Work, 130
Deportation, 9, 96, 158, 197 (n. 77)
Depression, Great, 66, 99
Detroit, Michigan, 101

Lescallett, Gary, 150
Levi-Strauss factory, 104
Lewis, James W., 70
Leyva, Francisco G., 60
Liberation: from above, 129; of *raza*
    people, 181; struggle for, 150, 178, 181
Liminality, 36, 186
Little Chile, 44
Little Parish program, 112
Liturgy, 80, 110–13
Local 261, Building and Construction
    Workers Union, 130
Lopez, Eduardo, 109
Lopez, Gio, 150
Lopez, Segundo, 146
Lopez, Yolanda, 176
Los Angeles, 14, 25, 34–35, 59, 73, 84, 90,
    92–93, 101–2, 121, 152, 161, 172
Los Siete de la Raza (Los Siete), 150,
    175–76, 178
Lucey, Robert E., 202 (n. 136)
Lucky Alley Gang, 167
*Lumen Gentium*, 110–11
Lynch law, 17

Magallanes, Chile, 55
Mahon, Leo, 112
Maine, 54
Maldonado, Dr. E., 60
Manifest Destiny, 3, 20
Manila, 156
Manzanillo, Mexico, 85, 90
*Maranos*, 176
Marginalization, 5, 64, 67, 74, 153, 185
Marin County, 196 (n. 68)
Mariposa Street, 104
Marquesas Islands, 42
Marshall, John, 23
Martinez, Ben, 119, 132–34, 137–38, 142–44
Martinez, Juan, 168–69
Martinez, Mario, 150, 176
Martinez, Tony, 150
Marxism: Marxist critique, 151; Marxist
    ideal, 131
Mason, Richard B., 21, 25
Mass, 52, 73, 75, 81, 97, 102, 109–15

Massachusetts, 54
Massey, Doreen, 13
Mazatlán, Mexico, 23, 56, 85, 89, 90
McAlister, James, 128
McDonnell, Donald, 108, 159
McGuinness, Aims, 67
McKinney, Peter, 48
McReynolds, John, 134
McWilliams, Carey, 28
Media, 162, 176, 178–79
Medical doctors, 92, 94; Chilean, 33;
    Spanish-speaking, 94
Melendez, Danilo, 150
Meléndez, Gilberto, 94
Mendocino County, 196 (n. 68)
Merchants, 40, 56, 63
*Mercurio, El*, 32
Mexican American Political Association
    (MAPA), 127, 172
Mexican American Students
    Confederation (MASC), 168–69
Mexican American Unity Council, 127
*Mexicanidad*, 74–75
*Mexicanos*, 52, 73, 79, 91
Mexican Patriotic Society of San
    Francisco, 73
Mexican Republic, 16–17
Mexico, 4, 9, 15, 17–20, 22–24, 27–28, 34, 36,
    44, 47, 52, 54–60, 65, 72–74, 79, 83–85,
    87–92, 94, 96–97, 102–3, 111, 138, 155, 189
    (n. 6), 198 (n. 5), 201 (n. 91); indepen-
    dence day, 142; Mexico City, 72, 94
Miami, 103
Michell de Rodríguez, Isaura, 113
Midwest, U.S., 9, 101
Miller, Mike, 134, 137, 139, 145–46
Mining: regions, 33, 35, 45, 48; skills, 25
Misión San Fernando Rey de España, 25
Mission Area Community Action Board
    (MACABI), 132–34
Mission Coalition Organization (MCO),
    115, 119, 167, 171, 178; decline of, 145;
    organized religion and, 203 (n. 171);
    Point System, 141
Mission Council on Redevelopment
    (MCOR), 131

Mission Dolores, 11, 64, 106, 202 (n. 124), 204 (n. 11); secularization, 25
Mission Eleven, 165–66, 176
Mission High School, 127, 149, 163–64, 174
Mission Neighborhood Centers, 124–25
Mission Neighborhood Health Center, 184
Mission Rebels, 135–37, 166
Mission Renewal Commission, 132
Mission Tenants Union (MTU), 127, 131, 137
Missouri, 99
Mitty, John J., 196–97 (n. 76), 198 (n. 101)
Mixed-race, 39, 47; couples, 156
Model Cities: agreement, 142; campaign, 143; funds, 133, 135, 137, 145; involvement, 137; opposition, 133, 137; phases, 133; program, 120, 133, 135, 137
Model Cities Neighborhood Corporation, 137, 142, 145
*Monitor, The*, 66, 107
Monterey Bay, 3
Montijo, Fernando, 58–59, 62–63
Moreno, Dorinda, 105, 171–74; family of, 100
Multinationalism: features of, 16; multinational collective, 77; multinational unions, 99
Murguía, Alejandro, 190 (n. 31)
Murphy, Charles J., 78, 80, 196–97 (n. 76)
Murray, George, 168
Musicians, 95, 98

Napa Junior College, 173, 210 (n. 106)
Napa Valley, 88; wine producers, 160
Napa Valley College, 210 (n. 106)
National Association for the Advancement of Colored People (NAACP), 153
National Guard, 163
Nationalism, 31, 40, 42, 77; Chicano, 181; ethnic, 79; Latin American, 75
Nations, 1, 28, 54, 72, 125, 162, 164; Central American, 90, 101–2; Latin American, 101; Mexican, 72, 90
Native Americans, 20, 22, 34, 134; American Indian Movement, 178; women, 42, 155
Natural disasters, 10

Navarro, Ramón Jil, 40
Neighborhood Youth Corps, 129
Neoimperialism, U.S., 4, 90, 151, 185; vision of, 87
New England, 19, 24
New Granada, 27
New Haven, Connecticut, 30
New Jersey, 8
New Mexico, 8, 100, 178
New Orleans, Louisiana, 92
Newspapers, 10, 28, 55, 92–93; local, 25, 32, 57; major, 46; Mexican, 26; Spanish-language, 55, 72, 89, 91–92; strength of, 57; U.S., 24
Newton, Huey, 161, 176–77
New World, 3
New York, 8, 24, 44, 54, 59, 87, 103, 152, 156, 178
Nicaragua, 12, 74–75, 85, 88, 100, 102, 114, 138, 201 (n. 91); celebrations, 75; Nicaraguan-born, 107; Nicaraguans in San Francisco, 84, 102, 116, 180; population of, 75, 114, 138
1930s, 95, 98, 122, 197 (n. 77); late, 94, 104; mid-, 103
1960s, 13, 111, 114, 126–27; early, 163; mid-, 162; late-, 144, 152, 162, 165, 172, 175, 182, 184
1970s, 13, 173; early, 120, 172–73, 182, 184
Noe Valley Improvement Club, 126
Nonwhite population, 17, 152
North American continent, 29
North Americans, 15, 30, 32
North Beach, 69, 71, 93–94; barrio of, 84, 93–94, 103, 156
Northern California, 11, 20, 171–72, 210 (n. 107); Mexican nationals from, 158
North Mission, 104, 180
Nuestro Señor de Esquipulas, 114
Nuevo León, Mexico, 90

Oakland Diocese, 196 (n. 68)
Obama, Barack, 9
Office of Business, Education and Community Advancement (OBECA), 132

Ohlone College, 210 (n. 106)
Oklahoma, 99
Oral histories, 11
Oregon, 23
Orella, Captain, 41
Orendain de Medina, Hipóleta, 59–60, 62
Osgood, J. K., 36
Our Lady of Guadalupe Church (Guadalupe Church), 51–53, 69, 71, 73, 75, 77–82, 103, 108, 114, 156, 196–97 (n. 76), 198 (n. 101); construction of, 60, 72, 78–79; decline of, 80–81; Mexicans and, 73, 75, 97; neighborhood surrounding, 71–72, 77, 92, 96; non-Mexican Latinos and, 77
Outer Mission, 105
Overland passages, 29
Ownership, 43; collective and communal, 150; continuity of, 96; cultural, 185; racialized perspective on, 36; transfer of, 22; U.S. citizens and, 22; working-class and, 120

Pacheco, Maria, 156; family of, 156
*Pachucos*, 207 (n. 14)
Pacific Gas and Electric, 115
Pacific Mail Steamship Company, 53
Packard, Alberto G., 56
Padilla, Felix, 6
Palm Sunday, 107, 116
Panadería Española, 72
Panama, 29, 34, 67, 201 (n. 91)
Panethnicity, 5, 52, 186, 190 (n. 17)
Pan-Latin America: community, 23, 32, 51–52, 72, 80; efforts, 99; ethnicity, 6; population, 26; sensibility, 40, 57, 96
Paraguay, 103
Parish Historical Report, 80, 198 (n. 105)
Parishioners, 70–72, 74–75, 78–81, 106, 109, 111–13, 122, 131, 159, 196 (n. 76), 198 (n. 101), 202 (n. 123)
Pastor, Manuel, 4
Patriotic clubs, 58
*Patrones*, 16, 41
Paul VI, Pope, 203 (n. 147)
Pennsylvania, 9, 24, 54

*Peones*, 16, 27–28
Pérez Rosales, Vicente, 28–29, 33, 39, 41–42
Periodicals, 56–57, 96–97
Peru, 27, 32, 34, 103
Peruvian, 15–16, 28, 32, 42, 97, 203 (n. 168)
Petrini, Josephine, 105, 201 (n. 109)
Petroni, John, 111–12, 115
Philippines, 90, 156
Plan de Aztlán, El, 181
Plan de Santa Barbara, El, 181
Planning and Development Committee, 142
Pluralism: possibility of, 8, 16; white supremacist encounters with, 38
Police Narcotics Bureau, 165
Political prisoners, 150
Polk, James K., 24
Polyglot culture, 37
Poor, 27, 97, 115, 125, 130–32, 152, 162; nonwhite, 163, 170; Spanish-speaking, 159; students of color as, 168
Porfiriato, 90–91
Portelli, Alessandro, 11
Portolá Expedition, 3
Ports, 15–16, 18–19, 27, 29, 31, 90; Bay Area, 87; Caribbean, 29; Central American, 88; Chilean, 15–16; European-controlled, 30; Latin American, 23–24, 27, 67, 87; Mexican, 15–16, 42; Pacific, 85, 88; Peruvian, 16; southern, 55, 90; U.S., 29, 90
Posadas, Las, 115
Potrero Hill Boosters, 126
Potrero Police District, 162
Poverty, 65, 96, 100, 156, 166; antipoverty programs, 115, 129, 166; politics of, 161
Presbyterian Church, 130–31, 134
Priests, 80, 107–11, 113–14, 130–31, 159; Mexican insistence on, 79; Spanish-speaking, 67–68, 78–81, 107–11
Prisoners of war, 58
Prisons, 96
Pritchard, Miguel G., 60
Processing plants, 94, 99
Progress, 20, 73, 131; economic forms of, 124, 126, 184; potential for, 30

intraethnic forms of, 81; legacy of, 184; limits of, 51, 77; multiracial forms of, 158, 169, 174; need for, 67; pleas for, 1; voice of, 11

University of San Francisco, 93

Urban studies, 7

Ures, Mexico, 25

Urrea, Manuel J., 72

Uruchurtu, Antonio, 26-27, 192 (n. 50)

Uruguay, 103

Valencia Gardens, 155

Vallejo, Mariano Guadalupe, 17-18, 194 (n. 153)

Valparaíso, Chile, 25, 27, 31, 44, 46

Vargas, Roberto, 176

Varigny, Charles de, 41

Vasco, Señora, 81

Vásquez, Frank J., 94

Vasquez, Manuel, 155

Vatican II, 110-11, 203 (n. 147)

Venezuela, 103

Veracruz, Mexico, 57

Vietnam, 150, 178

Vietnamese, 178

Villanueva, Francisco, 196-97 (n. 76), 198 (n. 101)

Villanueva, Rosendo, 196-97 (n. 76)

Villaseñor, Rosendo, 78

Virgin of Guadalupe, 52, 73-74, 108

*Voz de Chile, La,* 55

*Voz de Méjico, La,* 55, 57-58

Walgreens, 183

War on Poverty, 128-32, 166

Washerwomen's Bay, 42

Washington, D.C., 58

Washington Hall, 44, 46

Watts Riots, 161

Wealth, 28, 43, 87, 121; competition for, 33; distribution of, 16; familial quest for, 41; instant, 15, 24; mineral, 26; prospect of, 26-27, 35; seeking of, 16, 18, 24

West Coast, 18, 35, 120; Mexican, 89

Western Addition, 125, 131

Whaling, 3, 18; ships for, 19

Whiteness, 17, 34, 40; *californios* and, 34; Mexicans and, 60, 155

Whites, 9, 22, 36, 61, 99, 112-13, 121, 126, 137, 152, 162, 175, 197 (n. 77), 208 (n. 57); liberal, 161; racist, 170; students, 165; yuppies, 183

White supremacy, 37, 164

Wind, James P., 70

Woodward's Gardens, 62

Women, 15, 33, 62, 96, 105; Chilean, 44; church roles of, 75, 109; classes for, 172-74; groups for, 97; importation of, 42; lack of, 41; Latin American, 41-42, 48, 116, 173; majority of, 197 (n. 93); movement of, 174; Native American, 42, 155; Peruvian, 42; political consciousness of, 173; reproductive economy and, 42; Spanish-speaking, 41-42, 109; strategies of, 62; working-class, 11; young, 173

Wonder Bread, 140

World War I, 88

World War II, 14, 99, 121, 152, 185; antifascist debate during, 154; governance during, 22; and housing, 100; and industrial expansion, 100; laborers during, 100; post-, 5, 80, 99, 163; pre-, 77, 93

Xochimilco Café, 73

Yerba Buena, 4, 19-20, 22, 44, 64

Yorke, Peter C., 107, 115

Young Lords Party, 178

Zacatecas, Mexico, 92

Zaragoza, Ignacio, 58

Zaragoza Club, 73

Zermeño, Alex, 129

Zoot suiters, 207 (n. 14)

Lightning Source UK Ltd.
Milton Keynes UK
UKHW041814080319
338774UK00002B/206/P